Alan Parsons' ART & SCIENCE OF SOUND RECORDING

THE BOOK

Alan Parsons' ART & SCIENCE OF SOUND RECORDING

THE BOOK

Alan Parsons
and
Julian Colbeck

Hal Leonard Books
An Imprint of Hal Leonard Corporation

Copyright © 2014 by Alan Parsons and Julian Colbeck

All rights reserved. No part of this book may be reproduced in any form, without written permission, except by a newspaper or magazine reviewer who wishes to quote brief passages in connection with a review.

Published in 2014 by Hal Leonard Books
An Imprint of Hal Leonard Corporation
7777 West Bluemound Road
Milwaukee, WI 53213

Trade Book Division Editorial Offices
33 Plymouth St., Montclair, NJ 07042

Printed in the United States of America

Book design by Damien Castaneda
Book composition by Bill Gibson

All images in this book are taken from the *Alan Parsons' Art & Science of Sound Recording* DVD series or from the authors' personal collections, except as noted below or with the images themselves. Any inadvertent omission of credit brought to our attention will be remedied in future editions.

Artwork by Cliff Mott on pp. 76, 106, 167, 177, 205, 218, and 233
Technical illustrations and graphs by Bill Gibson on pp. 9 (fig. 2.1), 10, 14, 15 (fig. 3.5), 16 (fig. 3.7), 20 (fig. 3.16), 23, 60, 63, 89, 107, 153, and 226

Library of Congress Cataloging-in-Publication Data

Parsons, Alan.
 Alan Parsons' art & science of sound recording : the book / Alan Parsons and Julian Colbeck.
    pages cm
 Includes bibliographical references and index.
 1. Parsons, Alan. 2. Popular music–Production and direction. I. Colbeck, Julian. II. Title.
 ML429.P335A5 2013
 621.389'3--dc23
                    2013021717
 ISBN 978-1-4584-4319-9

www.halleonardbooks.com

CONTENTS

ACKNOWLEDGMENTS vii
INTRODUCTION ix

1 A BRIEF HISTORY OF RECORDING 1
2 STUDIO ACOUSTICS 5
3 MICROPHONES 13
4 CONSOLES AND CONTROLLERS 31
5 DIGITAL AUDIO AND COMPUTERS 45
6 MONITORING 53
7 MIDI 65
8 EQ 73
9 COMPRESSORS AND LIMITERS 87
10 NOISE GATES 99
11 REVERB 105
12 DELAYS 113
13 A BAND TRACKING SESSION 119
14 VOCALS 129
15 INTERNET RECORDING 147
16 DRUMS 153
17 KEYBOARDS 165
18 BASS 177
19 GUITAR 185
20 RECORDING ACOUSTIC GUITAR WITH VOCALS 203
21 RECORDING A CHOIR 207
22 APPROACHES TO LIVE RECORDING 213
23 MIXING 217
24 DEALING WITH DISASTERS 235

GLOSSARY 241
INDEX 255

ACKNOWLEDGMENTS

A great debt of thanks is owed to many people who inspired, contributed to, and helped behind the scenes on both the *Art & Science of Sound Recording* video series and this book that is based on it:

Chuck Ainlay, Scott Austin, Erykah Badu, Andrew Barta, Delia Bernal, Athan Billias, Niko Bolas, Gary Boss, Bob Bradley, Will Bright, Tulsi Briones, Dave Bristow, Tony Brown, Paul Buff, Pat Caddick, John Cerullo, Steve Clarke, Abi Colbeck, Annie Colbeck, Cameron Colbeck, Victoria Cole, Kim Copeland, Sharon Corbitt-House, Ben Cruz, Rachel Dean, Richard Dodd, Thomas Dolby, Jack Douglas, Jimmy Douglass, Roxana Drexel, Nathan East, John Fields, Ian Gilby, Brian Granfors, Susannah Grant, Jackie Green, Ashley Greer, Norm Hajjar, Danny Hakin, Gavin Haverstick, Taylor Hawkins, Rami Jaffee, Ashley Jones, Raymond Jones, Carol Kaye, Kevin Kennedy, Peter Kerns, Hal Ketchum, Chris Killen, Andrew Kitchenham, Kaz Kobayashi, Dale Krevens, Miguel Lazaro, Ledfoot, AJ Lemos, Patrick Leonard, Lisa Liu, Michael Logue, Tim Martin, Steve Marcantonio, Sylvia Massy, John McBride, Michael McDonald, Megan McDuffee, Angel Moon, Robin Moore, Spencer Nilsen, Paul Nugent, P. J. Olsson, Greg Ondo, David and Stacy Pack, Lisa Parsons, Chris Pelonis, Joe Perry, Simon Phillips, Tim Pierce, Jack Joseph Puig, Bill Putnam Jr., Coley Read, Record One Studios, Simon Rhodes, Tony Rita, Lisa Roy, Craig Russo, Sami Ryan, Chris Sampson, Elliot Scheiner, Margaret Sekelsky, John Shanks, Terry Shields, Allen Sides, Brad Smith, Dave Smith, Robin Sones, Karyn Soroka, Charlie Steves, Craig Stubblefield, Shinichi Takenaga, Bruce Tambling, Phil Taylor, David Thoener, Martin Thomas, Terry Thomas, Billy Bob Thornton, Matt Ward, Jason Ware, Tom White, Russell Wiener, Josh Wimmer, and Casey Young.

We'd also like to add our special thanks to two people in particular whose contributions form crucial parts of the book: Tim Pierce, whose guitar playing and observations thereon are simply in a league of their own, and Simon Phillips, who is to drumming what Bill Nye is to science.

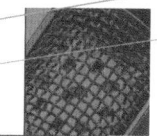

INTRODUCTION

Hello there!

Is this hello for the very first time, or have you got the video series as well? If the former, we also produced a video series entitled *Alan Parsons' Art & Science of Sound Recording*, and this book is both based upon and an extension of territory we covered in the videos. We hope you will find one to be a good companion to the other.

Alan Parsons' Art & Science of Sound Recording—The Book is a complete rewrite and reappraisal of the original video version. Because it is a book and not an audio-visual experience, we've been able to examine all of the topics in greater detail. With the videos we strove to keep you visually and aurally entertained. Now, you can be reading this at home, or in a busy Starbucks, or on a plane . . . you can read one page at a sitting, or one chapter, or just dive in here and there using the index or the glossary. Ingest the words, look at the pictures and diagrams, and if something is not clear first time around, well, read it again. It'll make sense eventually; promise.

The great thing about a book is that you can go at your own pace. Plus it's the ultimate in nonlinear formatting. You can flip from here to page 145 in less than a heartbeat. Eat your heart out, modern media! (Readers of the *ebook* version possibly have the best of all worlds, of course.)

For the book, we have kept the same basic tone as the video. We hope it is both intriguing for the newcomer to recording and interesting to the seasoned professional. We've dug a little deeper into all aspects of recording technology. Chapter 1, "A Brief History of Recording," may still be a relatively brief version, but it's now not quite so "on a pinhead."

A question that often cropped up on the video series was, "How do I use the videos? What order should I view them in?" Sensing potential for the same line of enquiry here, here's what we recommend you do.

This book does have a logical flow of chapters. First we look at how sound is created and how it behaves, before moving onto the different sources, components, and equipment involved in making and reproducing sound recordings. With these pieces of the puzzle in play, we then look at all the processes involved in *manipulating* sound recordings, such as EQ, reverbs, delays, compression, and so on. Then we look at how the various types of sound sources respond to the various processes and how they are best applied for particular sonic needs.

The rubber truly hits the road when human beings are tossed into the mix and we actually have to record real live musicians sitting there right in front of us. We look at drummers, guitarists, bass players, singers, choirs, keyboard players . . . all of whom can have very different mindsets, roles, temperaments, and functionalities.

Finally, even though the word "mix" is now more of a formality than the "performance" process it used to be in the days of analog technology, the mix is still the point where decisions and choices have to be made. And that, in itself, is an art and a science.

So if you can, read this book from here . . . right through to the end—at least once.

Learning anything—especially something as nuanced as sound recording—is a journey, and that journey is half the fun. You can fly from Paris to Istanbul, or you could take in the delights of Lausanne, Milan, Venice, Belgrade, and Sofia along the way by traveling on the Orient Express—same destination, but a very different experience.

As with the Orient Express, a top-to-toe read of this book will introduce you to topics you may not fully appreciate the first time around. But you can always come back to Venice and look at its sights and virtues. Although we will try not to dazzle you with clever-sounding words and concepts, important messages can be missed if you speed by too quickly.

Finally, a great debt of gratitude is owed to the many engineers, producers, and artists we interviewed for the video series, whose words of wisdom are included here. Music is so often best when it's a team sport, and although there are actually some incontrovertibly bad ideas (e.g., don't try recording a kick drum with a ribbon mic), sound recording is definitely NOT a place for closed minds.

Experimentation—within some context of tried and tested sound practices—should always be on the menu.

You're in good company. So enjoy your journey.

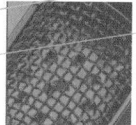

A BRIEF HISTORY OF RECORDING

Ever since we've communicated using speech, we've been able to hear our own voice reproduced in the natural world through echoes—sound waves that travel to and bounce back from hard, reflective surfaces like a canyon or rock face. But the ability to capture and store these waves is a surprisingly recent invention.

Thomas Edison started it all with his invention of the phonograph in 1877, a process immortalized with the inventor's own voice narrating the nursery rhyme "Mary Had a Little Lamb."

If we could travel back in time, imagine how difficult it would be to explain to someone in the late nineteenth century what "sound recording" was. We could say it's the sound equivalent of how the camera, which was invented just a couple of decades earlier, stores an image. Or we could say it's a bit like a mechanical parrot that squawks back exactly what we said to it at the press of a button.

When Thomas Edison first publicly displayed his phonograph it was to huge acclaim, and it instantly made him world-famous. Interestingly, Edison hadn't foreseen that one of the principal applications of his invention would be for the reproduction of music.

At the Grammy Museum in Los Angeles, they've assembled exhibits and artifacts that trace sound recording from the days of the tinfoil cylinder through to the iPod.

The rotating cylinder on the phonograph developed into the flat disc on Emile Berliner's Gramophone that was patented in 1887. In 1900, Valdemar Poulsen of Denmark patented the first magnetic recorder, the "Telegraphone," using steel wire. But it was a long time—some four decades—before the basic principle was adapted into machines using magnetic tape.

Soon after the turn of the nineteenth century, flat discs had largely superseded Edison's rather short-lived cylinder technology. Mass production techniques for cellulose and shellac records made the hand-wound gramophone a common household object.

The development of electrical recording spawned the concept of the sound recording studio, and recorded music as an art form burst into life. Celebrated

British composer Sir Edward Elgar recorded the London Philharmonic Orchestra at the grand opening of Abbey Road Studios in November 1931.

For movies to contain sound, audio was recorded optically by a photographic process onto the edge of 35mm film, adjacent to the picture. Incredibly, the soundtrack for Walt Disney's *Fantasia*, made in 1939, was recorded stereophonically on eight such optical tracks.

The Development of Tape

The Ampex company started making magnetic tape recorders in the 1940s. Tape, in countless incarnations and variations, became the standard recording and playback medium from the 1950s through to the turn of the century.

The technology of magnetic tape opened up sound recording to a whole new generation of artists, and along with them a new breed of professional technicians, engineers, and producers.

But it's not just the technology—it's what you do with that technology that counts. One can't really live without the other.

The Beatles had a big influence on how recording technology developed. Their entire debut album, *Please Please Me*, was recorded in a single day. (As George Harrison famously quipped, "The second album took even longer.")

In those days the Beatles recorded on 2-track 1/4-inch tape. To make an overdub (or a "superimposition," as Abbey Road Studios called it), they would copy one tape to another while adding the new material. The rhythm track or instruments would usually be on Track 1 and the vocals on Track 2. These two tracks were then mixed down to mono for the final master. Somewhat hilariously, the 2-track tape was also released as a so-called stereo version, where the backing was on the left and the vocals were on the right. Right up to *Sgt. Pepper's Lonely Hearts Club Band*, stereo was just an afterthought. But *Pepper* was a big turning point. Four-track had arrived by then, along with the ability to overdub new material onto the same tape and remain in sync, a previously impossible feat.

The complexity of the *Sgt. Pepper* album involved huge engineering challenges, and Geoff Emerick received a well-deserved Grammy for his work as engineer. It's still hard to believe it was recorded on 4-track.

Alan:

> By the time I started working at Abbey Road, we were recording the Beatles on 8-track. Then came 16-track, the format we used to record Pink Floyd's *Dark Side of the Moon*. Then 24-track. "Will it ever end?" we asked. The answer was no, it probably wouldn't, because before long, digital technology came along and allowed us to have an unlimited number of tracks at our disposal.

Digital Days / Daze

Pioneering work in digital recording had been going on in laboratories in the U.K. and USA since the before the Second World War. But it wasn't until 1981 that the word "digital" really made any impact on the recorded music community. Japanese electronics giant Sony, founded just a year after World War II, must be given credit for two major developments: First, the PCM-F1, a recording device initially intended for consumers but which was quickly adopted by professionals as an affordable digital recorder for mastering. And then, of course, the compact disc, developed in conjunction with Philips, which first trickled into the market in 1982. The CD was soon followed by the DAT, or Digital Audio Tape, format, which became a studio standard for several years not only for stereo mixing but also for the delivery of masters.

Alan:

> I was an early adopter of the first Sony PCM stereo formats and mixed a couple of albums recorded to analog tape to the PCM 1610 [later 1630] formats. I was also one of the first to commit to the Sony DASH 3324 format and owned a pair of weighty (and expensive) PCM 3324 24-track tape machines. Soon, ADAT on VHS tapes gave us unlimited batches of eight digital tracks, as did their competing format, the TASCAM DA-88 series on smaller videocassettes. It's interesting that in the early days of digital recording, we were still dealing with tape—but tape disappeared so quickly as hard disks took over that it was almost frightening.

The Learning Curve

Almost all the great engineers and producers from the 1960s onward spent years learning their craft in great studios like Capitol in Los Angeles, the Record Plant in New York, and Abbey Road in London.

Alan:

> Unfortunately, only a handful of large commercial recording studios exist today, which makes it very difficult for a young engineer to get the experience I had: recording an orchestra one day, a pop band the next, an opera singer the next, and so on.

Reading a book or watching a video—or even attending a recording school—is not going to turn you into Quincy Jones or George Martin. But what any good teaching medium will help you do is develop the most important skill an engineer and producer should have: the ability to listen. That covers judging sound quality, sound balance, knowing when something is lacking, and knowing when enough is enough. Too many producers tend to be "over-producers."

The Recording Academy's full name is the National Academy of Recording Arts and Sciences. That name was, naturally enough, an influence on the title of this book and the DVD video series that inspired it. The Recording Academy has always embraced and acknowledged the countless composers and artists that form our musical heritage. It also acknowledges the producers, engineers, and technologists without whom music would simply not be the same. This book peeks behind the curtain and unveils the tools and techniques music lovers don't normally get to see. Our main objective was to make a "how-to," practical encyclopedia for those interested in the technical side of recording. Although you will read about knob twiddling and parameter adjusting, sound recording is not just a modus operandi and hard-and-fast rules. It's about developing an understanding and a feel for both the artistic as well as the technical.

The greatest technological stride in recent years, for everyone, has been the Internet. In recording, the concept of reality has been stood on its head, encompassing everything from *virtual* equipment to *virtual* spaces available in ever-increasing numbers on mobile devices.

In a relatively short space of time, the ability to record sound has gone from a mechanical curio only the privileged could set eyes on, much less use, to a wireless slice of silicon open and available to all.

Read on as we look at the tools, tasks, and techniques of sound recording in detail. Onward!

STUDIO ACOUSTICS

Up until the 1990s, if you wanted to make a record, someone had to pay for you to go into a professional recording studio. Needless to say, cost and complexity kept all but the lucky few out of these temples of technology.

The door cracked open in the 1980s with the advent of semipro home recording, using 4-track cassette tape, initiated by Tascam's Portastudio recorder. By the beginning of the next decade, home recording had morphed into the Digital Audio Workstation or DAW, the name we use for a recording environment based on hard disk storage on a computer. Suddenly high-quality audio had reached the masses—or had it?

This revolution brought new people into recording, but it also created a whole new world of untrained recording engineers and acoustically untreated spaces. Today, a studio is not so much Abbey Road as it is a laptop in the kitchen of 34b Main Street.

This democratization is healthy in many ways, but while it may now seem possible to fix anything digitally, you shouldn't underestimate the value of getting the best-quality recordings in the first place. Unless you're working entirely from pre-recorded material with loops, samples, and plug-ins, at least part of your recording will probably involve a microphone. Anything recorded by a microphone in a real space is going to be affected by the properties of that space, be that the acoustics of the room or having to deal with interference from extraneous noise.

Less obviously, the room in which you are recording may emphasize or disguise certain frequencies or characteristics, which will invariably lead to your recording or mixing your material based upon false information. Big deal? Well, yes, because it's a bit like commenting on the quality of a fine wine through a mouthful of chocolate chip cookie! If you record music in a room that falsely emphasizes or reduces certain tonal or spatial characteristics, then when you take it out of that room, the recording is going to be unbalanced. In other words, it may have too much or too little bass, or result in a mix that is too bright or too dull.

If a recording *only* sounds good (and by good we mean "how you intended it to sound") in the studio where you recorded it, either something is wrong with the studio or something is wrong with the way the recording was engineered.

Acoustic Principles

You may neither wish nor need to study acoustics per se, but acoustic principles are real, and some appreciation of them will enhance your ability to record accurately and achieve your recording goals, whatever they may be.

Whatever your budget and whatever physical options are open to you, following some of the following basic guidelines, which we discussed with acoustician Gavin Haverstick during the building of a modest single-room recording studio for the *Art & Science of Sound Recording* video series, can only help.

Gavin said there was a saying around Auralex (the company he worked for at the time): "In the beginning there was perfect sound, and then man created rooms."

Sound is created by changes in air pressure transmitted to our ears by sound waves. The length and intensity of the waves govern a sound's pitch and volume. The shape of a wave determines its tone, and the characteristics of a wave determine whether we interpret it as simply noise or something musical.

Low-frequency sound waves have extremely long wavelengths, and so small rooms just can't reproduce low frequencies naturally. All sorts of things can skew the response of the low frequencies.

In the open air, sound goes its merry way until the waves peter out, so the sound fades and then dies. But if sound encounters a hard and reflective boundary, it bounces back as an echo. In a room with hard and reflective boundaries like walls, floors, and ceilings, sound also bounces around, but not in quite such a discrete and obvious way. When you are recording, you just want to create an environment where your music is not going to disturb the neighbors—and a passing jet is not going to fly into the chorus.

Acoustic Terms

Isolation is the practice of separating your environment from extraneous sound and vice versa. Sound isolation effectively equates to soundproofing.

Absorption refers to soaking up the sound waves so they don't bounce back when they hit a boundary; an analogy would be how a sponge absorbs water. When you absorb sound, you deaden it.

Diffusion is the redirecting of sound waves—breaking them up, so they don't produce undesirable artifacts, especially in a confined space like a home studio.

Acoustic Issues

Gavin Haverstick explains why small rooms pose special problems:

> Sometimes you run into things called *room modes*. Typically, room modes are cancellations and buildups across the frequency range. Low-frequency issues are a huge concern in small rooms, due to the fact that low-frequency wavelengths are much longer than most of the dimensions in small rooms. Small rooms just can't reproduce that information as well as a larger space can. You want to avoid dimensions that are divisible by the same number or each other.

Such dimensions to avoid would be rooms measuring 12 by 12 feet, 6 by 12 feet, or 15 by 10 feet, for example.

When first looking at a space you'd like to improve or treat acoustically, you have to look at two problem areas: (1) problems in the *frequency domain*—which will affect frequency response or, in other words, the ability of the room to reproduce the entire sound spectrum faithfully; and (2) problems in the *time domain*—caused by reflections that might give a false impression of the perceived acoustic being recorded.

As Gavin explains:

> The frequency response of the room, or how it represents different frequencies, is going to vary depending on the size of the room and the materials used in it. A drywall room will react differently than a concrete room. If you have a frequency problem at 80 Hz [abbreviation for *hertz*—see glossary] going side to side in that room, you're also going to have it going floor to ceiling, and then an octave higher going front to back. Time-domain issues concern how quickly reflections come back to you, which are also governed by the size and shape of a room, plus its surface materials.

Gavin again:

> If you have a highly reverberant space, this can smear intelligibility. It can also cause you to adjust your decision making during a mixing process, to where if you hear reflections coming within 50 milliseconds of the direct sound, our brain actually factors that in as *part of the direct sound*. Reflections can essentially be summed [added together].

These are the issues and their consequences. If you are assessing and treating an existing room, solutions are largely going to be exterior—things that will help mask or minimize problems.

If you have the chance to start from scratch—to, say, convert an existing room or build a room within a room, you should be aware of a number of basic design and construction techniques that will help you create a space you can trust for recording.

Approaches to Studio Construction

Chris Pelonis has built studios for Skywalker Sound, Disney, Jeff Bridges, and Jack White, to name but a few. When we spoke during the making of the *ASSR* video series, he was quick to point out that there is no universal solution.

Chris Pelonis:

> If you've got nothing but money, you can fix anything and you can make anything as perfect as it can be. But oftentimes you have to cut a corner. You might have to say, well, you're not going to have the isolation you think you need (sometimes you really don't need it anyways). Do you really want that console or these speakers, or do you want the room to be this true or have this kind of an ambience?

It's good to hear from a top studio designer like Chris that compromises are acceptable, so let's look at what you really need in a studio environment. The single most important consideration when building a studio is to create an environment where you know and trust the sound you hear without being tempted to "fix" sounds in a mix that are perfectly fine.

Gavin Haverstick:

> Essentially, what you want to do is create a very consistent low-frequency response at the mix position in a control room. If you happen to be sitting in one of those cancellation points around 60 or 70 or 80 Hz, that's right in the kick drum range. And so if you're sitting in a cancellation point and you cannot hear that frequency very well, you'll keep boosting it and boosting it, until it sounds good in your room. But your room is really lying to you, because that's not how it was recorded; it's just how your room sounds. And so after you adjusted it and boosted it, and then you burn a CD and take it out to your car—all you can hear is the kick drum. And that's because you've artificially boosted the low-frequency range to compensate for your room problem.

We shouldn't, however, fall into the trap of thinking a studio should be some sort of dead-sounding space with no reverberant qualities. A completely dead room with no reverberant characteristics would be very claustrophobic, like recording in a closet.

Traditionally, the studio's performing area and control room are separate rooms with their own acoustic characteristics. These can vary enormously and be tailored to a particular type of music or performer. An orchestra might want an acoustic more like a church, while a rock band might look for more of a club-like acoustic. To take the studios at Abbey Road as an example, Studio One is a vast reverberant hall, whose natural acoustics are ideally suited to orchestral and classical recordings. Studio Two, as favored by the Beatles, has some liveness to it, but if close-miking and screening techniques are employed, it can be made to sound fairly dead. Studio Three is more geared to rock and pop and is the most dead acoustically of the three. Control rooms are generally designed around good frequency response in the entire room and pleasing reflective properties.

For many people nowadays, the control room and the recording studio are one and the same place: a single environment where the roles of writer, musician, engineer, and producer are often combined.

Ideally, you want a room that's comfortable to work in audio-wise and atmospherically, and that offers you some kind of flexibility. An ideal situation would be a room that is fairly dead in one area—when you want to record an intimate vocal—but quite lively and inspiring in another—say, when you want to record an acoustic guitar.

A few years ago, the phrase "live-end/dead-end" came into use to describe a room that has different acoustic treatments at different positions, in order to create some different acoustic environments—something we were mindful of when building our own single-room studio during the making of the *ASSR* video series.

Gavin Haverstick feels that live-end/dead-end can give you the best of both worlds:

> The dead end is typically where you put your control and mix position, somewhere where you don't have a lot of reflections. But then in the back part of the room, you have diffusers and other materials that reflect the sound, so that you can set up an acoustic guitar or even a drum set and it'll still sound natural and will be able to breathe in a room like that. You have to walk the tightrope between what's going to be best for monitoring and what's going to best for recording, and live-end/dead-end works great for that.

Ideally, a studio should have a floating floor (see **figure 2.1**)—in other words, a floor that is not in direct contact with the floor joists or the foundation, but is cushioned by rubber pads or some other highly absorptive material. Alternately, it can be suspended in midair from above.

If you're constructing your own space, the other thing you can plan for is nonparallel walls. There's some debate about how nonparallel you need to be to reduce what we call *flutter*. In the studio we built for the *ASSR* video series, wall-to-wall and ceiling-to-floor were approximately 5 percent off true, and to be honest we did encounter some flutter echo problems initially, which had to be corrected with surface reflectors. One thing that did work well in terms of isolation was the use of staggered studs for the wall joists (see **figure 2.2**), and this is a relatively simple technique you can use to reduce points of contact.

The corners are particularly important in a small room because of room modes that can result in what we call "standing waves." These bounce back and forth in a room, distorting the appearance of not only the low frequencies themselves, but also related harmonics. "Trapping" the bass to prevent this is vital in a small room. Here in our studio, "bass traps" (see **figure 2.3**) have been built directly into the corners. You can also construct or purchase off-the-shelf bass traps to cure this problem.

FIGURE 2.1. **Floating floor principle: Absorbent pads made of dense sponge material placed between the hard wood surfaces of a floor to help soak up vibrations.**

FIGURE 2.2. **Wall joists with staggered studs.**

FIGURE 2.3. **Bass traps. Photo courtesy of Auralex Acoustics.**

Issues to bear in mind with ceilings include how load-bearing they need to be and how much weight of construction material can be used. It's best to avoid making the ceiling dead parallel to the floor, which is why you often see sloping ceilings in commercial studios. (Sloping floors may be a concept too, though we are not sure that's been done anywhere other than a cinematic dubbing theater.)

Soundproofing

You don't want sounds from outside invading your recording. You need the room to be isolated from the outside world—both to keep noise from coming in and music from going out to your neighbors—so you can work when you want, how you want, and as loudly as you want.

Sound doesn't only travel through the air; it also gets transmitted via the vibrations of the surfaces between spaces. So if we can isolate those surfaces from each other, or at least minimize the points of contact between them, we can substantially improve unwanted transmission or vibration (see **figure 2.4**). We call the practice of isolating surfaces from each other *decoupling*. The mass of a surface can substantially affect how it transmits sound vibrations.

Track lighting is a good idea because you'll have fewer "holes" going out into the outside world above. Windows and doors are two obvious potential weak points in terms of isolation. Windows should be sealed, double- or triple-glazed on both sides, and angled away from each other, and should have as little direct contact with the framing as possible.

Doors should be constructed from dense material and need to be airtight. Ideally, use double-thickness or pairs of communicating doors.

The thickness of the absorptive material you use particularly affects low frequencies. You can compensate for low mass in your material by not attaching it directly to the walls, but rather mounting it two or more inches away. A room that only cuts down on the high and mid reflections will produce a totally false bass picture.

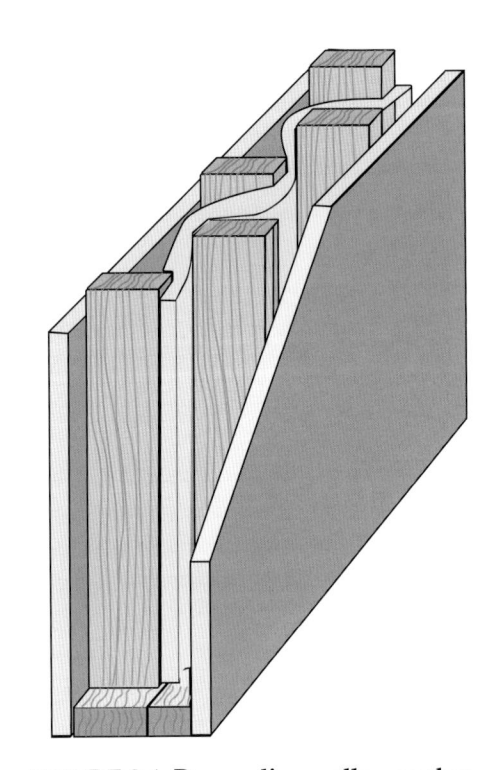

FIGURE 2.4. **Decoupling walls—so that points of contact are minimal or possibly absent altogether—helps reduce the transfer of sound from one surface to the other.**

A measurement you might want to familiarize yourself with is STC or "*sound transmission class*," which measures how much sound penetrates the materials you'll use to construct your studio surfaces.

Different materials—like drywall (called plasterboard in Europe) or a relatively new rubbery compound you can sandwich in between layers of drywall, called SheetBlok—come with different STC numbers. The higher the number, the greater the soundproofing. In total, you should aim for an STC rating of more than 45. This might sound simple enough, but it's not a question of adding up different materials' STC numbers. It doesn't quite work like that. Use the STC as a basic indicator from which a reasonably accurate prediction can be made.

Gavin Haverstick puts it nicely:

> It's a two-way street with sound isolation, because you have sound that you're trying to keep within your room so that you don't disturb other people outside of the room, but you also have external noises like airplanes, train tracks that are nearby or a busy street . . . or even noise coming in from other rooms . . . even through the HVAC system. There's all sorts of paths for sound to come into the room. If you're trying to soundproof your room, it's very similar to trying to waterproof your room. If you can imagine filling your entire room up with water and finding the areas where it's going to leak out, that's very similar to where sound is going to leak out. So if you see daylight around the door when it's shut, then sound is going to zip right underneath the door and travel out to other places as well.

Even if you are only working on a single multi-application room, a lot of what we have discussed here can get expensive. What can you do for a few hundred dollars? Well, a bookshelf (with some suitably dense reading matter—Dostoyevsky works especially well!) can make a good and inexpensive sound diffuser.

Freestanding bass traps and wall-mounted diffusers are perfectly acceptable in a far less custom-built environment.

Alan:

> I have one tip on studio construction where there is a separate performing area and control room. Watch the height of the window between the two—I've seen a number of studios where all you can see is the top of the performer's head when everyone is sitting down.

Placing Your Equipment

Having spent so much time and effort getting the physical space constructed, you want to make sure the equipment layout of the room is right as well. You don't want your working position to be in the center of the room. One third of the way back is ideal. Most crucially, the speakers need be aligned so that an equilateral triangle between the two speakers and the listening position is created, with the tweeters at approximately ear level. You don't want speakers too close to walls, and never in a corner, unless the speakers in question are specifically designed for it—or you can place them in a specially treated area.

If you plan a one-man operation, you'll want to make sure the gear you use most is at your fingertips. Many studios arrange equipment in a U or L-shape, so that the computer is directly in front and keyboard instruments, for example, are at one side.

It also never hurts to run some tests in your room. You can do this on your own using test tones and a sound level meter, or you can go to a company like Auralex, which uses software to analyze problem areas and provide solutions.

Whether you have the budget for a custom build or simply a few bass traps in your garage, what we've just covered should help you optimize the acoustics in your recording environment. In terms of isolation, which is probably the number one issue for most people at home, a lot depends upon how problematic external noise may be, and the consequences of waking the neighbors when you're playing music at fifty billion decibels at three in the morning.

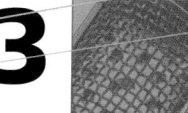

MICROPHONES

3

A microphone wouldn't have any purpose without the existence of a device such as a loudspeaker to reproduce what it picks up. Interestingly, microphones and speakers are to some degree interchangeable.

Microphones are the beginning of the recording chain. They pick up audio sources and vibrate just like the human eardrum. Each mic is, in a way, like a mono "ear."

The time-honored childhood game of using two tin cans joined by a piece of string to both "talk" and "listen" to your friend on the other end, ably demonstrates the ambiguous world of sound capture and reproduction (see **figure 3.1**). When spoken into, the tin can funnels or focuses your voice into sound waves that are carried along the string and are then converted back into the movement of air by the receiving tin can, which is now effectively a loudspeaker. Switch from mouth to ear and the mic becomes the speaker and vice versa. Ah, the magic of audio!

An extension of the tin can and string idea was used in Thomas Edison's early phonograph recordings. One day, he shouted the words "Mary had a little lamb" into a cone-shaped horn, which caused a needle at its narrow end to vibrate and cut a groove into a rotating tinfoil cylinder. When the process was reversed, the rotating cylinder caused the needle in the groove to vibrate, and much to his delight, the horn reproduced the stored vibrations of his voice as a sound output. This is another example of the process being reversible.

The invention of the microphone is generally attributed to Alexander Graham Bell, and it was initially a very impractical contraption involving liquid acid. The so-called

FIGURE 3.1. The classic game of tin can telephone—a simple example of the relationship between loudspeaker and microphone.

"carbon microphone" was invented by Emile Berliner and virtually simultaneously by Thomas Edison in 1876. The carbon microphone was used in early telephone designs and, somewhat surprisingly, survived in telephones into the late twentieth century. It relied upon the change in resistance caused by sound pressure and the consequent change in current between a metal diaphragm and two metal electrodes separated by a layer of carbon particles.

Later designs used what became known as the moving coil principle, which relied on electrical pulses being generated by a diaphragm attached to a coil surrounding a magnet. Present-day devices using this principle are called "dynamic" microphones (see **figure 3.2**).

Just as with the tin cans and the phonograph, the moving coil process is reversible, and we use the principle for the modern loudspeaker (see **figure 3.3**). Electrical pulses cause a coil between magnets to move back and forth. The moving coil is attached to a cardboard or plastic cone, which causes the air in front of it to move and thus generate sound that we can hear.

Sound, after all, is just the movement of air.

The close relationship between loudspeaker and microphone continues to this day. Headphones can actually be used as microphones if you're in a real jam.

Before there were microphones, music performances had to be tailored at the source to compensate for the differences in volume between different instruments and voices. Orchestras traditionally positioned quiet instruments at the front and the noisy ones at the back—and actually, they still do.

Opera singers require a phenomenal technique to sing loud enough to be heard above an orchestra. The design of an opera house, plus the positioning of the orchestra in a "pit" below the stage, both work to enhance the singer's chances of being heard.

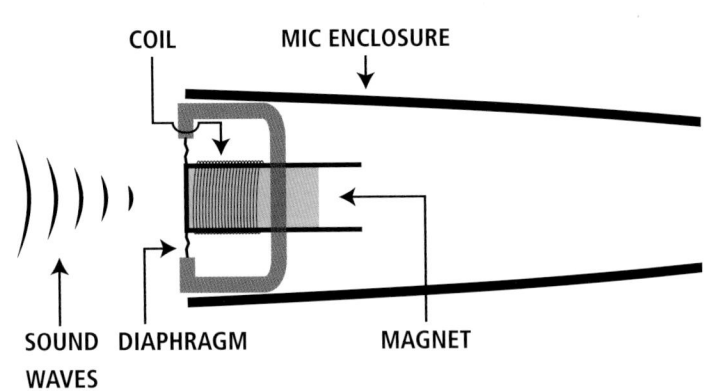

FIGURE 3.2. **Principle of the dynamic microphone: Sound waves cause the diaphragm attached to the coil around the magnet to vibrate. These movements are then turned into electrical pulses.**

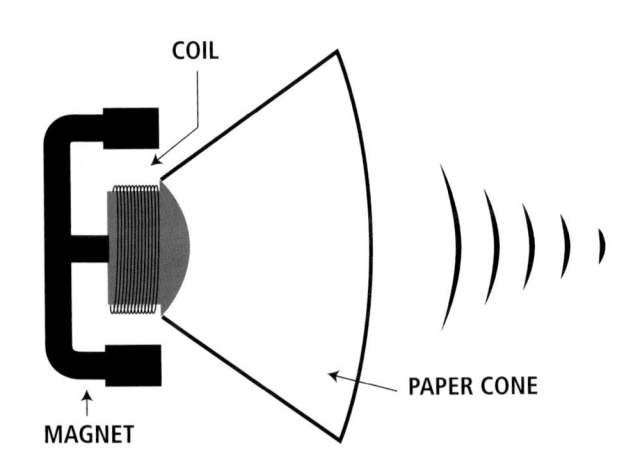

FIGURE 3.3. **Principle of the loudspeaker: Electrical pulses are applied to the coil, which is attached to the paper cone. This then vibrates, producing sound waves.**

The microphone and its buddies the amplifier and loudspeaker turned the tables on these natural balances created in symphonic, chamber, and big-band music and enabled new genres to develop. With their help, untrained human voices or very quiet instruments could easily keep pace with a brass section, a drum kit, or an electric guitar cranked up all the way to 11: This artificial, *un*natural balance between performers became the entire basis of rock and pop music.

What Do Mics Actually Hear?

The job of a microphone is to turn sound waves into electrical pulses that can be recorded or amplified. This can be done in several ways.

But first, what is the sound you're trying to capture? Is it the immediate, close-up source of the sound? Or is it the sound as a human ear normally perceives it in a room or space? Musicians can balance themselves (Oh, no, they can't! —*Ed.*), taking the loudness of each instrument into account and positioning themselves around one microphone—as in fact they often did in the early days of recording and radio. If a performer had a solo, they would move closer to the mic.

But since the 1950s, on most rock and pop records, different instruments on the recording have been acoustically isolated and recorded via separate microphones. That way, the engineers and producers can adjust the level between the instruments and create an ideal "sound balance" to record to tape.

At Abbey Road Studios back in the 1970s, recording engineers were in fact called "balance engineers" and there's some real truth to the notion that the art of recording is still the art of balance. Nowadays it's the mix of levels between mics that produces the balance, and each mic is usually recorded on its own individual track.

Modern recording is a distortion of time, creating the illusion of a simultaneous performance that never actually happened. All the different elements were most likely recorded at completely different times and even in completely different spaces. This is relevant because the microphone is the bridge between the actual sound-event and a recording. How a mic absorbs that information will color everything that is done with it.

For instance, you can set up a single mic in front of an entire band and get a pretty decent result. This is borne out by the countless available live concerts recorded on the internal mic of a pocket recorder (see **figure 3.6**). But for a professional recording of a live band, you'd also want to mic instruments individually, which could probably require as many as twenty mics or more recorded to individual tracks.

The choice and placement of a microphone dramatically influences the sound you're recording. Even if you are using a sample, someone has

FIGURE 3.4. **The Moss Landing Band, carefully "balancing" themselves around a single microphone.**

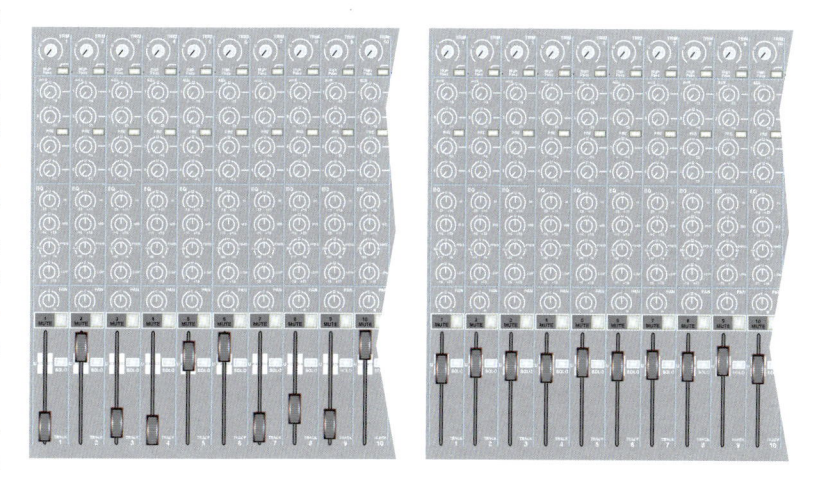

FIGURE 3.5. **A problematic-looking sound balance** (*left*) **and a good-looking balance** (*right*).

recorded it at some stage with a microphone, which would have affected its tonality, presence, and character.

Finally, it's helpful to understand a little about the much bandied-about term "frequency response," which is essentially a measurement of the consistency across the audio spectrum that a microphone is capable of "hearing" and thus passing on.

On the one hand, a "flat" (undistorted) frequency response would seem to be the goal of any mic, and to some extent it obviously is. But award-winning mic designer Jackie Green, from Audio-Technica, provides this refreshing alternative viewpoint.

Jackie Green:

> Frequency response is important. These are exaggerated cases in point, but if we record with a mic lacking above 3 kHz, it might sound dull . . . And if the mic is lacking below 500 Hz, it would sound very thin . . . And a mic lacking both high and low frequencies has an effect we put up with every day of our lives (it's called the telephone).
>
> On the other hand, if one mic has a response quirk you like, or that makes a particular audio source sound good, then go with it. It's all down to individual taste.
>
> If there was such a thing as the perfect mic, that would be the only one out there.

FIGURE 3.6. **A Yamaha Pocketrak PR7 handheld recorder. Photo courtesy of Yamaha.**

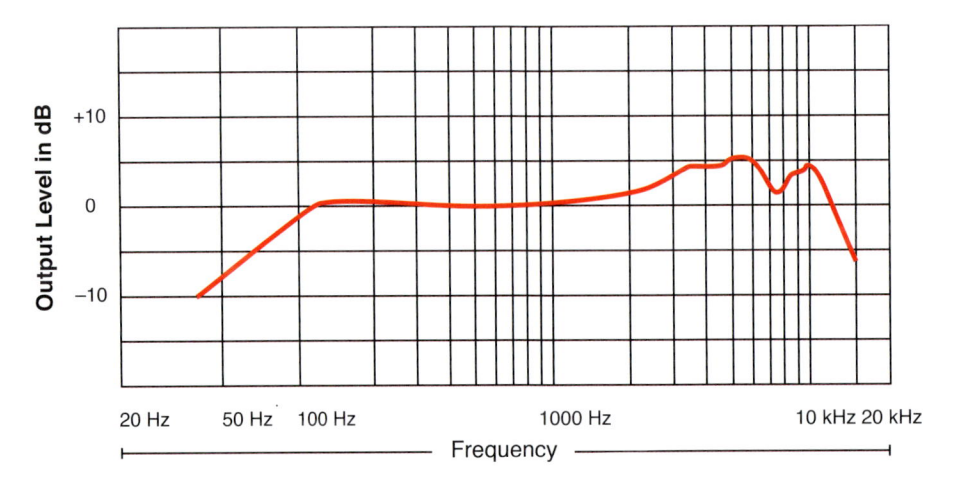

FIGURE 3.7. **The frequency response of a classic dynamic microphone. This tells you that it's not going to handle ultra-high frequencies very well but it is solid in the mid and high range. This should be good for live vocals . . . and indeed this is the graph of a Shure SM58—a classic choice for live work.**

Microphone Types

Sound can be converted into electrical pulses in many ways, which is why there are several fundamentally different types of mic in existence, each operating on different principles. In simple terms, almost all current mics fall into one of three main types, based upon the technology they employ:

The *condenser mic* (see **figure 3.8**) relies on the change of capacitance between a diaphragm and a fixed electrode. Condenser mics are sometimes called capacitor mics. The sound source causes the diaphragm to vibrate, changing the capacitance. This causes a variation in an externally applied electric current, which is then converted into electrical pulses.

So condenser mics need to be powered. This can be with an external power supply or an internal battery. Most commonly, power is supplied by the console or recording hardware via the mic's own cable. This method or system is called "phantom power" (see **figure 3.9**).

Condenser mics have excellent frequency response with low distortion and noise. They used to be considered rather fragile, largely because they contained valves or tubes, but modern solid-state designs are much more robust and are even suitable for live work.

Condenser mics fall into two broad categories: *polarized* and *electret*. Mics using the polarized principle include the classic vintage valve or tube microphones by Telefunken, AKG, and Neumann (see **figure 3.10**). The electret was developed in the early 1960s and is often associated with low-cost mics for use in modern telephones and communication devices. Interestingly, the electret principle is also used by manufacturers of very high-quality studio microphones, notably AKG and Audio-Technica. The large diaphragm on this type of condenser mic gives it a better signal-to-noise ratio than a typical "small" diaphragm design offers. Large diaphragm condensers have more mass, tend to sound smoother, and are generally associated with higher quality.

Small diaphragm condensers, on the other hand, react very quickly to sound changes; in other words, they are good at handling transient or "attacky" sounds, which is why you often see them used on sources containing a lot of detailed high end, such as cymbals and acoustic guitar.

The Audio-Technica AT4033 is a great general-purpose mic. With a higher output level than many other condensers and a slightly enhanced top end response, it's great for many vocal applications.

The Neumann KM 84 (see **figure 3.11**) small capsule condenser mic has been a favorite of mine for years, particularly for snare drum and acoustic guitar. Its small size makes it easy to squeeze into tight spaces on a drum kit.

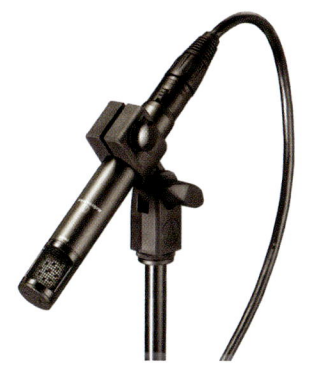

FIGURE 3.8. **An Audio-Technica condenser mic. Photo courtesy of Audio-Technica.**

FIGURE 3.9. **The phantom power button on a console.**

FIGURE 3.10. **Neumann U 87 and U 89 condenser mics. Photo courtesy of Neumann.**

FIGURE 3.11. **A Neumann KM 84 small capsule condenser mic. Photo courtesy of Neumann.**

FIGURE 3.12. **An Audio-Technica boundary mic, which uses the electret principle. Photo courtesy of Audio-Technica.**

FIGURE 3.13. **A Shure SM58 dynamic mic. Photo courtesy of Shure.**

An extension of the condenser electret principle is the so-called boundary mic (see **figure 3.12**). These somewhat strange-looking mics are designed to be surface-mounted and can be used on anything from pianos to kick drums or attached to walls, windows, or floors in a theater. They thrive on high sound-pressure levels. Crown developed the first boundary microphone in the 1980s and trademarked the name PZM, which stands for "Pressure Zone Microphone."

A pair of Radio Shack PZMs were used to record the grand piano on *Gaudi* by the Alan Parsons Project. Both mics were mounted under the soundboard and held on with trusty gaffer tape (duct tape). PZM or boundary mics shouldn't be confused with piezoelectric pickups commonly used for acoustic guitars, which aren't strictly speaking microphones.

Dynamic mics work on the electromagnetic principle mentioned earlier, where the movement of a coil around a magnet translates into an electrical output. Dynamics are generally more rugged than condensers.

Although dynamic mics are used for studio recording, they are still very much the staple for live work and none more so than the SM57 and SM58 from Shure. The SM57 dynamic microphone has become the industry standard snare drum mic, both live and in the studio. Its brother, the SM58 (see **figure 3.13**), is an extremely versatile mic—Shure used to claim you could even hammer nails with it, but less controversially, the 58 is a fail-safe favorite for live vocals. Even in this age of accessibly priced large capsule condenser mics, some people swear by the SM58 for studio work too. At $100 or so it's a real bargain.

Engineer and producer Sylvia Massy once told a wonderful story about her experience with an SM58:

> I have a fantastic Telefunken U 47, which I love for vocals. However, I find one of the greatest mics made is an SM58.
>
> I was working with Rick Rubin on some Smashing Pumpkins music, and Billy Corgan wanted to try some different mics for his voice. So we rented and brought in about thirty different choices of mics, including my Telefunken. We had a Telefunken 251, we had an M 49, we had U 87s, U 67s—the whole thing, including a SM57 and a SM58 and a Sennheiser 421.
>
> We put them all in a row and had him sing the same verse with each mic on a separate track, and then did a blindfold test and listened to each of the mics afterward. And the winner was the SM58 out of all of them. There were, you know, $30,000 worth of mics, and the best mic for his voice was the $100 mic.

Moral of the story: Trust your ears. The right mic for the job may not always be the expensive one.

In the studio world, as far as dynamic mics are concerned, the Austrian manufacturer AKG has a huge range of excellent options, which are very popular, particularly for the recording of drums. (See **figure 3.14.**)

Ribbon mics operate on the principle of a thin, metallic membrane or "ribbon" vibrating between magnets producing an electrical voltage. Like dynamics, ribbon mics do not require a power source, but their sound output level is relatively low. They are also inherently rather fragile. The reversible principle applies as with dynamics, but don't try it—you'll almost certainly fracture the ribbon.

Alan:

> Trust me. I inadvertently plugged a ribbon mic into an output socket and blew it to pieces!

FIGURE 3.14. An AKG D190E dynamic mic.

Even though they've enjoyed a big resurgence in recent years, the heyday of ribbon mics was in the 1940s, when the image of large, desktop-mounted mics, predominantly made by American manufacturer RCA (see **figure 3.15**), became synonymous with radio broadcasting. To some extent, ribbon mics were overshadowed by condensers, largely due to the ribbon mic's somewhat limited high-frequency response. When a warm sound is called for, they're wonderful; but in general, they lack top end, even if, to some extent, this can be compensated for with EQ. Ribbons have what has come to be thought of as a "vintage character." The polar pattern of a ribbon mic is usually figure eight, and we'll come to exactly what that means in a moment.

Polar Patterns

The distance between a microphone and the source you want to pick up has a considerable influence on the sound. If it's too far away, it may pick up sounds you don't want, like other instruments or the neighbor's vacuum cleaner; distance also affects the tone (see "Mic Characteristics," below). If it's too close, it may sound characterless, or certain frequencies may be unnaturally boosted. All microphones inherently have directional characteristics—in other words, the field which they will "hear" and pick up sound from. Some pick up from all around, some just from the front, others from in front and behind . . .

FIGURE 3.15. An RCA 44-BX ribbon microphone, which was ubiquitous in 1940s radio. Photo courtesy of Dave Josephson.

This directional characteristic of a microphone is called its *polar pattern*.

It seems obvious to say that you want a mic to pick up only the sound you want to record, but microphones aren't choosy. They'll record anything they hear.

Fortunately, the microphone's polar pattern gives you fairly decent control over what that is. A polar pattern defines the region or field around the mic where it is most sensitive. Anything outside the most sensitive area in the polar pattern—or "off-axis," as we say—will either be reduced in level, or at times literally rejected.

There are four main types of polar pattern, all of which have rather nicely descriptive names: cardioid, hypercardioid, figure eight, and omnidirectional (or "omni" for short). A polar diagram (see **figure 3.16**) is a graphic representation of a microphone's polar pattern, displaying its output level at positions all the way around its center axis.

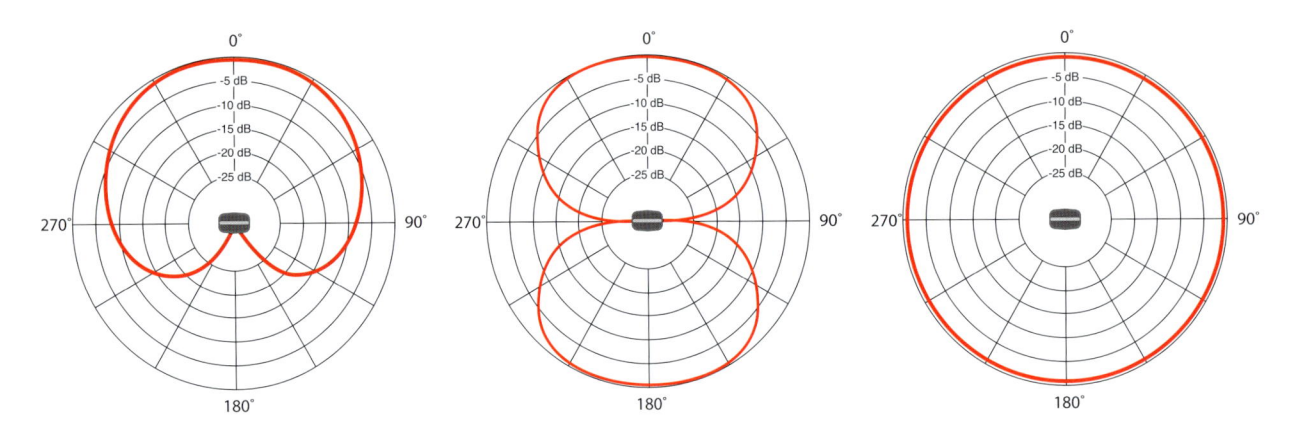

FIGURE 3.16. Polar diagrams for three kinds of mics/polar patterns. A cardioid mic/polar pattern (left) shows maximum output at the front, decreasing as the source moves sideways in either direction. Its minimum output is when the source is at the back. A figure eight mic/polar pattern (center) shows equal maximum output level at both the front and back, while sources at the sides are minimized. An omni mic/polar pattern (right) has an equal output no matter which direction the source comes from.

Cardioid mics produce a loosely heart-shaped polar pattern, as the name suggests. They are loudest at the front and quietest at the back, and their sensitivity will gradually reduce almost to nothing as you move off-axis from the intended pickup area. As you go toward the mic's more sensitive area at the front, the level will increase again to maximum.

Dynamic mics are generally cardioid. Condenser mics can be fixed cardioid or switchable from cardioid to omni or figure eight, which can substantially enhance the range of applications the mic can be used for. The Audio-Technica 4050 is an example (see **figure 3.17**).

Hypercardioid mics are similar to cardioid mics, but offer extreme rejection off-axis. The so-called shotgun mics you see around TV news camera crews and bird-watchers have hypercardioid polar patterns. Sometimes a parabolic reflective dish helps produce a clear focus on the chosen direction. The hypercardioid polar pattern normally offers an inferior frequency response, but this usually isn't a problem for the intended applications.

Figure eight mics pick up sound from the front and back, but reject sound from the sides. You'd look for a figure eight mic if you wanted to capture both the direct source of a sound and its reflection. Ribbon mics are normally fixed at figure eight. A figure eight pattern also works well for two singers standing opposite each other.

Omnidirectional mics pick up sound from all around. These mics tend to offer the best frequency response. If you wanted to record a group of singers gathered around the mic, or capture room ambience, or a live audience, you'd most likely want to use an omnidirectional mic.

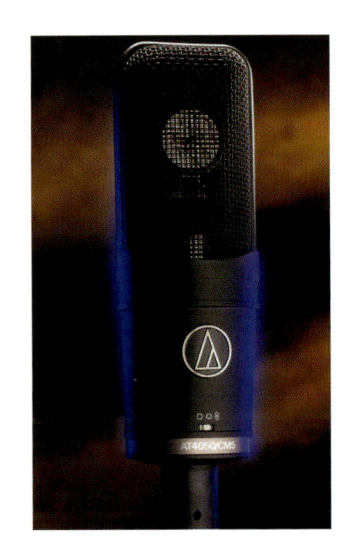

FIGURE 3.17. An Audio-Technica 4050, a condenser mic that can switch among cardioid, omni, or figure eight polar patterns. Photo courtesy of Audio-Technica.

The polar pattern is a very important consideration both when using and, crucially, when buying a mic. If you're buying a vintage mic with no documentation, you can probably go online and find information about its polar pattern including its polar diagram.

Dynamic Range and Sensitivity

Dynamic range is the ratio between the softest and loudest signal detected. Human ears have an accepted dynamic range of about 120 decibels (dB). That covers the difference in level between an explosion and a pin drop. It's a somewhat sobering thought to consider, then, that rock music typically has a dynamic range of around 12 dB. Heavily compressed material might only vary by 2 dB, a barely perceptible amount.

Under most circumstances we want a microphone to be capable of recording the softest and subtlest of sounds, but not to curl up and die if it hears something cataclysmically loud, like a bombastic cymbal crash combined with a fortissimo thump on a bass drum.

Condenser mics generally offer the best dynamic range and frequency response. The length and quality of mic cable you use can influence both. Long cable runs—and this goes for a guitar cable as well as a mic cable—will invariably result in the loss of high frequencies. A very good rule is "Keep your cable as short as possible."

In general, condenser mics produce a higher output level than dynamic mics. Another way of putting this is to say they have high sensitivity. This makes them particularly suitable for recording quiet sounds or sounds that vary drastically in level. If you simply turn up a dynamic mic to compensate for low volume at the source, you're going to add a lot of noise along with it. In other words, the *signal-to-noise ratio*, as we call it, is going to be worse. Orchestral music tends to have a much wider range; you'll almost never see a dynamic mic on a classical recording session, because of their limited dynamic range and signal-to-noise ratio, compared with condensers.

Condenser mics often have switchable pads or attenuators (effectively, volume reducers) that prevent overload at the mic's internal circuitry when they are exposed to a very loud sound source. If you're using a condenser mic on a snare drum, you would definitely want to apply the pad, which effectively reduces its sensitivity.

Dynamic mics, on the other hand, are very tolerant of high sound pressure levels. However, if they're recording a quiet instrument, you'll have to make up the gain elsewhere, thus increasing the noise.

What comes with experience is knowing which mics have the right sensitivity and dynamic range for the intended purpose. Audio-Technica mics tend to produce higher outputs than their Neumann or AKG counterparts and are therefore eminently suitable for sources with large dynamic ranges. Wide dynamics can also be reined in by the performer's own mic technique—in other words, moving closer to the mic for quiet passages and away for loud ones. Another solution is the application of audio limiting and compression (see "Compressors and Limiters," Chapter 9).

Mic Characteristics

The relationship between a microphone and its distance from the sound source is critical and complex. Not only will the distance between mic and sound source affect the mic's output level, it will also affect its tone, sometimes in quite surprising ways. When a microphone is positioned very close to its source, it will tend to accentuate the low frequencies, producing what is called the "proximity effect."

Designers often try to compensate for the proximity effect in their products, although sometimes this very intimate close-up effect is exactly what we want—say, for the "In a world . . ." movie trailer voice or the deeply personal radio DJ, when the desired effect is to sound superhumanly warm and enveloping.

There's another related, but almost always unwanted, close proximity recording phenomenon called "popping." This is when sounds that have hard front ends—particularly P's, where air gushes out of your mouth in a sort of audio explosion—can produce an exaggerated thump or "pop" that is very uncomfortable to listen to.

There are various ways to avoid this. One is simply to place a finger in between your mouth and the mic, which is not really very practical, of course, on television, but incredibly effective in the audio recording studio. Try this: Say "Peter Piper" with the back of your hand six inches in front of your mouth. You can feel the pops on your hand, right? Now try saying "Peter Piper" again, with a finger held three inches in front of your mouth. In reality, a quarter-inch dowel suspended in front of the mic works well in the audio studio. Another solution is to place a purpose-made foam or metal mesh pop shield over the mic grille (see **figure 3.18**).

There are many types of pop shield, from the commercially manufactured circular frame holding a layer of acoustically transparent nylon mesh, to the equally effective rough and ready, hastily removed pantyhose stretched over a coat hanger (see **figure 3.19**). If you don't have any additional paraphernalia available, sing or speak slightly across the mic as opposed to directly into it, especially on a problem word or phrase, but without moving any further away. Microphone designers try to reduce popping artifacts in their products—especially for mics intended for live use. Some condenser mics produce such severe pops that they are virtually useless for vocals.

Another unwanted artifact is rumbles produced by foot tapping or other extraneous vibrations. In recent years, elasticated cradles have become quite the fashion, effectively isolating the mic from the stand.

Pops and rumbles can be dealt with "after the event" with the use of high-pass filters, which you can read about in Chapter 8. But as ever, it's better to nip the problem in the bud if you can, so you don't have to deal with a problem later.

FIGURE 3.18. **A commercial mesh pop shield. Photo courtesy of Shure.**

FIGURE 3.19. **A homemade pop shield, made from repurposed pantyhose and a hanger.**

Phase

Another important characteristic of a microphone is its phase relationship (see glossary) with other microphones. Two microphones might be totally or partly out of phase with each other, causing a drop in level at certain frequencies, or a "phase cancellation," as we call it. When in phase, the outputs of two mics at the same distance from the source, and panned hard left and right, will be added together, and the sound will appear to be coming from the exact center between the speakers. Pressing the phase button found on most consoles or workstations on one of the mic channels produces a very strange effect: the source will now seem to be coming from outside the speakers. Trained engineers can spot this a mile off.

In the *Art & Science of Sound Recording* video series, we provide a demonstration of this. If you switch the mics to mono, you'll get an entirely different effect when you reverse the phase. The phase reversal is canceling out all the low frequencies, producing a very thin result.

In-phase/out-of-phase can also be used practically and creatively. If you have one or more mics with a phase difference between each other—on drums, for example—you might find that you get a good result by switching the phase relationship between the mics. Sylvia Massy once described her favored process thus:

Sylvia:

> When I'm miking toms, I like to have a mic on both the top head and bottom head and flip them out of phase, and use the top mic for the attack of the drum, and the bottom mic for the body of the drum.
>
> I think if you're not really paying attention to the phase of the drums when you're recording, there is a hollowness in the sound of the drums and the relationship between the different mics. If you want the best, punchiest sound, it's much more than just the microphones and the mic pres and the EQ; it's really the relationship between each individual mic on the drum.

Alan:

> During our conversation, I wondered whether there is any particular relationship between the phase of, say, the kick and the snare and the overheads or other drums?

Sylvia:

> After I set up my miking scheme for a drum kit, I'll carefully go through each mic, starting with the kick drum and muting all the other mics on the drum kit. And I'll listen to that kick drum along with one of the overheads put into center in mono, and I'll compare phase in and out, the phase button on the channel, just to see which way sounds better.

So, deliberate phase inversions are one thing, but accidental reversals are probably not going to produce a good result, so be aware that a reversal of phase can also happen in a cable. In this case, the phase button on your console or DAW is the quickest solution. That said, it's a good idea to make sure all the cables in your studio are wired the same way (see **figure 3.20**).

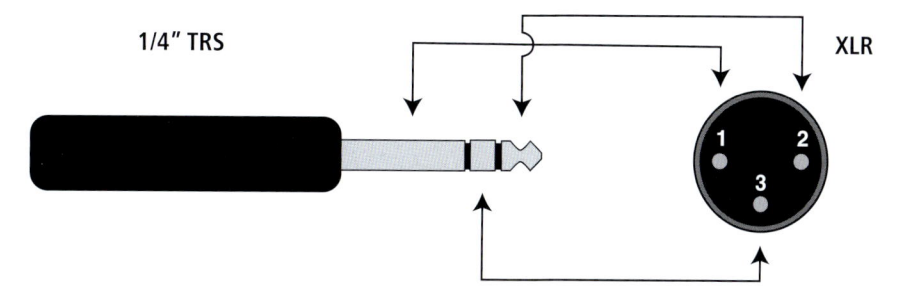

FIGURE 3.20. **Diagram showing how cables can be wired. Be consistent in your wiring to avoid phase reversals or, in some cases, loss of output. This XLR wiring to the US is standard—pin 2 "hot." There is also a pin 3 "hot" standard which can cause unwanted phase reversals or even complete loss of signal.**

Philosophies of Mic Placement

Mic placement is one of the most important skills a recording engineer needs to learn. You need to consider not only the inherent sound of the instrument or group of instruments you want to capture, but also whether you want to reject other instruments playing at the same time, or extraneous noise.

The ability to exclude or reject unwanted sounds is what engineers call "separation." Good separation means the mic only picks up the intended source, while bad separation means other instruments or sources will, as we say, "bleed through." A tried and tested technique for improving separation is to place screens or "gobos" between instruments. Screens are normally made of absorptive material and sometimes contain glass panels so musicians can still see each other.

Close-miking will increase the chances of getting good separation, but it might also yield a lifeless sound that doesn't breathe. Quieter instruments like acoustic guitar against a hell-for-leather drum kit will always be a problem, and that's when we might consider putting the guitarist into his or her own "isolation booth." Virtually all commercial facilities will offer one or more isolation areas for this purpose. In a home studio, you might want to consider putting a quiet instrument in your sister's bedroom or the bathroom or whatever. You can also consider adding the problem instrument later as an overdub. Whether to close-mike or to mike at a distance to take the natural ambience of the room into consideration is a matter of taste and fashion.

The sound you hear from a drum kit acoustically might be very different from the sound you want to hear on the recording. If you only use close mics on a kit, it will sound relatively small and intimate. If you want to increase the size of the sound, you'll need to add artificial processing, such as reverb or delays. Or . . . you could simply move the mics further away, but that might be result in a separation problem with other instruments. Whether this is important or not is where taste and fashion comes into the picture.

On a drum kit, overhead mics not only serve the purpose of picking up the cymbals, but will also add ambience and "size." If we were in a cathedral-like reverberant building and wanted to capture the sound and atmosphere of that environment, a mic placed close to the source would not give us a true representation of that environment. We either need to move the mic or mics far enough away to capture both instrument and environment, or alternately, to add a pair of "ambience" mics to record the room sound separately in stereo. We'd then have the option of mixing the close and ambient components to achieve the best blend for the recording.

One advantage of overdubbing (adding an instrument or part at a later stage) is that the separation problem is eliminated, because all previously recorded instruments are only heard over headphones and not acoustically. In some cases, overdubbing might compromise the feeling of the interaction between a number of instrumentalists playing together. The counterargument is that a clean overdubbed part with the mic in an ideal position will sound better and improve the overall sonic experience.

Many bands will insist that the basic backing track be captured live. This was the case on *Let It Be*, where the Beatles' intention (at least in the original sessions, until Phil Spector got his hands on the tapes) was to record absolutely everything for each song, including vocals, in a single take. Mic placement was absolutely crucial.

Alan:

> I remember Glyn Johns, the engineer on those sessions, explaining to me why he had angled George's guitar mic and amp away from the drums. It seems obvious to me now, but at the time it was "Wow—will that really make a difference?"

> Most of the basic rhythm tracks for *Dark Side of the Moon* were recorded with the four members of Pink Floyd in the live room together, while I remained in the control room on my ownsome. Some of the basic parts got replaced, of course, and there were endless overdubs, but I maintain that some of the magic of the album was created as a result of four people playing and interacting together.

How Many Mics Do We Need?

Some of the best orchestral and choral recordings have been made with just a single stereo pair of mics. There are special mounts for what we call a *stereo coincident pair*. In its most basic form, a stereo pair picks up the left signal from one direction and the right signal from the other. The two directions are commonly 90 degrees apart, and the mics are mounted right next to each other (see **figure 3.21**).

Some manufacturers make mics with a pair of mics in a single enclosure (see **figure 3.22**). Most engineers believe pairs of mics should be closely matched.

Another equally minimalist approach is the Mid-Side miking technique, or MS for short. It's an interesting way of recording an ensemble or a group of singers. This technique involves one mic being aimed at the center front of the ensemble and a figure eight mic directly above it or below it, at an angle of 90 degrees to the front mic. Once the audio is recorded, we combine the signals of the two mics added together and panned to one side with the same signals *subtracted* from each other by reversing the phase relationship and panned to the other side. This produces an amazing stereo spread effect. We used the MS technique when recording a choir for the *ASSR* video series, and you can read more about that in Chapter 21.

For rock and pop recording, is the more the merrier? Or do we really need so much choice? It's a question we put to Audio-Technica's Jackie Green.

Jackie:

> You don't need a hundred thousand different types of microphones, and a more experienced engineer can do a lot more with few mics. The price more or less represents what you're getting, but not necessarily. I've heard some really expensive microphones that I really was disappointed with, and I've heard some very inexpensive microphones that we said, "Wow, that actually sounded pretty nice—that actually did some pretty cool stuff."

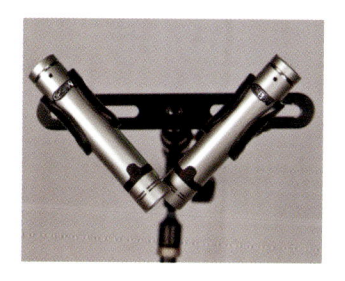

FIGURE 3.21. **A stereo coincident pair of mics. Photo courtesy of Miktek Audio.**

FIGURE 3.22. **An Audio-Technica stereo mic. Photo courtesy of Audio-Technica.**

During the making of the video series, we also visited self-confessed gear junkie John McBride at his legendary Blackbird Studios in Nashville. In addition to recording his wife, Martina McBride, there John has seen his studio and equipment emporium frequented by such varied acts as the White Stripes, Bon Jovi,

Carrie Underwood, Mariah Carey, Kid Rock, Faith Hill, and many more. John's mic closet—and actually, he has several—would surely be the envy of any engineer or producer. But does that mean you have to have this type of collection to make good records? This is what John has to say on the subject:

> We look at the engineer or the artist and the producer as painters, and I want to be able to give them every color on the palette. If there's a certain sound they're looking for, I want them to be able to achieve it here. I don't want them to ever be limited by the studio. So that means thousands of different pieces of outboard gear, if they're ever looking for suggestions. You know, we can say we've tried this and this and this, or you know, they'll ask about a particular record that was cut here, what did they do on the kick drum there, and we're able to say, well, they used an RCA 44 with a Telefunken mic pre or an RCA mic pre and such and such an EQ, and there you have it.

Necessity is almost always the mother of invention, and it's extremely important to grasp the fact that recording rules are always made to be broken. Especially mic choices. Jackie Green again:

> We had one guy who wanted to know why we discontinued one of our drum mics. And I said, "Well, we've got this other microphone now. It's good." He said, "Oh, but it was the best voice-over mic I ever used." And I said, "That's a kick drum mic!"

The old school would say, if it's a mono source, you only need one mic. But with the advent of stereo in pop and rock, it became important to make a stereo picture "better" than early stereo Beatles releases, for example, where the instruments were on the left and the vocals on the right—almost laughable by today's standards.

The demands of the stereo-hungry consumer and now the surround consumer might influence our decision to record instruments with multiple microphones, to spread the sound throughout the listening environment. You can have a dream mic cabinet, but if you don't know how to use it, you'll get nowhere. Similarly, you can have a very modest inventory of mics, but if you are knowledgeable and creative, you can work wonders. If you're going to be recording a lot of vocals, it's always worth spending money on a high-quality condenser, which you can always use on other instruments as well.

Many companies make copies of classic mics, which may well be an economical way to get close to their sound. Secondhand mics are also a possibility, and it's well worth searching on eBay if you are looking for a particular model.

If a mic has a good reputation, it's probably justified. Check magazines for what the popular mics of the moment are. If you have a good relationship with an audio dealer, he will probably lend you a mic so you can try it out.

There are more SM58s out there than any other mic. Ask yourself why. Modern mics are unlikely to perform badly. If it's working, it's working.

Alan:

> Not like my early years at Abbey Road, where it was almost a certainty that a mic or its preamp would go noisy, or we would lose a power supply at some point on a session.

However, it's wise to look out for excessive moisture buildup on a close-up vocal mic, which can adversely affect the sound and in fact do permanent damage. That said, there are always replaceable components to bring a mic back to top-notch performance. Mics (and headphones) often grow legs. Always check your inventory and keep them locked up.

So what constitutes a good mic?

The textbook answer is a flat response: a mic that picks up every frequency without being selective and that doesn't emphasize any particular frequency and has no distortion.

Jackie Green's definition is:

> A good mic actually lets you get the sound you're expecting to hear. It lets you capture whatever it is you're trying to capture. We've got a little microphone. It's a little omni thing, and maybe it costs ten dollars. It's a good mic because it's very good under certain circumstances to do a specific thing.

Generally speaking, with the passage of time we have increased the number of mics we use to record with. Alan:

> The console on which the Beatles recorded *Sgt. Pepper's* [on 4-track tape] only allowed for eight microphones. When 8-track and then 16-track and 24-track came along, accompanied by much bigger consoles with more inputs, we were more inclined to use more mics.

Drums could now justifiably put into stereo, and each individual instrument could be separately recorded with its own mic, rather than being lumped in with other surrounding instruments as a section. Vocal harmonies could get recorded with one mic per singer, instead of the group gathering round a single mic.

More control equals more choices, and more choices equals more time needed to make those choices. So whether this is unequivocally "progress" is the subject of endless debate.

Mic Choices

Miking technique is an art if not a book in itself, and we spoke about this with several highly successful engineers and producers, amongst them David Thoener, whose credits include AC/DC, Santana (David recorded "Smooth"), and Bon Jovi.

David Thoener:

> I started in a time before all this technology existed, and you had to tune the instrument, mic the instrument properly with the right microphone, and start there. And that's still how I work—not: immediately go to the equalizer, just throw any mic in front of the instrument, and then go to the equalizer and make it sound right. Never. I go to the equalizer absolutely last. If it doesn't sound right, I change microphones, I change mic placement, change the instrument, change the amp out.

Multiple pop hit producer John Fields had this to say:

> We all know there's a difference. When you sing, if you want to sit there and A/B five vocal mics, one of them is going to be the best. But I'd rather have already finished the

> song by then. I mean, not to say that I don't experiment, but I know that it's not that big a deal and that you can EQ out. If something is too bright, just turn down the treble, and if something is not bright enough, turn up the treble. I have been backed into a corner sometimes, when you're with, like, a superstar vocal and you only have an hour. You can't A/B, you don't have time. You'd rather spend that five minutes getting vocal takes on maybe a mic that's not sufficient, but will work.
>
> I'm the guy who says, "What's the closet mic? We're going to record a dobro, take that upper tom mic, and just swing it over."

There's certainly nothing wrong with experimentation if the artist or session can accept that. If you're in a high-pressure situation, or your budget is limited, then you'll probably have to make choices based on past experience. There's nothing worse than disrupting a session because of indecision over a mic choice.

Alan:

> I've certainly spent many hours with finicky artists trying different vocal mics, all of which sound remarkably similar, and I have to say I felt it was a waste of time. Some people feel they need to go through every mic available, but I venture to suggest otherwise. OK, I'll come out and say it: That's ridiculous!

Mic Pres

Mic pre is short for microphone preamplifier. The electrical voltage produced by a microphone is very small and has to be amplified from a few millivolts up to about half a volt to be useful to the console or interface. The amount of amplification needed depends on the type of microphone. As we said earlier, condenser mics are inherently the loudest.

Consoles normally have the ability to accept mic inputs directly with their own onboard mic pres, but in recent years there's been a movement to sell mic pres as external boxes. Manufacturers are very quick to claim their product will sound better than the one already built into a console, or maybe to say it is a clone or copy of one built into what is now considered a "classic" console. This has increased the number of choices we have to make. Now, not only do we have to choose the mic, but we also have to choose the mic pre.

Alan:

> I personally feel that using a lot of external mic pres at the same time is a nuisance, as it gives you too many knobs to twiddle, which can detract from other things you should be thinking about, such as the original sound or the performance.

If you don't have a desk, then obviously a stand-alone mic pre does becomes a vital link in the chain. Some consoles might have an insert point bypassing the console's own preamp stage. The nice thing about external mic pres is that you can carry your favorite mics and mic pre combinations around with you from studio to studio. Some mic pres also contain high-quality analog-to-digital converters, which again might have particular characteristics you like, so you won't be stuck in a studio with a converter that you don't like.

Mic/Instrument Choices

If a mic delivers the result you want or were looking for, then you made the right choice. But it's hard sometimes to know where to begin, so here are some hopefully useful starting-off points:

- **Vocal:** Neumann U 47, U 48, U 67, or for lower budgets, Audio-Technica AT4033, AT4050, or even a Shure SM58.
- **Piano:** Neumann U 87, AKG C12. You might consider a dynamic mic if you're going for particularly hard sound.
- **Acoustic Guitar:** Neumann KM 84, Neumann U 87. Avoid dynamic mics unless you want a hard sound.
- **Electric Guitar Cabinet:** Shure SM57, Neumann KM 86, Audio-Technica AT4050.
- **Bass Guitar Cabinet:** AKG C12 (a classic Abbey Road choice).
- **Solo Sax:** Neumann U 87, 86. Don't stick the mic on the horn—get the whole instrument from a couple of feet away.
- **Brass Section:** Neumann U 87, U 86 (or a ribbon mic: STC/Coles 4038).
- **Solo Violin:** Any large diaphragm condenser: Neumann U 47, U 67, Audio-Technica AT4050. A dynamic might make strings sound tinny.
- **Violin/Viola (section):** Neumann KM 86 or KM 84.
- **Cellos/Double Basses:** Neumann U 87, Audio-Technica AT4050.
- **Woodwind and Percussion:** Neumann KM 84, Audio-Technica AT4033.
- **Drums:** For rock, you generally want to use at least as many mics as there are drums. For jazz (and light music like Broadway musicals), maybe you can use just three or four.
- **Kick Drum:** AKG D20, D112. (The crucial thing is the punch. A dynamic mic has a better reputation for this.) You need a mic that can handle transients.
- **Snare:** Neumann KM 84, Shure SM57.
- **Toms:** AKG D190. D202. (A lot of Beatles recordings used the D19, the predecessor of the D190.)
- **Overheads:** STC/Coles 4038, AKG 414.
- **Hi-Hat:** Neumann KM 84, KM 86.
- **Steel Drums:** Good luck! These are legendarily hard to record, as the sound is inherently distorted and you can't get any bite. Often they sound like they're coming through a wall of cotton wool.

CONSOLES AND CONTROLLERS

Alan:

> One day when we were filming the *Art & Science of Sound Recording* video series, I'd been interviewing the young and extremely successful producer John Fields, when at the end of the interview, he said: "Would you like to see the board you used on *Dark Side of the Moon*? It's just down the road at my friend's studio."
>
> Not having seen it in thirty-five years, I leapt at the chance to reacquaint myself with this classic console, now living in a Los Angeles studio some six thousand miles away from Abbey Road Studios, where once its circuitry had indeed injected magic into the sound of Pink Floyd, Paul McCartney, and a host of legendary artists of the 1970s and 1980s. It was quite a moving experience to see it again.

There's endless speculation as to why these artists and those records sounded the way they did. Was it the analog tape machines? Was it the desk? The studio? The engineer? The songwriting? The playing? Of course, the truth is, it was a combination of all these things.

One certainty is that as soon as multitrack recording became widely available in the 1960s, the only way those multiple tracks could be mixed down to a mono or stereo tape for duplication was to use some form of track combining on a mixing desk or recording console—the terms are fairly interchangeable. "Board" and "mixer" are also sometimes used, but a "mixer" can also be a piece of DJ gear, or Bob Clearmountain, of course.

Analog Versus Digital Hardware

You can still find analog consoles in major recording studios, although they are tending to become analog/digital hybrids these days. In some studios, you'll find an all-digital console or possibly a Digital Audio Workstation controller. All of these tend to look similar, with row upon row of faders and knobs, and indeed they do perform many of the same functions. But there are crucial differences.

The biggest difference concerns how the audio is being processed and then output. On an analog console, the audio is a series of analog electrical pulses (a microphone's output or a guitar pickup, for example, passing through the circuitry), which remains analog all the way to the final output.

On a digital console, those electrical pulses get digitized as soon as they are received and converted into what we call "the digital domain," as a stream of ones and zeros.

As digital recording developed, it wasn't long before the recording of audio reached the world of the personal computer, complete with graphical representations of mixing desks or virtual consoles on the screen—thus, the Digital Audio Workstation was born. This was particularly attractive and very cost-effective for home studios, but it wasn't so practical in terms of the challenge of mixing hundreds of tracks of audio with a mouse.

The DAW controller simply acts as a front-end control surface—a set of dummy knobs and faders, if you will—for the processing that's actually taking place inside the computer. Unlike the circuitry of an analog console, no audio actually passes through a controller.

Controllers communicate with the computer using either basic MIDI or, more commonly, their own proprietary high-resolution control language. However they communicate, what's important is that the control data can be recorded along with the song file, which means the various functions it controls can be recalled and used for automation.

Automation in some form has become a standard part of the mixing process. In the old days, before automation, you might have seen three or four people at a mixing desk, adjusting levels and tweaking effects in real time as the individual tracks were mixed down to a stereo master. If those three or four people happened to be members of the band, invariably the fader they'd be moving up (rarely down) would be their own instrument! As individual faders went up, the engineer would be pulling down the main stereo bus fader. Chaos was inevitable!

Green Day and John Mayer producer Jack Joseph Puig feels you can't overestimate the importance of recall and automation:

> Automation has become very important, because at this point in time, "recall" is something that everybody in the world wants to do and does. I think I would give the Grammy to [console manufacturer] SSL. I'd give two Grammys to SSL.

Not surprisingly, Jack works on a massive SSL.

> The one beautiful aspect of this console is the fact that it's recallable—every button, every switch, every knob, every send, etc. And that's the whole reason I'm working on this particular desk at this point.

Nowadays, countless records are made, as we say, "in the box." Because of the automation possibilities, it really is possible to mix a complex record with a mouse. But having said that, if you've ever experienced mixing on a large surface controller or a full-blown console, it's hard to go back. There's just something about that touchy-feely experience that suits music recording.

"Mixing in the box has its beauty," says Jack. "There's a certain sound to it. But it's not the same thing as mixing through an analog console. Given the choice, most people would probably pick analog if they could."

David Thoener shared his own thoughts as well:

> If you're going to do a great mix, it can be done in Pro Tools. It can be done totally with plug-ins. It's not the technology that dictates the sound of the record—it's the guy

CONSOLES AND CONTROLLERS | 33

FIGURE 4.1. **Alan at an EMI TG Mark IV console used on the recording of** *Dark Side of the Moon*.

working the technology. Just because it's an analog console doesn't mean you're going to get a great mix. It's the guy working the console.

Wise words indeed.

Analog Versus Digital Consoles—A to D and D to A Converters

The process of how audio gets into an analog desk is fairly straightforward: Mics or instruments are connected directly or via a patch bay. It's easy to see exactly how many inputs you have in front of you. Still, most engineers still label all the sound sources on a strip of masking tape for clarity. Smarter engineers can do without the masking tape and work on fixed conventions—for example, bass always on channel 1, rhythm guitar always on channel 9, and so on.

On digital consoles and controllers, we type in the source names and have them displayed electronically—both on the work surface and on the screen.

However, on a digital console what you see is not necessarily what you get. The issue is where and how the analog-to-digital (A-D) conversion takes place.

A digital console may or may not offer its own A-D converters. If it doesn't, you will have to use external converters; and even if it does, you may still *prefer* to use external converters, some of which have now become highly prized, as well as highly priced.

The quality of your converters will affect the quality of your digitized audio, but as with all recording equipment, your decisions tend to have to walk the tightrope of fashion, budget, and common sense.

There are several so-called "front-end" rack-mount units that offer a mic pre stage, EQ, limiting, compression, and gating in various combinations. They also often include A-D conversion, as well as a regular analog output.

All manufacturers tell you that their front-end box is cleaner, more transparent, and more accurate than anyone else's. In general, you get what you pay for, but beware of salesmen who tell you their box will give you a "night and day" result. The differences will in most cases be subtle. Let your ears be the judge before you commit hard-earned cash to devices based on promises of magical properties. You may find that the same amount is better spent on a good mic.

> *It's a good idea to always place stereo tracks with the left on an odd-numbered track and the right on an even-numbered track. Avoid "Guitar Solo Left" on track 14 and "Guitar Solo Right" on track 23.*

Adding yet more murk into the pond, instruments—notably keyboard workstations—might provide some form of stereo or multichannel digital audio output themselves, using FireWire, USB, or other interface connections.

And here's where you need to be careful: A 24-channel digital console might have twenty-four faders on it, but only, say, sixteen mic inputs and therefore only sixteen A-D converters. Even more extreme, some hybrid digital/analog consoles may offer eight or sixteen analog inputs, but only offer two channels of digital audio conversion into and out of a DAW.

The moral of this cautionary tale is that when looking at any digital or digital-encompassing console, you need to be clear about exactly how many A-D converters it offers and whether it has enough for your purposes. If you are making music essentially by yourself, you may not need many independent converters, because you're only recording one thing at a time. Likewise, if you are comfortable working mainly "in the box"—in other words, adjusting EQs and levels within your computer and DAW—then two channels may be fine. It may be perfectly sufficient for your console to offer only two D-to-A channels that you can configure as an analog stereo output from the DAW to listen to. If you want to mix on an analog console, you'll need as many D-A converters as you have tracks, or groups of tracks.

If you want to record a live backing track, say, or a live drum kit, then you'll need multiple A-D converters to record the output from multiple mics simultaneously. If you want to make use of a lot of outboard processing equipment, or want independent channel control from physical faders, you're looking at multiple channels of conversion. That way, each source can be heard and adjusted independently.

"In the Box" or Analog Summing?

For mixing, a digital console or DAW is quite capable of combining a large number of tracks, remaining in the digital domain for all EQ, effects, and level changes. But analog traditionalists insist that combining tracks together should take place in the analog domain. This is referred to as analog summing.

The counterargument is that the conversion process needed to get the tracks "undigitized" so that they can be combined or mixed in the analog domain, only to be "redigitized" for the final mix is, as we Brits say, a swings and roundabouts situation. In others words: You win some, you lose some.

In the *Art & Science of Sound Recording* video series we conducted an experiment to see how much difference there was between these two approaches. One of the tests at the end of this chapter explains what we did, should you want to come to your own firsthand conclusion.

And not only is it personal, it can also be dependent on the type of music you're recording. Top classical engineer Simon Rhodes, from Abbey Road, had this to say about a similar experiment he conducted:

> I'm afraid there was a certain transparency and depth of the "virtual," which to my mind, for this orchestral recording, was just a hair better than having all the converters and all the summing amps, which for some people are an advantage. But for non–rock 'n' roll recordings—i.e., nice acoustic recordings—it really helped to maintain that pure nemesis that we're heading for! So, I am a fan of working inside the box.

Layouts and Functions of Analog and Digital Mixers

The purpose of both analog and digital mixers is to receive multiple inputs, process each of them individually, and create a recipe that balances them into a unified whole.

Continuing with the cooking analogy, a mixing console takes multiple ingredients and combines them, in what the engineer or producer feels are the correct amounts, in order to serve up a tasty meal. Within each main audio ingredient is a set of its own preparation details, plus seasonings and spices.

Although mixing desks look forbidding to the untrained eye, there's a lot of duplication. For example, a 24-input console typically has twenty-four horizontal "channel strips," as they're called (see **figure 4.2**).

A channel strip is a row of controls that all relate to one input channel. So we don't have to learn what every single button and knob on the console does, because for the most part they are just duplications. Since each channel strip functions the same way, once you've learned one, you've learned them all, and even the most complicated desk won't seem so daunting.

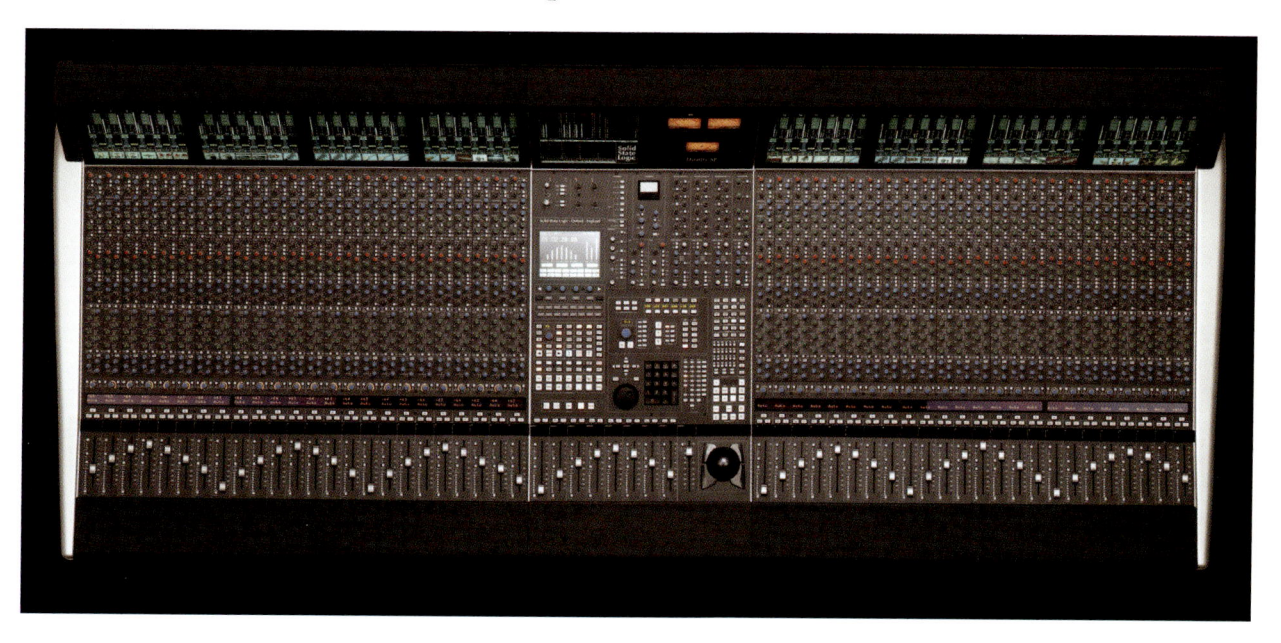

FIGURE 4.2. **The SSL Duality: A large-format analog console. Photo courtesy of SSL.**

Each channel strip offers a quick snapshot of the current state of that channel: namely, its input gain, pan, EQ, and dynamics settings, and whether it is being sent to reverbs or delays, and finally, at the end of the chain, where it is being routed—typically, to tracks on a DAW or tape machine, or to the main stereo bus for a final mix.

Alan:

> The great thing about working on a big analog console is that it gives you a constant stream of information. You can see everything that is being done on every channel. On some digital consoles, you may only get that information one channel at a time.

Channel Strip Layout

Figure 4.2 shows a fairly standard analog console. Here's what each knob on the channel strip does and is used for:

1. **Mic/line switch.** This determines whether we are accepting a signal from a microphone or a high-level source such as a keyboard, effects unit, or tape track.

2. **Phantom power.** This switch will usually be found on channels intended for microphone inputs, to activate the necessary 48-volt power supply to condenser mics and occasionally ribbon mics. It's called "phantom power" because, rather cunningly, the power to the mic is actually carried down the same wires used for its output signal. Some equipment is sensitive to having voltages fed into it, so it is best left switched off if it isn't needed.

3. **Input gain.** This control is a coarse control that determines how much amplification is needed for the console to raise the input source to a volume level it can deal with. We call this the microphone preamp stage or mic pre for short.
   Microphones are low-level sources and need a fair amount of amplification or gain to get them up to the operating level we need. Other low-level sources include the output of a guitar or bass pickup directly off the instrument itself. Of course, a mic on an instrument like a flute will need more gain than a mic on a loud brass instrument. Mic pres can also be external devices, which means they can be fed directly into the console as a line input.

4. **Phase switch.** This reverses the phase of the input. It is required very occasionally to switch the phase relationship between two or more sources, or to correct a signal path that is wired out of phase (two guitar amps with out-of-phase speakers, or a balanced cable wired with the "hot" and "cold" conductors reversed, for example). See Chapter 3 for more about phase.

5. **Dynamics controls.** Controls that govern dynamics—which include limiting, compression, expansion, and noise gating—are a relatively recent addition to consoles. You may like the convenience of being able to rein in dynamics quickly and simply directly on the console itself, or you may prefer to use external devices or plug-in software. (See Chapters 9 and 10 for more info on compressors, limiters, and noise gates.)

6. **Track output.** Bussing or routing switches determine where the channel's sound source is going to end up or where it will be output. Typically, we'll go out to an individual track on a recording device, or to the main stereo bus in the case of a mixing session.

7. **EQ controls.** To the layperson, these are treble, middle, and bass "tone controls." Many of the knobs on a console will be dedicated to equalization, because these are very fundamental adjustments, but adjustments you will probably want to make without too much interruption to the work flow. It is common to find three sets of controls (loosely: low, mid, and high) for frequency, level + or –, and Q (the shape of the EQ curve) in a cluster for each band. There are usually additional controls for high- and low-pass filters. See Chapter 8 for more info on EQ.

8. **Aux Sends.** We usually want to send a signal to other places, as well as to a record track or a stereo mix. Aux sends, or sometimes "echo sends" or "cue sends," are a set of knobs that send the signal out (often, especially on analog systems, via an external patch bay) to reverbs, delays, and effects, for example. Sends are also used to create dedicated mixes for performer's headphones.

   Headphone mixes are important because the performer will most likely want to hear a different balance from what the engineer is hearing. In fact, every musician in a band might want a different balance, which is why many well-equipped studios now tend to put this directly under the control of the individual musicians, with a small headphone mixer. This is a good thing, because the engineer has more time to consider the overall picture without having to worry about getting everyone's mix exactly right.

   Sends are also likely to be used for setting up "stems" for a film dubbing session.

9. **Pre/Post switch.** Both the dynamics and the Aux send sections will have another set of switches marked "Pre/Post." These allow us to send a signal to its designated destination either before it gets to the channel fader or after. This gives you control over whether adjusting the channel fader will alter the amount of signal going to the Aux bus. That's important, because you don't want, say, a monitor mix to change just because a particular sound has been increased or decreased in the main mix. On the other hand, we might want it to do just that—i.e., by increasing the fader level, we might want to also increase the reverb.

10. **Pan control.** The Pan control determines the stereo positioning between far left, far right, dead center, and anywhere in between. Obviously, this needs to be to a stereo destination—for example, a pair of mono tracks panned L and R, a stereo track, or the main stereo mix bus. "Pan" is short for panorama. We can leave sources in one position or, as was fashionable in the seventies, move them around in real time as we did on countless guitar solos at the time.

11. **PFL or Pre-Fade Listen.** The PFL switch allows you to instantly hear a particular channel on your main monitors or in your headphones, regardless of whether the channel fader is up or down. The signal path is arranged so that we can PFL a channel during a recording or mix without affecting the mix itself or the tracks being recorded. PFL activity, in other words, will only be heard during the time it is activated and won't spoil the recording.

12. **The Solo button.** The Solo button is designed to cut all the other channels, so that one or more can be isolated from the rest of the mix or the channels being sent to tracks. Under certain conditions, if you press a Solo button during a recording, it will be reflected in the result at the outputs and will probably ruin the take or broadcast, or confuse a performer. Some consoles allow the Solo buttons to be configured "safe"—in other words, they will behave more like a PFL. Consoles can also offer a "Solo with effects" facility so that we can isolate a single instrument but not remove any effects that have been applied to it.

13. **The channel fader.** The channel fader controls the source's output level to its chosen destination. On many consoles, a second, smaller fader or knob will control the monitor level only (see **figure 4.3**). The functions of the big and small faders are usually interchangeable. If the monitor controls are included on the channel strip, the console is said to be an "in-line" design. If the monitor controls are elsewhere on the console—sometimes together on their own separate panel—the design is called "split."

FIGURE 4.3. The smaller faders in the second row on this console are the monitor faders.

Faders are designed both for smooth changes in level and also to give you a quick visual indication of the current balance.

Alan:

> I remember a session with a German classical engineer who would insist, "I vant all my faders in a straight line." It's true to say that if all our monitor faders are equal and we are hearing a good mix, then we can pat ourselves on the back for recording everything at an appropriate level.

On a multitrack recording we will adjust all our input faders to give us a comfortable recording level at the meter for each track, or at the stereo output meter when we are mixing. Sometimes we will deliberately under-record certain instruments, so that they don't drown everything else when played at a normal level. A tambourine is a perfect example of something that doesn't need to be recorded at peak level.

Let's now look at metering in more detail.

Meters

Meters are a vital tool for the engineer. Without metering, we have no indication of the level of the signals coming in or going out. Mechanical meters with a needle have for the most part been replaced these days by bar graph–style meters or even graphic representations of these on a computer screen.

There are two types of meter in common use: the PPM (Peak Program Meter) and the VU (Volume Units). Many consoles and DAWs allow you to switch between the two.

On a PPM, the rise time—the time it takes to show the level of a sound—is much faster than on a VU meter, which makes transients like drum hits much easier to measure. Conversely, the fall time of a PPM—the time it takes the meter to indicate to a lower reading—is much slower.

These rise and fall times come under the heading of *meter ballistics*. Books could be written about metering and ballistics, and strong opinions have been expressed about what type of meter gives the best results. With VU meters there can be a tendency to over-record or record at too high a level on transient material like drums and percussive sounds. On the other hand, PPMs tend to display transient sounds as much louder than smoother sounds—like strings, for example—and that can create a tendency to under-record nontransient audio.

With analog tape, the recording level and how you meter it has considerable importance. If you record to analog tape too quietly, tape hiss will be an issue. If you have to turn up a track, you'll as a consequence turn up the hiss.

At the other end of the scale, tape has a tendency to compress sounds recorded at too high a level; "tape compression" is often regarded as a pleasant artifact and is one of the reasons for a resurgence of interest in tape at the present time. Plug-ins are of course ever on the heels of a trend, to provide a modern and more controllable alternative.

Drums are sometimes recorded to analog tape specifically to get the slightly compressed result, whereas everything else might stay digital.

The good news is that in the digital world, we have a much greater available dynamic range. Provided our meters are not reading too low on the scale, and that at the top of the scale nothing overloads or lights up the red "clip" light, you are probably recording at a good level. But if you choose to under-record, you are sacrificing some of the *bit resolution*. In other words, you might only be using twenty of your available twenty-four bits.

On a mix we want to record at a level that makes our recording sound at least as loud as the next person's—or do we?

If you're using a console, it's important that the meters are calibrated to match the levels of your tape machine or DAW. What's the use of reading the meters on the console if the recording device is treating everything as being 6 dB louder than the console meters are telling us?

On VU meters, we normally accept that zero VU is the maximum comfortable level we will allow a signal to reach. On analog equipment, we would be careful not to exceed this, although an occasional brief excursion into the red might be acceptable. On digital media there's a level we call *digital zero* (or zero dB FS, or full scale), where theoretically all the binary bits are ones rather than zeros and it physically cannot get any louder. If we do try to exceed digital zero, the results can be distinctly nasty.

So we need to allow what we call "headroom," to make space for unexpected louder sounds, particularly transient peaks, so that they don't clip or distort. So we establish our operating level—zero VU as being a safe amount under digital zero. There are various standards from −12 to −20 dB, but we've found a comfortable operating level is 14 dB below digital zero.

Calibration

So how do we go about calibrating our console and other equipment to our workstation?

The easiest way is to have a digital test tone available to us, one known to be at our precise chosen operating level. A good way to get this is from an audio test CD, such as the one on this page, which appears to have someone looking remarkably like Alan Parsons on its front cover (see **figure 4.4**).

If we feed track 33 from the Sound Check 2 CD—which is a 1 kHz tone at −14 dB FS, or 14 dB below digital zero—from the digital output of a CD player into a DAW as a digital input, we'd then adjust the calibration of all the inputs on the audio hardware (or in some cases, we'll have to do it within the software program), so that the DAW sees that incoming level as zero VU. Now we have a reference level to match our whole system to. A tone at digital zero is very loud. You'll find it as large as life on the Sound Check 2 CD, so be very careful not to damage your ears or your sound equipment.

FIGURE 4.4. **Sound Check 2 CD.**

Now when we send a test tone from the console's or DAW's onboard signal generator at zero VU, it should be calibrated to be received by the recording device—which could be an internal mix bus within the DAW's software—at −14 dB. This way, even strong peaks that exceed zero VU slightly will not overload, or give us what is called in the digital world an "over level," where the red indicator lights up. VU meters, calibrated as above, will have a tendency to show higher levels than would be acceptable in the analog world. But there again, they were invented long before the word "digital" was coined!

Viewing the Information

To cut down on the number of switches and buttons, many digital mixers divide the faders into *banks*, and only allow us to view or modify channel parameters one at a time. We can switch the viewpoint from one channel to another. So, effectively, channel strips do still exist, but only in a virtual sense.

Sometimes a further duplication of controls or layers will allow other functions to be viewed and modified. For example, on a typical digital console, the fader positions can switch from the channel's output level to the echo send outputs. Another layer might show us the headphone send levels.

Why would we need to have all these channel strips, when in the digital world all we need is one channel strip or possibly even one fader? The answer is *information*.

Alan:

> On a large console I can see the entire snapshot of my current recording configuration without touching anything. I can see by the position of the faders, the settings of the knobs, and whether lights are on or off for a particular function exactly what is going on. It makes the engineer's job much easier when everything can be seen at once. On a compact console where I can only see one channel at a time, I am going to have to a lot of button presses just to get to the channel or layer that I am interested in. A lot depends upon your budget, the space you have available, and your preferred work flow. But if time is money, then the speed of access to information afforded by a large console is a factor you should take into consideration.

How Sound Leaves the Console

All mixing consoles will have at least one set of outputs that carry the required monitor signal out to the main monitoring system. This output will depend on the setting of the *monitor level*.

So this is an important knob! It's also important to understand the signal path within a console and to realize that, for example, pushing the channel faders or the main stereo bus fader will affect the monitoring as well as the recording.

However, only the monitoring will be affected by changes in the monitor gain of a source or by activating PFL or Pre-Fade Listen.

Other dedicated monitor outputs may be switchable to feed—for example, secondary speaker systems and headphones.

FIGURE 4.5. **Master section of a large-format console.**

Other faders, knobs, and switches, aside from those that run along our channel strip, control functions relating to effects and monitoring different sources. This area of the mixing console is often referred to as the master section (see **figure 4.5**).

Controllers: Giant Mice?

What differentiates a controller from either an analog or a digital console is its inherent flexibility, its ability to link or assign certain knobs or controls to certain functions on your DAW. Assignability was a big word in the early days of digital consoles and controllers.

Different consoles and controllers will offer more or less assignability, of course. Some controllers are also more aligned with a particular DAW, and some are truly "agnostic" or transparent.

A large console or control surface that is dedicated entirely to controlling the functions of a DAW could be considered just a giant mouse.

All control changes are virtual. It is important to remember that controllers do not have any audio signals passing through them. That's the job of analog hardware, which translates our sources into the digital domain.

The Value of Physical Equipment

Alan:

> Because I'm an old-school engineer myself, I got very used to the idea that every mic or every tape track had its own fader. The other controls were a bonus, but lots of faders was a key factor. The level of a source is the most likely thing I'm going to want to change. Level changes are just so easy on a console or controller that gives me a fader per channel. I can grab a fader on a whim and make a level adjustment, instead of having to search a screen or go through several button presses to find the right channel or layer that gives me the fader I am interested in at that moment. That's why the ergonomics of a controller are very important. Its operation has to be intuitive. A well-planned track layout will also help me instantly locate a track I want to adjust without having to search for it.

Many keyboards and other musical instruments contain their own digital interfaces and can be connected to a digital console or computer directly through a dedicated digital input (or by USB or FireWire, for example) and could contain multiple individual tracks of information.

So where does this leave the role of consoles and controllers in a modern recording rig? The functionality and real estate price per square foot is a big issue, but in the home studio world, compactness is a must. A big surface means instant accessibility. A small compact surface can offer just as much flexibility, but at the expense of the time you must take to find the right button or switch "hiding" in a complicated menu.

Alan:

> I've said many times that recording is a balancing act, and with consoles and controllers the equation might be, as much as anything else, your ability to balance your bank account as well as balance your mix.

Perhaps the best reason hands-on equipment is so valuable to the recording process is that its physicality and immediacy helps create the magic, as producer and songwriter Patrick Leonard describes working with one of his favorite engineers, Bill Bottrell:

> When we started an Elton John record, on the first mix he did at the end of the day, I said something about brightening the cymbals, and he goes, *Oh, yeah, yeah, OK*, and he pushes in the equalizer on this Neve console, and then the mix is finished and it's stunning; it sounds amazing. And then, the legend goes that we left, and all the engineers in the building wanted to come in and see the console, like what had Bill done, because

> this guy is really revered. There was nothing in the patch bay, there were no compressors, there were no equalizers, there were no effects, no EQs pushed in. So, he uses the console to compress, he uses the ratios between things to equalize, literally. And you listen to this thing and it just sounds stellar.

The immediate power of a physical console was also ably described by engineer Niko Bolas, as he recollected one of his earliest sessions with legendary engineer Glyn Johns:

> I said, "Oh, you've got to mix it, because I want to learn how to sound like Glyn Johns." And, he looked at me like I was out of my mind, and he sat down at the console and pushed up a few faders, and it sounded like Glyn. Then he got up and he said, "Now mix it." And I had no idea what he did. All he did was turn up the shit that he thinks is his favorite stuff, and he filled up the speakers the way he hears music, which is not what he wanted. He wanted to see how I hear music.

Test: Analog Summing Versus In the Box

Take four audio sources—say, bass, drums, guitar, and keyboards. On a DAW it's a simple matter to set the fader levels and simply output the result to the stereo bus. If we were finishing up a record, the whole thing would remain in the digital domain through mastering, CD production, and duplication. Interestingly, it only actually leaves the digital domain in the consumer's stereo system or iPod, where it undergoes its first and only digital-to-analog conversion process. We call this mixing "in the box."

However, we could also take those same four tracks and convert them individually to analog, using one D-to-A converter for each source, and then mix these analog signals together using an analog console. We call this "analog summing." We'd then reenter the digital domain by sending the stereo analog result into an A-to-D converter. So what would be the difference between these two methods?

In the *Art & Science of Sound Recording* video series, we devised a scientifically accurate comparison for demonstration purposes, where four digital tracks were combined at exactly the same levels with no other processing—first in the digital domain and then in the analog domain. In theory at least, both the stereo results should sound exactly the same. But unfortunately, to hear it on the DVD, we had to reconvert the analog result back into digital or there would be no soundtrack on the DVD player or computer. For the full "analog experience," the analog version could of course be recorded directly to analog tape for a vinyl disc transfer or compact cassette (whose predicted demise might be premature in these days of "Anything old must be good!").

If you hear a difference at all, it's probably subtle—and you may say there's a difference, but you can't actually say whether one is definitively *better* than the other. Rather than try to influence your opinion, we'd like you to try to discern what the comparison represents: whether you hear an overall difference or a difference that affects only one instrument, for example. The art of recording has a lot to do with learning how to listen, so we'd like you to make up your own minds on this issue. You'll probably want to listen to this in a more controlled environment and for a longer period, so we have posted the full length result of this experiment on the *ASSR* website. These are of course uncompressed files and are formatted at 44.1 kHz at 24-bit resolution.

5

DIGITAL AUDIO AND COMPUTERS

When you hear a great song today, can you really tell whether it was recorded in a professional studio or on a laptop? The problem for commercial recording studios is that you really can't. In the right hands, a Grammy-worthy recording can be made in the most humble of environments.

Obviously, if you're recording a symphony orchestra, a jazz quartet, or even possibly a rock band that wants to do everything live, then space, acoustics, and getting separation between instruments are areas where a professional recording studio is still the best choice.

But if you're making a pop record, a dance track, or certainly any type of production that can be recorded one track at a time, or that's based around loops, samples, or MIDI parts, then you can build your own highly portable recording studio on your desktop or laptop computer for pennies on the dollar.

Differences Between a Pro Studio and a Laptop

Interestingly, today's recording media are largely the same, whether you're working on a laptop at home or in a professional recording studio. Except in the case of analog purists, all recordings these days are stored on hard drives—either onboard the computer or on external, removable FireWire or USB, solid-state, or flash drives. With cloud-based storage on the rise, the sky literally does seem to be the limit in this constantly evolving segment of the market. The "front end" of modern recording systems, in the form of Pro Tools, Cubase, Logic, Ableton Live, or similar software, is both available to and relatively affordable for pros and enthusiasts alike.

The most obvious differences between a pro studio and a laptop are essentially environmental: how large and how acoustically friendly are your recording spaces? We also shouldn't underestimate the "service" offered by commercial studios in the form of large collections of microphones and equipment, food and drink, runners, technical engineers, assistants, and so on. Portable or home studio systems can comprise anything from one or two mics and mic pres, and some interfaces that convert analog sounds into digital audio files, all the way to a full-blown recording console and monitoring system. All components in the modern recording chain are, at least theoretically, accessible to all, even those on very modest budgets.

It can just be down to the budget of a record, but if the opportunity arises, it's usually best to still record in a professional recording studio. That said, countless records are made in home studios using a personal computer with music software, plus one or two key external pieces of equipment that allow the recording of audio into the computer and offer control over the various tracks of music coming back out. This combination is now generally referred to as a Digital Audio Workstation, or DAW for short. DAWs are often used in conjunction with "plug-ins."

> *Plug-ins are separate applications (often designed by third parties) that, when used with a DAW, offer a wide range of synthesized or sampled instrument sounds, and sound processors, including EQ, delays, reverb, and limiting or compression. Plug-ins can be free downloads from the Internet or cost literally thousands.*

This chapter looks at all the components of a computer-based recording environment, how they fit together, and how to get the best results from them.

Main Components of Digital Audio Recording

A DAW normally comprises three major components: a computer, a digital audio interface, and recording software. There's no standard model. You can buy all-in-one packages, of which Avid's Pro Tools is the best known, or you can mix and match, choosing your software and hardware from different manufacturers.

All Apple computers are currently delivered with an entry-level DAW called GarageBand. You can simply connect a mic to the computer (or even use the built-in mic) to record and mix music, without the need to use anything else. You can also survive on frozen pizza, but most people, if they can, probably can see the advantages of buying their own ingredients and cooking at home, or going out to a decent restaurant as well.

The Computer or Terminal

First let's look at the host computer. A Mac or a PC will work just fine for digital audio recording.

Macs and PCs both come in tower and laptop versions, and towers can also be rack-mounted. Laptops are obviously more portable, but they're normally not as powerful or expandable as a tower. It depends on what kind of work you're doing and whether you have a purpose-built studio space or just want to record whenever and wherever you find yourself.

With desktops and towers, fan noise can be an issue. In a permanent studio setting, you might want to consider encasing your computer in some form of soundproof housing. Some computers are better than others for generating noise. Some are whisper-quiet when the fan is not running, but if you are pushing the machine to its limit, the fan will be on and it may cause problems.

DIGITAL AUDIO AND COMPUTERS | 47

At the time of this writing, we live in the age of the seemingly ubiquitous iPad and other tablet computers, and it seems quite likely that networking will soon challenge the current imperative of any "computer" with its attendant processing and speed capabilities. Records have even been made on smartphones!

Digital audio recording applications or programs will always be needed. No matter how your recordings are being processed, you will still need some form of on-screen workspace—not only to run the programs, but also to run instrument and effects plug-ins and to carry out processing and editing tasks.

A computer is the mainstay of most modern recording rigs, and it's best to use one with the largest possible amount of power under the hood—in other words, the fastest or most powerful central processing unit or CPU (which can be thought of as the brain of your computer) you can afford. If you're using some form of tablet, then, again, speed of access to your software and content remains the issue. Music production does not take kindly to delays of any sort.

RAM (random access memory), the real-time memory where data lives as it is being processed, is also important. Although applications publish their "minimum" RAM requirements, new computers tend to have more RAM installed than, say, last year's model, so this shouldn't be a problem. In almost all cases, the more RAM you have, the better.

Memory is relatively inexpensive, and this also applies to permanent hard disk storage space, or cloud storage, where your applications along with the music you make may be stored.

Although it's now perfectly possible to record on an external drive, it's better practice to record on an internal hard drive and then to back it up to an external drive. The subject of backups in covered elsewhere, but it's worth mentioning here that backups should be stored in a different location—ideally, in another building. Cloud storage is also a good backup option.

Generally speaking, save your various projects and backups onto different drives. Put another way, just because you have a multi-terabyte drive that can hold every track you've ever recorded, backing up to other drives is a good protection against drive failure or insurance company failure. Fire, floods, earthquakes, etc., are seldom predictable (see Chapter 24, "Dealing with Disasters").

Alan:

> I remember in the late eighties, when I had been using an Atari computer with a MIDI sequencing program, I used to store each song rather inconveniently on a separate 3 1/2 inch floppy disk which held 360 KB of data [see **figure 5.1**].
>
> I soon invested in a rather fragile external hard drive with a capacity of twenty megabytes, and I said to myself, "I'll never need all that space." It's ironic that the average USB stick you can buy in your local office supply store now has a capacity of a hundred times that amount.

One-terabyte drives, which are fairly standard at time of this writing, provide fifty thousand times the capacity of a floppy disk. Storage capacity is a movable feast or famine, but no matter whether you are using hard drives, digital tape, the cloud, or some new wonder material like graphene, the underlying moral of all storage media and systems is: Make backups, and don't "wholly" trust any piece of technology. Don't forget that human error can also be a factor—no one's perfect!

FIGURE 5.1. **A 3 1/2 inch floppy disk—a popular storage medium for music/MIDI data in 1984–1996.**

Computer specs and software requirements change on a seemingly daily basis, so there's no point in going into detail about any particular type of motherboard, for example. Since music applications are becoming increasingly graphic, it's as well to make sure the system's video card can support the use of two monitors and that the audio card has the appropriate connectors for the audio interface being used.

In terms of the exact computer hardware or terminal that delivers the best performance du jour, you are but a click or tweet away from that type of information.

Anything coming from a microphone, guitar, keyboard, turntable, or any other audio source will need to be fed into a digital audio interface. This not only converts those analog signals into digital data you can manipulate on the computer, it also converts the digital data you're working on back into analog audio so you can hear it.

What is generally known as an "interface" actually encompasses two things: it converts analog into digital and also forms the link between the now digitized data and the audio application on your computer.

Interfaces can accomplish both of these tasks. But not all do. There are in fact "converters" whose sole job is to convert analog into digital—A-to-D converters or ADCs. Then there are pure "interfaces" that only take digital data and introduce that to your recording application—D-to-A converters or DACs. It's probably true to say that separate devices like this are in the upper echelons of power and sophistication. All-in-one devices are more common.

You might now be wondering where MIDI—the technology that inspired computer-based recording—sits in all of this? MIDI In and Out may be offered on an audio interface, but it isn't always, some manufacturers taking the view that those interested in recording MIDI will want more MIDI Ins and Outs than can feasibly be placed on a device whose primary purpose is, after all, audio. Other interfaces may offer simple MIDI connections quite sufficient for most people's way of working.

As with all things surrounding DAWs, it pays to keep a close eye on exactly what each component is and what it can do.

Digital Communication Formats

It is important to understand how converters and interfaces communicate because, frankly, there are so many of them. Into this category fall the connectors, the cables, and the information being passed through them.

One of the main stumbling blocks to a happier state of understanding are all the complex sounding, acronym-based words and phrases used to describe formats and data streams.

Here are the prime candidates (see the Glossary for details):

- AES/EBU
- S/PDIF
- ADAT
- TDIF
- Ethernet
- FireWire
- USB
- MADI

Each of these has different specifications as to number of channels, sample rate limitations, connector types, and the type of cable that carries the data stream. An important point to understand is that you can't always use any old cable to transfer digital data. You may need to use cable manufactured to an exact specification.

Digital audio can be recorded with the following possible variables:

Sample rate. Currently a choice between 32 kHz, 44.1 kHz, 48 kHz, 88.2 kHz, 96 kHz, and 192 kHz.

Bit depth. Usually 16-bit or 24-bit or 32-bit or 64-bit and so on. Check back in ten years for the number to be in thousands of bits.

A higher value for both sample rate and bit depth translates to better quality. But high values mean you will need more storage space. It's vital to make sure that everything on a project is recorded at the same sample rate. Mixing sample rates is asking for trouble.

Word clock. For digital recordings to be recognized by all the devices within a system, they need to be driven or synchronized by a series of high-frequency pulses we call the word clock. There can only be one word clock driving the entire system. If different clocks are driving each piece of gear, it will almost certainly end in tears. The stability and purity of the clock will have a significant effect on the quality of the audio. A bad clock will introduce what is known as jitter, which is not a good thing and will have a subtle but nonetheless adverse effect. Speaking of subtlety, the difference between the sound of one mic pre, interface, or digital converter against another will be perceived by many as negligible, but some of us have better ears than others.

We talked to producer John Shanks during the making of the *ASSR* video series, and he revealed Sheryl Crow to be one such person:

> Sheryl can hear the difference between an API or a Neve. There was a night she came in, and for some reason the API got plugged in as the mic pre, and we were using a [Telefunken] 251 [mic] into an LA 2A into an API, and it's usually a Neve. And, she kept saying, "John, you have me plugged in through the API." Her ears are that sharp.

Digital recording quality has come a long way since the early days of CDs. As digital audio has developed, more importance has been attached to the quality differences between interfaces, converters, master word clock generators, and the virtues of using higher sample rates.

Alan:

> Back in the early eighties I remember my impressions of early digital systems being, "Wow, it's very clean and there's no tape hiss!" As technology improves, we develop an ability to listen for different elements within audio recordings and to become sensitive to certain previously unnoticed artifacts. I would react very differently now to a recording made on eighties equipment played against a recording made today.

Dongles and Authorizations

Software piracy remains a major problem for manufacturers of audio applications, which is why they are constantly developing new ways to protect themselves against unauthorized use of their products.

The most common type of authorization is typing in a serial number and a password. But this method is relatively easy for a hacker to crack. Much harder to work around is a physical object that contains a license—either a "dongle" (see **figure 5.2**) from companies such as iLok and Syncrosoft, or what is effectively a

FIGURE 5.2. **An iLok USB dongle for Nuendo, a high-end DAW used mainly in post-production.**

giant dongle, such as dedicated Pro Tools interfaces, or a Mac computer, which is the only device that will run GarageBand!

Making the Connections

Armed with all the necessary component parts to record and process audio on your computer, there are one or two settings or decisions that still need to be made before you're quite ready to roll. The first concerns which point in the audio chain you are going to hear your audio from. And the second is how to deal with certain discrepancies in timing that will naturally occur as a result of digital processing.

Computer processing causes delays, which we call "latency." "Direct monitoring" is the term used for hearing the outputs of your audio interface "directly"—in other words, before it gets to your computer. Some interfaces have a mix knob to control whether you are hearing more input or more software output. Sometimes this is controlled within the software.

The downside of direct monitoring is that you can't insert software-based processing into the signal path.

For any real-time musical performance, anything but the smallest amount of latency is completely unacceptable, so we want to make sure that when we're working with real players, doing overdubs and so on, latency is kept to the absolute minimum.

We asked singer Michael McDonald how he dealt with latency. His reply is worth paying full attention to because it also goes to the heart of so many problems in the studio (frankly, ancient or modern), where art sometimes doesn't meet science so much as collide with it.

Michael McDonald:

> For the longest time, I guess I just put up with it, but then as I started to understand it—what was wrong and what it was doing—I really hated it. I remember with Pro Tools in the first few years, I learned that engineers—when they're not musicians—don't really hear latency of a fraction of a second. But because I've played it, I know how it's supposed to feel.
>
> That was kind of a terrorizing element of Pro Tools early on. You'd hear your piano and you'd be going, "That just doesn't feel right."
>
> One time we worked with an engineer and we were mixing something, and he goes, "Look, let me get the mix up and you guys come back, and when I get it where I think it should be . . ." And we're going OK. So we left, which I never did. I don't know why I did it, but we went and got lunch. I guess we were hungry or something.
>
> We came back, and the piano was just way out, way out, you know what I mean? He had put it through some look-ahead mastering software. I tried to explain to the guy that that's way off. He goes, "It couldn't be." You know, it's the old artist versus engineer: "It's impossible. You couldn't hear that. It's forty thousandths of a second." And I'm going, "Trust me, it's way off."

An alternative to direct monitoring is to use a hardware mixer with its own reverbs and effects that are perfectly adequate for live overdubs. You can always use your preferred plug-ins once you've got your master takes. This might also be the justification for investing in some outboard processing.

Latency is dependent upon buffer size and sample rate, both of which can be adjusted in your software. Very low latency values can be achieved with modern interfaces, drivers, and a fast computer. But as we've said, don't change your sample rate once you've started a project. Low latency can sometimes be at the expense of computer performance and nasty fizzes and crackles.

As a final thought and not to counter Michael McDonald's experience, which is totally understandable in the modern age, it's interesting to consider that for generations, church organists have had to deal with latencies measured almost in seconds. The pipes can be as much as a hundred feet away from the player, and it takes time to get the information to the pipes in the first place.

For most of us, the concept of recording music on tape is a thing of the past. But most of the basic operational functions of tape machines have been imported into the new world of recording bits and bytes onto a hard drive.

All recording software rather quaintly allows buttons to be pressed to control what we call the transport: play, record, fast-forward, rewind, and of course, stop. The difference is that tape is a linear format, whereas DAWs allow us to access any piece of audio at any time. Now it's point, click, and hit the space bar.

Alan:

> When I came into the studio industry at Abbey Road Studios, my job was as a tape operator, which was a separate activity from the engineer. With DAW recording we often have the engineer doing both jobs, and he or she has to be computer-savvy. Many producers—myself included, who used to engineer everything on a session in analog days, working with an assistant—have found that working with a computer whiz is an essential. You can only wear so many hats, especially if you are a performing producer!

DAW recording gives us effectively unlimited tracks, cut-and-paste audio, nonlinear recording, multilevel undo and redo, and virtually unlimited audio processing and plug-ins for any effect or fixit your heart desires. Anyone who predates DAW recording will tell you what a very different experience recording used to be. One example is the time spent waiting for a tape to be rewound to the top (beginning) of a song. Wasted time? Absolutely not! Those were precious moments to contemplate the meaning of life, take a sip of coffee, or even a hit of tobacco or non-tobacco products . . . we digress. Next, we move on to . . .

Recording Software

Keeping software up to date equates to oiling the bearings on the tape machine. It's essential, and very much goes to the heart of your recording experience, whether you're talking about computer operating systems, drivers, or the latest application or plug-in.

Software has replicated if not replaced many pieces of studio equipment, tasks, even entire job descriptions. These computer applications have also ballooned into what no musician or engineer in past decades could ever have imagined might fall into their work flow.

- Multitrack recording
- MIDI sequencing
- Scorewriting
- Mixing
- Mastering
- Sampling
- Sound design
- Audio processing

- Audio restoration
- Forensic audio analysis
- Live performance
- DJing
- Game audio
- Music education
- Music therapy

The list simply goes on and on.

The software you use probably has the greatest impact on your life in the studio, be it a real studio or a virtual one, and there's a lot to choose from. Some is entirely and legitimately free; some is expensive. Some is Mac-only, some cross-platform, with many price points and versions.

What matters is not so much which you choose or use, but that you get to know it, keep it updated, and investigate all potential avenues of an easy recording life. In this category you should include:

- Learning all the shortcuts
- Maintaining all updates and upgrades
- Organizing your files so you don't have widowed and orphaned files floating about in random folders
- Developing a naming convention you stick to—a date in the title can be an invaluable search word
- Backing up. Even in these days of cloud storage, inexpensive physical media accidents can and will happen. It is said that if you don't back up your data three times, you're not really serious about it. That's not a crazy scenario. Back up the backup.

Beyond Your DAW

Plug-ins—applications that run inside your chosen DAW to give you specialist tools or capabilities—mean you no longer have to have a room full of equipment. Plug-ins have been hugely liberating for music production. They range from shareware to programs that cost thousands of dollars. Some are tied to a card installed in your computer, such as the TC Electronic PowerCore series, or the UAD-2 system from Universal Audio. The questions are: How many plug-ins do we need, and how do we organize them?

We've referred to several specific plug-ins throughout this book. Now's a good time to look at the big picture and see how plug-ins best fit into your recording system . . .

You're realistically not going to be able to release your music in multitrack form. Eventually you'll need to finalize your song, produce a stereo or 5.1 mix, and probably create some form of data-compressed file that can be played on iPods, smartphones, or over the Internet.

Mastering is the final link in the audio recording chain. This is a specialist job and a huge subject. This book is not here to give advice on how you should master your product. However, software does exist for do-it-yourself mastering.

Alan:

> I've always resisted self-drive mastering applications. I've always taken the view that qualified mastering engineers offer the best service and do the best job.

6

MONITORING

The Development of the Loudspeaker

To create the sound of an acoustic instrument such as a piano, air needs to be excited by a hammer hitting a string. The sound is amplified by a resonating device—in the case of a piano, a soundboard. The surrounding reflective surfaces then direct the sound waves out into the open. When you see the lid of a grand piano open and facing the audience in a concert hall, this isn't just to look cool. It's so you can hear it better.

Clap your hands. A sound was generated. You heard it, and then it was gone forever. The development of sound "recording" allowed sound to be decoupled from its real-time, direct source and converted into stored vibrations representing the original sound waves—a bit like a camera stores an image. But a recording device isn't much use if you can't hear what has been stored, so some form of "all-purpose" resonating device became necessary to reproduce and amplify sound waves.

In Edison's phonograph (see **figure 6.1**), the device was a metal horn connected to a stylus that vibrated when sound was received at the horn. The stylus then cut a groove in a rotating wax cylinder. When the process was reversed, the stylus picked up the vibrations from the cylinder and made them loud enough in the horn to be heard in a room at more or less speaking volume. But with electrical recording came the invention and development of the loudspeaker.

FIGURE 6.1. Two phonographs à la Edison.

The basic principle of the moving coil loudspeaker is attributed to many inventors in many countries, but the first U.S. patent for the electrodynamic loudspeaker was filed by two gentlemen by the name of Rice and Kellogg (who were no doubt proud of how every snap, crackle, and pop was faithfully reproduced!). Their invention became known as the Radiola.

The basic principle is this: Electrical signals are applied to a suspended coil wrapped around a magnet: the voice coil. As a result of a well-known principle of electricity and magnetism, it is made to move backward and forward. The coil is attached to a diaphragm or "cone," usually made of paper or thin plastic. Like the horn on the phonograph, this causes the movement of air necessary to make sound.

A loudspeaker needs to be able to replay a huge variety of signals as accurately as possible, so violins will still sound like violins and pianos like pianos. It's actually rather uncanny that such a crude device allows such a clear distinction between, say, a tweeting bird and a volcanic eruption. To this day, research continues on loudspeaker design, still using the original moving coil principle.

Size Matters

Speaker enclosure design is very important. Bass frequencies reproduce better when the speaker is sealed inside a box. But the dimensions and acoustic properties of that box are tremendously important.

Speaking of dimensions, studio monitor systems have rarely been physically bigger or come with a higher price tag than those designed by engineer Allen Sides of Ocean Way Recording. During the making of the *ASSR* video series, we asked him to explain the whys and wherefores of good speakers:

> For me it is the definitive reference point. If I can hear clearly, I have no limits. When I sit down to mix, I don't want to think that I'm compensating for speakers.
>
> In this particular system [see **figure 6.2**], it's unusual, in that you have a low-frequency horn and a high-frequency horn that have identical flare rates. On most systems that use a horn, the woofers are just mounted in cabinets. The dispersional characteristics of those woofers are utterly different than the horns. As soon as you move off axis, the information below the vocal changes and, therefore, conceptually the most important thing is incredibly even directivity—as you walk across the room, the sound doesn't change.

FIGURE 6.2. **Allen Sides' custom Ocean Way monitoring system in Record One.**

> Some hi-fi guys are big on electrostats. The problem with electrostats is, they have awful dispersion. So if you're in the sweet spot, it's not so bad, but the second you get off axis, it sounds strange. These have superwide dispersion.
>
> And then, the tweeter is a direct radiating dome, 10 kHz and above. It goes up to 28 kHz and it basically has the dispersion of a dome. So this is an unusual system. Very, very low distortion and no horn sound.

We think he just said his speakers sound really good!

The Perfect Loudspeaker?

Alan:

> During the making of the *Art & Science of Sound Recording* video series, I dug out the speakers that I used to record *Dark Side of the Moon* [JBL 4320s]. *Dark Side* went on to become a landmark recording, but does that mean there's something magical about these particular speakers? Might they produce, or reproduce, some special characteristics?

There are literally thousands of speaker designs of differing shapes, sizes, and price tags, but what makes a great loudspeaker and what are the criteria for judging it so? Some basic attributes can certainly be identified: good frequency response, a lack of distortion, and good stereo imaging. No matter how much we spend on seemingly perfect speakers, if the room is not acoustically suited to them, they won't sound good.

Speaker designers spend a lot of time making sure all the frequencies reach the ear at the same time—this is known as time alignment and results in what we call *phase coherence*.

The science of speaker design is a huge and fascinating subject beyond the scope of this book. But in the end, choice boils down to some fairly unglamorous factors, such as cost, space, and simply being able to know and trust what we are hearing (a concept we discussed in Chapter 2).

Monitor Choices

In the professional studio there is likely to be a choice of full-size main or big monitors and a set of smaller *near-field* speakers that often sit on top of the console. A full-blown monitor system with its associated amplifiers for a pro control room can cost as much as $150,000 from someone like Allen Sides. These systems will almost certainly be installed and specially equalized or "tuned" to the room by the supplier.

Even if you're not in the $100,000-plus bracket, a substantial investment in your main monitors will be money well spent. They need to be of sufficient quality and clarity to hear the true nature of a sound and have sufficient power handling to satisfy musicians who have been playing their gear at "11" in the tracking room.

A studio's main or big monitors should generally be able to deliver top quality and detailed audio to a roomful of people situated, say, three or four meters from the speakers.

A good compromise if you're short on space—and on big wads of cash—is to get midfield speakers that sit on the floor or on stands, rather than being permanently mounted in a wall recess. Midfields should also be able to supply audio to the room and not just the engineer sitting in front of a desk or computer.

Some producers and artists prefer to listen loud and with deep, thumping bottom end, or else they don't feel adequately energized. That's fine, but be aware that listening loud for long periods can and will cause hearing damage.

Near-fields, as the name implies, are designed to be listened to at relatively close range, from a distance of as little as one meter. There are countless studios using near-field monitoring exclusively. Near-fields are usually much more within the reach of home studio owners, but there is still a wide price range from under $100 to several thousand dollars.

Alan:

> In general, you get what you pay for, and size matters—the bigger, the better. But no matter what budget you have, I wouldn't recommend committing to a purchase until you have spent a good amount of time listening to your future investment—ideally in your own environment, or one that is similar to yours.

Recent improvements in near-field monitor design have brought affordable, high-performance loudspeakers to thousands of home recording studios. The bass end of the spectrum in particular, once considered impossible to reproduce in a small cabinet, can be surprisingly big-sounding in modern designs.

However, many systems do also offer a separate subwoofer, which makes up for the inherent physical deficiencies of a cabinet that simply can't move enough air to reproduce low frequencies accurately.

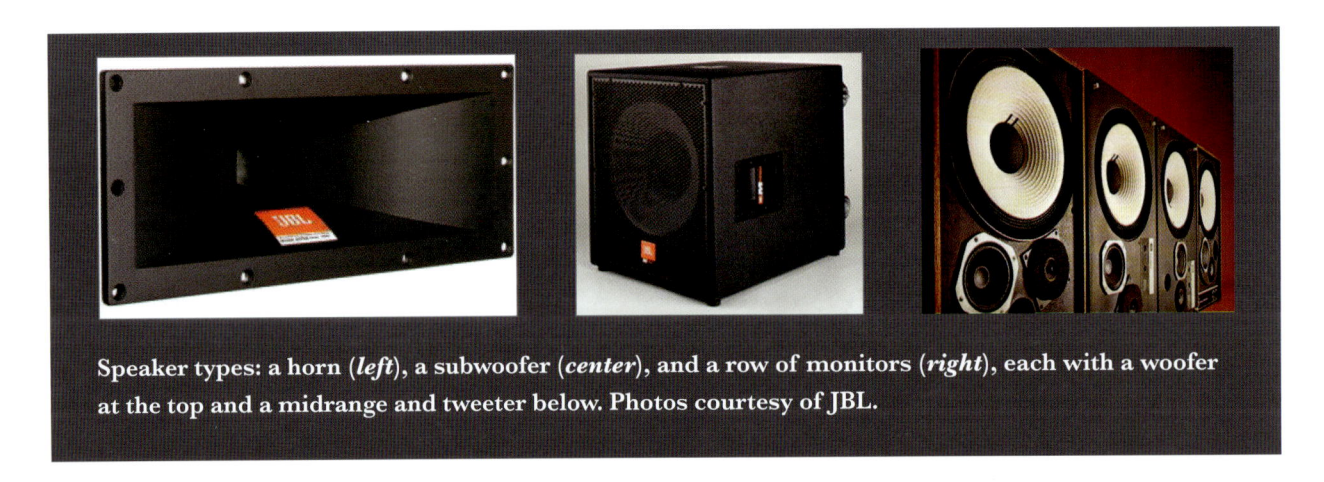

Speaker types: a horn (*left*), a subwoofer (*center*), and a row of monitors (*right*), each with a woofer at the top and a midrange and tweeter below. Photos courtesy of JBL.

Whatever system you use, the sound you hear in the studio—especially if you are working on big studio monitors—is going to be very different from the sound of the average domestic system. One of the skills of engineering is to assess how the sound we hear in the studio will "translate" to more modest systems out in the wonderful world of radio, television, and the Internet.

It's just a fact of life that we are never realistically going to hear our record the way it sounded in the studio—and the compromises we have to make to reach the masses can be hard to swallow.

Loudspeakers and Amplification

So-called "active" loudspeakers have amplifiers built in, so you can plug them in straight out of the monitor line output of your console or DAW. "Passive" monitors require external amplification. Most speakers made for the hi-fi world and also some pro audio speakers give us the choice of what amplifier to drive them with. Some engineers do prefer to have the choice of amplifier left up to them, rather than settling for what the manufacturer chooses as ideal for their speaker. Taste rules, but it's important to have the correct wattage at the amplifier, so as not to "underdrive" the speakers or, conversely, blow them up! Speakers will always carry a specified power rating, and likewise amplifiers will have a defined power output, so it's important to take heed of specs here.

How Certain Loudspeakers Became "Classic"

The Yamaha NS10, designed by Akira Nakamura in the 1970s, was initially marketed as a consumer bookshelf loudspeaker, but became a virtual must as a near-field monitor in pro studios in the eighties and nineties. Many producers still swear that if their mix sounds good on NS10s, it will sound good anywhere. That's why you'll still find these monitors in most studios to this day.

As with so much of the audio decision-making process, with loudspeakers it's a question of being able to "trust" that the sound you're hearing is an accurate representation of what the sound really is—i.e., will it still stand up anyplace, anytime?

Allen Sides recognizes the role of the NS10s but also their limitations in terms of providing you with detailed information:

> When I use a set of NS10s, half the time I'm looking to see how far the cone is moving to determine where my low bass is. That's not to say I can't make it work, but there's so many things you don't hear, particularly reverb trails and details, or sibilance that I'm not quite hearing correctly.
>
> I can mix on a set of NS10s, and I can make it sound quite good. I can then go to the big speakers and say, "Oh, no, that kick is not quite loud enough. There's not enough 40 Hz here. The low part of the vocal, there's a little resonance that I didn't hear that I need to get rid of. This is just slightly harsh. I've got to fix this little spot here."

Sometimes a baby pair of loudspeakers, like the ubiquitous Auratone, very popular in the 1970s, might be used to simulate the sound coming from a portable radio, a boom box, or a TV set—in other words, giving you a very useful audio reality check.

Sylvia Massy:

> I like using an Auratone, but not near the console. I prefer to have a single Auratone in the back of the room, maybe pointed to the wall and to monitor at low level, just to make sure I can, depending on the music, hear the vocal—if I need to hear the vocal for a television-style mix. But away from the console, off in the corner.

Most TVs and certainly home theater systems now deliver fairly sophisticated and powerful audio, so the days of needing this particular reality check may be numbered. Very few systems are mono these days.

Headphones

Another way to hear recorded sound, particularly important in the age of the iPod, is headphones (affectionately known in the industry as "cans") and their young sidekicks, earbuds.

There are several reasons for using headphones in a recording environment:

1. For musicians, when they are tracking with other musicians, so they can all hear each other
2. For a performer, to hear the instruments already recorded for overdubs
3. For the avoidance of feedback when recording vocals in the same room as the recording and monitoring equipment
4. As a simple alternative to monitors or loudspeakers

Headphone requirements for the recording musician are fairly basic. They need to be reliable, robust, and able to handle high volumes when necessary. They should have cables that don't get all snagged up (curly cables are not recommended) and should be long enough to permit the listener's free movement. Different headphone types suit different applications—see "Headphone Types" below.

For musicians, it can take time to get used to the claustrophobic world of headphones, and a lot of artists in smaller studios now choose to play "live in the studio," which, interestingly, harks back to the 1950s, before headphones became commonplace.

Top Nashville producer Tony Brown recalls:

> The first time I came to a studio, I was playing with a group called the Dixie Melody Boys, and we came to Nashville to record at the RCA . . . Studio B, the little studio. And that was a big deal for me. And I go back to that studio now, and it's like the size of a postage stamp, you know. And no one wore headphones back in those days. You had an upright bass, acoustic guitar, I played the piano, and we didn't even have a drummer. And we just sat in that room in a circle and recorded. It's changed so much since those days.

Or maybe not.

More common now perhaps is the need to record and engineer on headphones due to noise or space restrictions. In this instance, your selection should be made very carefully. The same criteria should be used as for loudspeakers: headphones that will deliver a sound you can trust. Make sure they are physically sturdy and comfortable, as chances are, they're going to be worn for long periods of time.

Headphones and earbuds both cover a wide range of designs and prices.

Headphone Types

Headphones come in a variety of basic designs.

Over-ear headphones completely enclose the ear and can be what we call a "closed" or "closed back" design, or be "open" or "open back"—or, as they're sometimes called, "open air."

An open design allows sounds from outside to enter and also sounds from inside to exit! This means you'll still be able to hear your significant other telling you dinner's ready. On the other hand, music spilling out from your cans might be picked up by an open mic and could cause feedback.

You might legitimately wonder whether this type of design really has a place in a studio, but if you mostly work alone, mainly with direct signals, and need to keep an ear out for the phone or the baby crying, then open headphones can be a perfectly acceptable solution and less claustrophobic.

A closed design headphone (see **figure 6.3**) is effectively a sealed system, like a speaker cabinet. This generally results in an improved bass response. This is probably the best type of headphone for most studio work—emphasis on "work." If you're just "listening," then an open design can be more appropriate.

FIGURE 6.3. **A listener wearing a closed design, over-ear set of headphones.**

Other closed designs may focus on near-total acoustic isolation from outside sounds, as worn by the guys you see waving a 747 toward the jet bridge at an airport.

On-ear headphones sit on the outside of the ear on a foam cushion. To some extent this type is slightly "open" by default. They won't totally exclude outside sounds, and most people find them less isolating. However, the problem with this design is usually a compromise in bass response. On-ears are often inexpensive, sometimes enough so that airlines will sell them for next to nothing or even give them away.

Noise-canceling headphones have also become popular. They use a nifty principle that electrically reverses the phase of outside noise, resulting in a substantial reduction in unwanted outside sound. Noise canceling does, however, adversely affect the overall sound quality.

Earbuds are familiar to the entire twenty-first-century world. Provided they fit snugly at the ear canal, surprisingly good bass response can be achieved. But loose buds can sound very thin and tinny. They don't really have a place in the studio, except possibly to provide a real-world reference for the countless consumers who will be listening to your music on an iPod or smartphone—the modern-day equivalent to the Auratone, perhaps.

Alan:

> I hate the damn things. They keep falling out of my ears and sound terrible. Don't ever think you'll get anything like the quality of a good professional pair of cans from those nasty white objects.

(C'mon now, Alan. Say what you mean. —*Ed.*)

In-ear monitors have become very popular nowadays with live musicians and occasionally studio players who like an "inside their head" mix. In-ear monitors are custom made for each user and require a mold of the user's ear canal, so it's a bit of a financial leap of faith to even try them. Their performance is very impressive compared with earbuds, and continuing research means they are improving all the time.

Monitoring Issues

The directional characteristics of mics and speakers, and the "spill" in and out of headphones, all come into play when trying to avoid feedback. If too much signal gets from a speaker or headphone back into the mic that's producing it, we will suffer the familiar squeal often heard everywhere from wedding bands to presidential speeches. Ironically, it seems to be particularly evident whenever a lot of pro audio people are around at trade shows, producing a lot of red faces at the console.

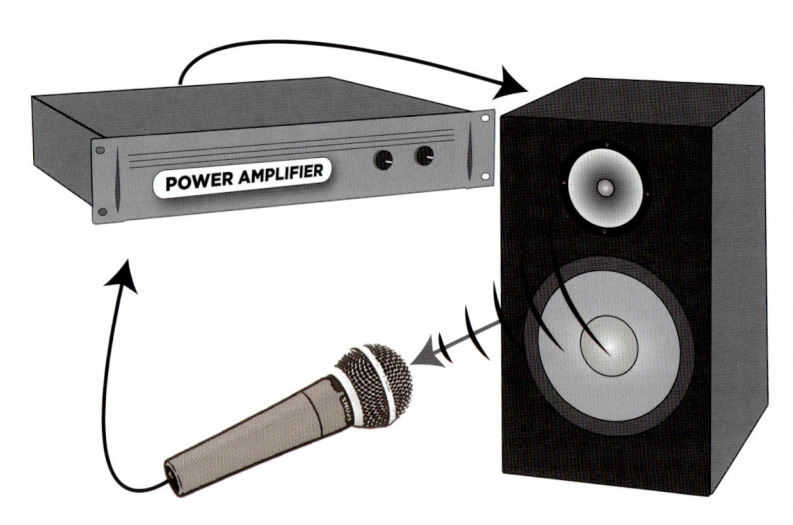

FIGURE 6.4. Feedback. The signal from the mic is amplified and then reproduced by the speaker, which is then "fed back" into the microphone . . . causing a chain reaction. If the signal gets louder each time it goes round the chain, it reaches a point where it cannot get any louder and the system squeals loudly to tell us how unhappy it is!

Although feedback is normally associated with live performance, it can occur even in the studio if the volume is loud enough, especially when the door connecting the control room and the performing area is opened. Vocals are nearly always the most likely source for feedback, because mics work hard to amplify the comparatively weak signal produced by the human voice. A mic on a guitar cabinet or a snare drum, for example, is much less likely to cause feedback. Another common cause of feedback is a vocalist who has his voice being sent to his headphone mix, and who then removes his headphones while close to his mic.

Smart engineers will sense when headphone feedback is about to happen and will jump to turn down the microphone gain or the headphone send level. Whenever and wherever feedback happens, it can range from unpleasant to damaging, so you should always be mindful and aware of the potential for feedback in a recording environment.

Few recording phenomena are wholly unwelcome, though, and feedback is a good case in point. Where would any self-respecting lead guitarist be without it? With apologies to guitarists (all of whom will surely know exactly how to create feedback), this effect is produced by holding the body of the guitar right up close to the speaker cabinet. The feedback effect can produce endless sustain as strings resonate when they "hear" themselves. But generally, guitar feedback can be a little unpredictable—which is, of course, the whole point.

Critical Listening

What a producer hears in the studio is invariably a million miles away from the lo-fi, overcompressed, and possibly distorted sound heard on radio, TV, or MP3s online. However, just because the final product may be compromised, we should still start off with the best sound we can.

Allen Sides again:

> I am a firm believer in making things sound bigger than life, and it's never been more important. If the end product is an MP3, if you've done a fairly meager job of the recording and it doesn't sound pretty good to begin with, by the time it gets to MP3 it will sound like it's broken. So, I think now it's even more important to make the most impressive recordings you can.

A key role of the producer is to discern what's important in the sound spectrum to make it transcend effectively into the real world, where audio quality is, inevitably, going to be compromised.

The quality of audio is all about information. If all the information is there on the recording itself, a good system can reproduce it, whereas a bad system will only give us some of it. However, a skilled producer will know how to ensure that the really important information will come through on even the most modest system. Without being too dramatic, this can make the difference between a hit and, well, not.

So what are we listening for? The balance of the mix is crucial. The stereo positioning of the instruments and vocals is important, as is the tonal or spectral balance between the constituent elements in a recording. Is the overall effect hard-edged, or is it smooth and easy on the ear? Is the emphasis on a thumping beat or the raw emotion of the performer? Is it important we hear every word of the lyric, or are the words just another element in the overall sound?

It's crucial that the monitoring system we use to make such judgments gives us a true impression of what the music really sounds like and how it will translate into the outside world.

Specifically, one issue for stereo monitoring is the center image, which is an imaginary focal point between the speakers. A good center image should give the impression that there is an invisible speaker between the left and right speakers. Pros refer to this as "the phantom center." The center signal is theoretically in the middle of your head when you're listening on headphones. Few consumers are even aware of this concept—they think mono is one speaker and stereo is two speakers, and there is no real comprehension of a stereo "picture."

A low-cost *sound pressure level* or SPL meter, available from your local Radio Shack or electronics hobbyist's shop, is a valuable tool for setting up speakers and amps at the correct levels. If the left and right speaker or headphone levels don't match, we will hear a phantom center offset to one side, which ultimately will mean we are hearing a different balance compared with what is actually there. You need to assess whether listening on speakers or on headphones is going to create any significant differences in your perception of the recorded information.

Why is the phantom center important? The lead vocal—in every style of music from rock to hip-hop to jazz, even operatic or classical music—almost invariably ends up in the center. In rock, so does the bass, the kick drum, and the snare drum. Why is this? If you want a snappy answer, it's because the beat and the melody are the key components of a hit record. If they're not coming out of both speakers, then the drums might be in the kitchen and the vocal in the living room! Some people just don't get stereo at all.

Another issue is monitor volume. At what level should we be making judgments about sound balance? There's definitely a perceived change in balance between music heard at different volume levels. Subtleties will be more apparent at lower levels, which is why many engineers and producers will spend a good deal of their mixing time listening at low level for subtleties of balance. At 100 dB (very loud), everything tends to sound good. When you're listening to music barely louder than the sound of your car engine, you're going to be very aware of the relative levels and the dynamic range of the tracks that make up the overall mix.

If you play one of your favorite records at ear-splitting level and then play it quietly—even with audio distractions—you'll see the difference in your perception of what the important features in the mix are.

Allen Sides once again:

> The other thing that I think is really important is that when you turn something up, if there's any one thing that's harsh or out of place, you can't enjoy it. Everything has to be in its place, so that when you turn it up, it sounds fun. And I think on a lot of mixes, it will hit a point where something is wrong and it ruins the whole mix, because you didn't hear it or it got by you.

Alan:

> When I'm mixing, I like to alternate between listening loud, then quiet, on the bigs, then on the near-fields, then on headphones, then from outside the room even! Somehow removing yourself from the studio environment and making yourself an eavesdropper can suddenly introduce thoughts on a mix that you might otherwise never have had. I remember Beatles engineer Geoff Emerick always checked the mix from outside the room.

The physical location or placement of our speakers is extremely important. Ideally, the left speaker, the right speaker, and the listener should form an equilateral triangle, with the tweeters level with your ears.

The directional axes of the speakers should be aimed directly at the listening position, and both speakers must be the same distance from the listener. Any slight variation would be a compromise. It's worth getting out a tape measure to be sure the distances match, rather than using the "That looks about right" method. Make your measurements from the tweeters, not your mid or bass drivers, as stereo information is predominantly carried by the higher frequencies.

Surround Systems

The same rules apply for the placement of multichannel surround systems, but there are a number of conventions for surround speaker placement (see **figure 6.5 A–B**).

Alan:

> People have been trying to create three-dimensional, immersive audio systems for years, Disney's *Fantasia* leading the charge back in 1940. In the seventies and eighties, two-channel, processing-based systems like Ambisonics, Hugo Zuccarelli's Holophonic system, or Roland's RSS abounded, and Quadraphonic sound, based on a set of four speakers, all came. And then went. Quadraphonic technology wasn't really ideally suited to vinyl records, but it wasn't that bad on 8-track cartridge. My "Quad" mix of *Dark Side of the Moon* was rereleased in a boxed set in 2012 and with a reasonable number of surround systems in consumer areas these days, particularly in home theaters, it's good to know my work was not entirely wasted, although I'm still waiting for the check to arrive.

Will surround "stick around?" The indications are that for music it won't—home theaters seem to be thriving, but music is the poor relation. It seems there is too much investment in technology by the labels and manufacturers, and then increased expense for the consumer. Sad.

There are several configurations for 5.1 sound. One forms a perfect square of speakers front and back, left and right (see **figure 6.5A**), which is the configuration Alan personally uses in his own studio. The center channel is recessed slightly behind the front speakers left and right, so as to be equidistant from the listener. Another format called the ITU configuration puts the rear speakers a little farther apart (see **figure 6.5B**). There is also a subwoofer channel that carries sub-bass information. The center channel originates from the film business for dialogue and has been the subject of endless discussions about its virtues for music only. Likewise, the "sub" channel was originally designed to make the room shake on movie explosions and earthquakes.

Surround sound is usually a mixing, as opposed to recording, process.

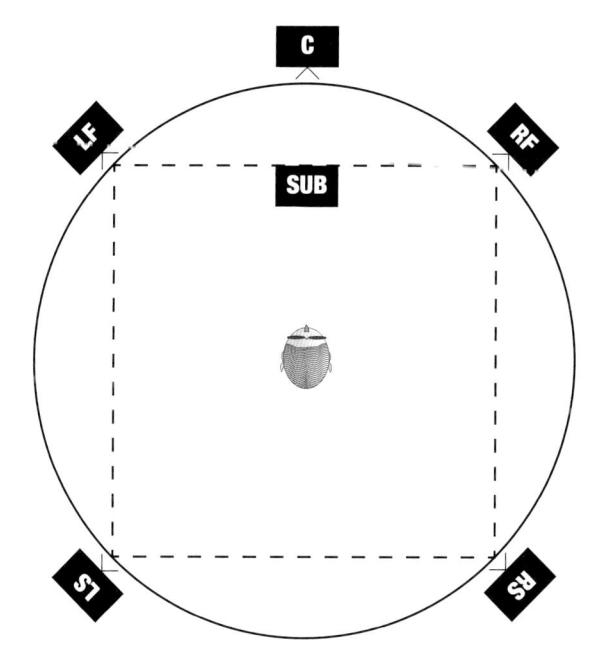

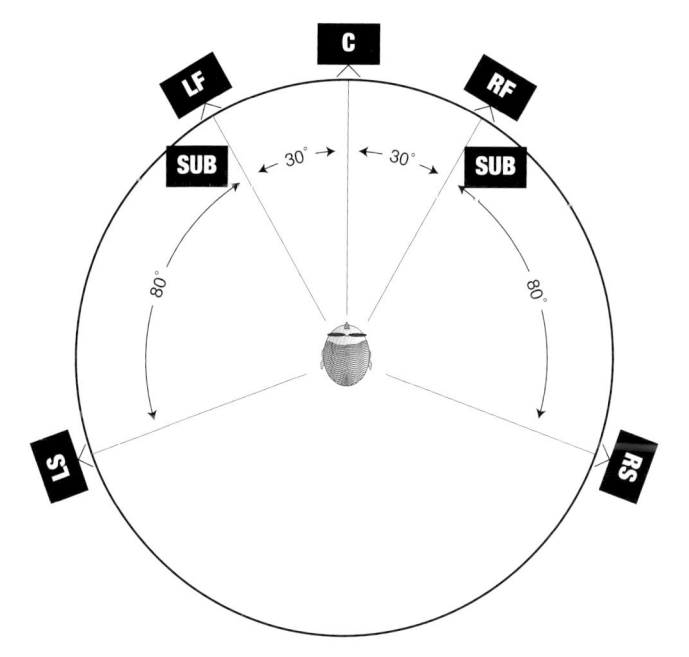

FIGURE 6.5A. **This placement shows the four main speakers arranged in a perfect square. All the speakers are equidistant from the listener. Note that the center speaker is recessed slightly in order to be equidistant. The subwoofer is normally in front of the listener but the placement is not critical and could be behind the listener or off to one side.**

FIGURE 6.5B. **This placement conforms to a standard known as the ITU spec. Again, all speakers should be equidistant from the listener, but in this configuration the surround speakers are toward the sides. Some systems use a pair of subwoofers, as shown here.**

Many surround music mixers will place the voice in the center channel. So if you remove the center channel, the artist is giving us a free karaoke version. When that channel is isolated, we can hear every breath or snort. For that reason, it's best to place vocals in the front left and right as well as the center.

Ideally, the subwoofer is at the core of the room, on the floor. Most pro audio engineers say the low frequencies are less directional, and hence the location of the subwoofer is not that critical. Another issue is what we call "bass management." This is an important but complex issue, and you'll find links on our website for further reading.

5.1 surround has progressed to 7.1 and even 11.1. Its potential? Hmmm.

Wrap

So as we've seen, there's a huge number of possibilities for monitoring audio. An interesting question in the age of mobile devices is whether we should be optimizing our sound mixes toward iPod users, or whether all great-sounding audio should strive to sound great wherever it goes. At time of writing it's too early to tell if Pono, with its lossless audio codec and range of dedicated high-end audio players, will reverse the trend in music delivery systems, but it's certainly a great and brave step in the right direction.

Another point worth noting is the great divide between the consumer hi-fi stereo world and the world of the audio professional.

Alan:

> Audiophiles will sometimes completely baffle pro audio people with their insistence, for example, that a CD player sitting on an ebony surface of a certain density with a $5,000 power conditioner and oxygen-free cables sounds better in some way. Pro audio people generally take the attitude that a piece of gear works for them, is reliable, and possesses sonic characteristics they can relate to. Better isn't necessarily better, if you see what I mean.

Consumer audio trade shows exhibit weird and wonderful speakers, amplifiers, turntables, and digital converters the audio pro hasn't even heard of. One interesting exception, which has manifested itself in recent years, are the loudspeakers from British manufacturer Bowers & Wilkins (B&W). Their 800 series has proved to be equally popular with audio pros and audiophiles. One difficulty B&W had to contend with were the power handling requirements in pro studios, and their Nautilus 801 has proved it can rise to that challenge in countless pro studios, including Abbey Road.

7

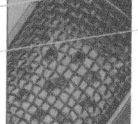

MIDI

In the early 1980s, a technology emerged that changed the entire face of musical instrument design and ultimately the entire basis of recording. That technology is called MIDI. MIDI stands for "Musical Instrument Digital Interface," and its origins were both humble in their original purpose and mind-blowing in what that original purpose would become.

MIDI grew out of keyboard technology and initially was just a means by which two synthesizers could be hooked up so that the keyboard of the first could control the notes heard on the second. Initially, this was done to expand the player's palette of tone colors. Back in 1983, though many companies saw the need for it and contributed to the idea, its final development was largely down to the designer of the revolutionary Sequential Circuits' Prophet-5 synthesizer, Dave Smith.

"We were looking ahead even then," says Smith. "Even the initial spec that we wrote at Sequential had pictures of computers in there and showed connecting up keyboards to computers. We were already looking into that in the future, even though the computer of choice at the time was the Commodore 64! We purposely kept the specification open enough so that things could be added later—things we weren't thinking about. For example, people started adding lighting control to it, or adding more timing information, or MIDI files for samples and that sort of thing.

"The amazing thing about MIDI is: Here we are, thirty years later, and it's still version 1.0, and you can still take any product that's built today and connect it to something that was built thirty years ago and it will work just fine. You don't find that anywhere else in electronics."

MIDI is a digital language, and its birth came alongside—and indeed became a significant player in the development of—the personal computer.

Companies such as Apple, Atari, IBM, and Microsoft all had strong ties with MIDI from the outset, and it's not fanciful to say that the concept of universal connectivity that MIDI embraces played an important role in the development of everything from the Internet itself to apps on an iPhone.

MIDI was established in 1983. By the end of the decade, MIDI-centric pop stars like Howard Jones, Thomas Dolby, and Ultravox and a generation of MIDI-file recording enthusiasts on their Commodore 64, Atari, or Apple IIe computers defined what modern DAW recording would become. It's an incredible achievement.

Although MIDI remains a feature within every recording device, from an Akai MPC groovebox to Ableton Live to the ubiquitous Pro Tools, the question remains whether one absolutely needs to understand MIDI to make sound recordings today. The answer to that . . . is a definite maybe.

Undoubtedly, understanding MIDI can turbocharge all aspects of your music production. Creating or customizing sounds and loops, hands-on and real-time control, mix automation, working in film, animation, game audio, and much more all owe a huge debt to MIDI.

The Difference Between Recording Audio and Recording MIDI

If you connect the audio outputs of a keyboard to an audio interface and DAW and hit "record," the WAV files you create can be edited to some degree, but the sound is fundamentally always going to be what it is: a piano, a string sound, drums, etc.

But connecting the keyboard via MIDI and recording the MIDI data means you have totally decoupled the "performance" from the "sound," in very much the same way a letter written on a word processor—as opposed to a typewriter—decouples the words you write from any particular font, or spacing, or layout.

The same part recorded into a DAW as both audio and MIDI should initially sound the same, whether you listen to the MIDI or the audio. However, at the press of a button, your MIDI-recorded guitar sound can be switched to a piano or a bass sound. It can also instantly be transposed without affecting the tempo, and sped up or slowed down without alteration of the pitch or tone.

Unlike with audio, where you are for the most part only able to see a waveform (with the notable exception of Melodyne at time of writing), a MIDI recording can be visualized as standard music notation. More magical still, each note can be changed or moved any which way you like.

FIGURE 7.1. Music recorded on a DAW both as MIDI, on a MIDI track (*top*), and audio, on an audio track.

What Is a MIDI Recording?

A MIDI recording is simply a series of commands that can be recorded and sent back to a MIDI-connected sound generating device such as a physical synthesizer or a software instrument on a computer. MIDI is simply a control language. It has nothing to do with sound per se.

MIDI instructions or "events" simply tell other devices what to do: In its simplest form: "Play this note, now! This loud, for this long." MIDI interprets each of these commands as an individual message sent out by a device designated as the controller and received by the connected sound-generating devices.

On a keyboard, if we play what is known as "middle C," the keyboard sends out a MIDI message: "Note #60 Note On." (See **figure 7.2.**) The strength with which we hit the note, and its resulting volume, MIDI calls "velocity," and it assigns a number or value to that as well. MIDI divides all its variable commands into 128 different values. So, in the case of velocity, a value of zero will be silent, a value of 1 extremely quiet, 10 very quiet, 30 fairly quiet, 60 medium, and 127 as loud as it can be—or maximum velocity.

When the key is released, MIDI will send out another instruction, this time a "Note Off" command.

If several notes are played at the same time, MIDI will see this as a series of commands in the form of packets of bits and bytes sent one after the other. MIDI is what is called a "serial" protocol.

MIDI allowed you to record multiple tracks of music on a personal computer for the very first time. The effect of this was dramatic. Being able to record and edit MIDI data directly on a computer meant that musicians could do everything from rehearsing a part to changing the arrangement and even sound design from the comfort of their own home, armed with just an Atari computer, some sequencing software, and a collection of synthesizer modules.

FIGURE 7.2. **The note being played is "Middle C," which MIDI refers to as "MIDI Note #60."**

MIDI recording had its limitations, of course—not being able to record vocals leading the pack—but it opened the door to professional-style recording without having to use professional-priced equipment in professional-priced environments.

What began purely as a solution for keyboard players ushered in the era of Pro Tools and DAWs, and a whole basket of magic bullets like Beat Detective and Auto-Tune to manipulate and even correct our rhythm and pitch. This all began back in the early 1980s with the invention of MIDI.

What's even more impressive is that from hardware keyboards to software plug-ins, samples, and beats, as well as underlying command and control, MIDI remains the lifeblood of modern recording systems. There is probably not a single pop record made in this time period that has been made without MIDI somewhere in its DNA.

Basic MIDI: Connections and Words You Need to Understand

Although MIDI is most commonly connected via USB, FireWire, or Thunderbolt, the original, most basic, and to some extent still the most flexible MIDI connection is a five-pin DIN cable coming from the MIDI Out socket of a controlling device being plugged into the MIDI In socket of an instrument or device you'd like to control. (See **figure 7.3.**)

To make it easier to connect a whole system of multiple devices, MIDI also offers a *Thru port*. MIDI Thru passes on information coming into its MIDI In and sends it through to another device's MIDI In. By this means, you can "daisy chain" a myriad of instruments or devices and just talk to whichever one you like at any given moment.

FIGURE 7.3. The most basic MIDI connection: A cable from a controlling device's MIDI Out (***bottom***) connects to a receiving device's MIDI In (***top***).

To be able to specify which particular sounds or instruments are doing what, MIDI ingeniously employs a system of channels, as with TV or radio, whereby you switch channels and tune into different stations. MIDI offers sixteen such channels, which allow you to tune into different instruments by setting up devices so they are both transmitting and receiving on the same MIDI channel.

To further specify a particular sound or program on a synthesizer, MIDI offers another parameter called a *Program Change* message. This tells a connected device communicating on a specified MIDI channel to switch to a particular sound or preset. There are 128 Program Change slots available. Because most synths offer more than 128 programs, MIDI can then further divide programs into *banks*. Theoretically, you can control up to 128 banks of 128 programs.

Sixteen channels might have been fine in the early days of MIDI, because you were unlikely to want to connect more than sixteen instruments at any one time. But as MIDI's reach extended into the control of individual parameters—not only on a synthesizer, but also within a computer or on a console—manufacturers needed a way to subdivide different types of MIDI data so that each could be sent out on its own "port," to streamline the flow of data. One "port" can then be reserved for sixteen channels' worth of musical functions—notes, tempos, etc.—another for a *separate* sixteen channels' worth of remote controller data, another for communicating with editors, and so on.

MIDI *Control Messages* fall into two basic categories: *system messages* that are not channel-dependent—for example, stopping and starting your DAW—and *channel messages* that let you specify, for each MIDI channel, certain aspects of a performance, such as filter movement, vibrato, volume, pan, and so on.

Local Control is an important system message to understand. Local Control has two states: on or off. This parameter lets you decide whether a device you are playing (typically a keyboard synthesizer) is outputting its own sounds via its own keyboard or is being controlled by another device (typically, your computer).

Here's a very common setup: You want to record parts you play on your keyboard *into* your computer and then have the computer play the parts back using sounds on that same keyboard. So, the keyboard gives the MIDI information to the computer and then the computer—not the keyboard itself—tells the instrument what to play.

With this setup, if your keyboard's Local Control is on, not only are *you* playing the sound on your keyboard, *so is your computer!* What happens here is that the MIDI commands from your playing are going to the synth's own tone generator, but also to the MIDI input of the computer. The information then comes out of the computer back into the keyboard, giving it a second set of the same information. The keyboard sees this as valid and sends it out again, both to the sound generator and back into the computer, in an endless loop going round and round. Not good.

This is called a MIDI loop and, rather like feedback, it'll slowly chew into your sound and eventually cause it to choke up. But if you set Local Control to off, then the keyboard will send data into the computer and only the computer will send the data to the keyboard's tone generator. The "local" controller—in other words, the keyboard's keyboard—is now decoupled from its own sounds. (Note that if you unplug the computer, you need to remember to turn Local Control back on, so you can hear anything. Ninety-nine percent of the times a keyboard seems to be "dead," it's because you or someone has forgotten that its Local Control has been turned off.)

MIDI not only looks at note and related parameter values, it can also handle timing. The so-named MIDI clock lets a device be in charge of the tempo, or optionally, lets it be controlled by another device and so remain in sync.

Many modern synths have their own built-in sequencer, where you can record and play back material entirely separate from a computer. But if you want to play back material recorded on the keyboard along with material recorded on the computer, then something has to be in charge of the timing so that both are in sync. As in everyday life, two bosses just gets complicated and out of whack. If you turn the keyboard's MIDI clock to external, it'll now respond to start, stop, and tempo controls coming from the computer. Alternately, we could set it up the other way around. It just depends on what you're doing, and which device you want to be the "master clock" or the boss of timing. Having said that, these days, most recording media are likely to be synced via a timecode, typically SMPTE.

As an extension to this, *MIDI Machine Control* (or MMC for short) is the name of a subset of the MIDI specification that provides specific commands for controlling a DAW or multitrack recorder from a remote control. This could be the transport controls on a keyboard or the physical controls on a dedicated controller. MMC is a standard, governing play, record, fast-forward, rewind, and stop.

MIDI Machine Control is a useful feature for everyday remote control over a DAW, but MIDI *continuous controller* messages are something else entirely. MIDI "CCs," as they are often called, are both handy and risky. The reason is the word *continuous*—due to regional variations from device to device, these channel messages provide incremental control over anything from a pan position to volume, modulation, pitch bend, or relative volume. The risky part is when one device is seeing a controller as a variable filter, for example, while another device might have that controller assigned to reverb level. It's important to "map" controllers correctly. Another controller is *After Touch*—where you add sound manipulation by holding down a key on a keyboard and varying the pressure. Using these parameters, you can inject a fantastic amount of life into recordings—in real time as you go, after the event as an overdub, or within a mix as automation. Be aware that after-touch information is data-hungry and in extreme cases could cause data overflow, resulting in timing errors. TMI applies here!

If undesired results occur and you end up with musical gibberish, MIDI thoughtfully provides a couple handy little panic buttons called *"Reset All Controllers"* and *"All Notes Off."* These messages are sent to all devices that are listening, and so restore order to the proceedings. If you find yourself using these a lot, though, you may need to dig in your MIDI event pages and see if excess data can be thinned out or even erased.

System Exclusive (Sys Ex for short) is the name applied to packets of MIDI data that relate to a particular make or model of instrument or device. Every manufacturer of MIDI equipment has its own MIDI ID number, so information can be stored that only applies to that device. A typical application of Sys Ex would be to store, transfer, and back up patch or program data.

Setting Up MIDI on Your System

In the early days of MIDI, setting up was as simple as plugging in a series of five-pin DIN cables connecting your instruments—or even your computer. Although hardware interfaces that solely distribute MIDI data still exist, a more common approach is to communicate MIDI data through USB, FireWire, Thunderbolt, or Ethernet ports.

The second "I" in MIDI stands for "interface," but MIDI most commonly describes a stream of data. It's strange how people say "MIDI interface," which translates to "Musical Instrument Digital Interface interface." Rather like a "PIN number" is a "Personal Identification Number number"!

As a rule of thumb, MIDI hardware devices need MIDI *drivers* to communicate with computers. Drivers are small programs that give computers instructions as to how to behave with specific applications. A driver may already be part of your operating system or—and this is probably the best course of action—you should check the website of your hardware manufacturer to see what MIDI drivers are available and install the latest one.

On some keyboards and other devices, you'll have a choice of using either USB or MIDI ports. Once the MIDI data is set to USB, you can forget the five-pin DIN connectors and take a USB cable out of the instrument and connect that directly to a USB port on your computer. When plugging in the USB cable from the keyboard to a PC for the first time, you should be prompted with the familiar "Found new hardware" dialog.

Be sure to download the right MIDI driver for your device, and then point the driver install wizard to the files you have downloaded. Once finished, you may be asked to reboot. After that, every time you start your DAW it should recognize the instrument's USB/MIDI ports.

Things You Can Do with MIDI

MIDI data is infinitely flexible, meaning you don't need to commit to a sound or a part until the mix. At that time, it makes sense to print your MIDI tracks as audio. Even though it used to be popular, recording in MIDI is now becoming more unusual in rock and pop. Perhaps producers feel it simpler to make all the decisions as they go along and stick to them.

Patrick Leonard, who produced many of Madonna's early, MIDI-driven hits, says:

> I'm a commit guy. With me and MIDI, because I'm a keyboard player, very rarely do I actually do any editing in it. I'm using it to record my Roland or my Prophet-5 that's been MIDI'd, I'm just using it to put that down, and sometimes using it because I can quantize or change velocities. But I'm not in there editing MIDI, because I'm just really recording stuff.

One area where MIDI is still widely used is in film, especially for orchestral scores, where it's not really practical to record cellists and oboe players during the initial recording or composing process. Music can be written, orchestrated, and presented to a director in demo form. If the material remains as a MIDI score, it can be edited and tempo-matched to picture in seconds. Once complete, the individual parts can be printed for real orchestral players.

Abbey Road classical engineer Simon Rhodes, who's recorded over 100 film soundtracks, including *Avatar* and *Skyfall*, says:

> The choice of staying with MIDI or realizing the MIDI into orchestral is very rarely a practical decision—it's always financial. And more and more, the MIDI is sounding really superb. Every few months, a new library comes out, and that just enhances the variety and the quality of sounds.

Nowadays, sampled or, in some cases, physical modeling-based applications and libraries such as Vienna Symphonic Library, Wallander Brass, Garritan, and the EastWest Orchestral Collection provide breathtaking realism for the orchestral composer to work with. Sometimes it's so real that producers stick with the MIDI version, rather than go to the time and expense of a full-blown orchestra session.

Simon Rhodes:

> The choice to use MIDI is a wonderful facility for directors really to get a sense of what they're going to have in their film, rather than just turning up at the scoring stage a couple of weeks before the dub and it's the first time you hear the music.

Anything from a Steven Spielberg movie to a simple song demo can benefit from recording in MIDI. Retaining control over your parts gives you maximum flexibility.

Back in 1984, British outfit Keyfax Software, which would later become the production company behind many music technology DVD and video projects—including the *ASSR* video series!—developed the idea of recording live musicians playing so-named alternate MIDI controllers such as MIDI drum pads, guitars, and wind controllers.

Keyfax recorded MIDI performances from a whole series of top-name musicians like Bill Bruford from Yes and Steve Hackett from Genesis and stored them as a library of MIDI loops called *Twiddly.Bits*. Cutting and pasting these short phrases and grooves can inject incredible realism and musicality into a MIDI recording.

Keyfax also developed *MIDI gates*. As you can see in the chapter on noise gates, applying the rhythmic opening and closing of a noise gate to a sustained pad sound makes a most effective "groove tool." A MIDI gate does exactly the same thing, but purely in MIDI: a series of pattern templates sending on and off MIDI volume messages can be applied to any MIDI chord or note. By superimposing this gate-effected rhythm onto your live playing or a recorded track, you have a highly flexible and almost limitless number of polyrhythmic textures at your disposal.

Most samplers, whether hardware or software, trigger samples via MIDI note-on messages. A simple software sampler called Groove Agent One, introduced in Steinberg's Cubase 5, allows you to just drag a series of bits of audio you have sliced and diced, and automatically distributes each one into a virtual drum machine–style "pad," which can be then immediately be triggered by hitting keys or pads on an attached MIDI controller.

Automation, as its name implies, is a way to store changes in volume, pan position, effects, EQ, and more within your DAW. Back in the day, all such changes within a mix would have to be done by hand, by real people!

MIDI remains a common control language for mix automation. All major DAWs, and most control surfaces, at least accept a standardized MIDI format even if they offer their own proprietary communication protocol.

MIDI remains the most common language for controller devices to communicate with their software counterparts or other devices. A knob or slider gives you a more immediate musical experience than a mouse, providing a more tactile interface between you and your music. Controllers range from very simple general use, to wild and wonderful customizable devices like Monome, to revolutionary new musical instruments on smartphones.

On a more down-to-earth level, MIDI control lies behind most knobs and faders on a keyboard workstation, giving you real-time control over otherwise static sounds. MIDI control like this lets you not only create a new performance but also edit it after the event.

MIDI's techie appeal has rarely been better served than by modular MIDI software applications that allow user-definable MIDI device routings and functionality. Spearheading this genre are Max/MSP, Reaktor, and Plogue. These applications are stand-alone or can work alongside a DAW. Despite their ability to reveal the outer fringes of MIDI control and synthesis, they do, ironically, tap into what "MIDI control" and "synthesis" have been all about since day one.

Although these applications tend to emerge within specific, possibly minority music genres, mainstream artists who want to remain on the cutting edge make sure they keep an eye and ear on what's being created with these new tools. MIDI also remains a powerful component within industry standard DAW software programs like Pro Tools, Logic, and Cubase.

For mixing consoles, processors like the Lexicon PCM96, and many synthesizers, software "editors" give you parameter-by-parameter control from the roomy setting of the computer monitor. Settings are generally stored as MIDI Sys Ex information, which is sent or received via a *bulk dump*—which, as its name implies, can transfer a whole raft of patch and setting information in one fell swoop.

Additionally, the individual parameters can themselves respond to MIDI controller messages created in real time—either built into the data of a song file on your DAW or initiated in real time via a performance controller. "MIDI Learn" is often implemented to allow for quick assignment of controller knobs or faders to a desired sound or FX parameter. The use of this is becoming ever more popular, as software is becoming more and more usable in live performance.

Many "software editors" simply choose to emulate the interface and menus of hardware devices, as with Yamaha's Studio Manager, for their range of consoles and synths. There are also many "VST" editors available for devices that use that technology.

The phrase "drum programming" arrived with Roger Linn's groundbreaking (and actually pre-MIDI) drum machine, the LM-1. Since MIDI, however, drum programming as an activity—even on later generations of machines, like the MPC series from Akai, which went on to effectively define hip-hop beats—have largely been based around MIDI.

Wireless MIDI devices have been available for a number of years and are primarily used to connect a MIDI controller such as a MIDI guitar or wind instrument to a MIDI system. A broad range of Wi-Fi or network devices can be used to work with MIDI. The iPhone and iPad are also popular front ends for many MIDI-based applications.

So it's clear that MIDI is a huge subject, and if you are interested, you can visit countless websites. But we would like to recommend one site, run by the MIDI Manufacturers Association: midi.org.

We hope you and MIDI have a long and meaningful relationship!

8

EQ

Without processing, sound recording would be more science and less art. Processing is the art of man-made manipulation, which can be necessary or sonically attractive for a variety of reasons.

All sound is produced by combinations of waves of varying frequencies moving the air around us. When we record, one measure of how faithfully we reproduce all the component sound waves is called *frequency response*. A good frequency response in a recording device is one way to assess its quality. What we call a "flat" response in a device or system is normally ideal. Also, we usually strive to have the recording as clean as possible without any distortion. But sometimes distortion and a modified frequency response *are* desirable. That's where audio processing comes into play.

Processing can be used to make sound seem more realistic and alive, or it can be used to make sound seem dramatically different and artificial. In this book, we look at a variety of processing tools and techniques, including compression, reverberation, delays, and compression. The name the pros give to tone control, or more precisely, processing the *tonal* characteristics of a sound, is *equalization*, or EQ for short.

Equalization was the first recognizable form of modern sound processing. It was developed at the birth of telecommunications to make up for quality losses in long cables as a way to rebalance or "equalize" the compromised sound and make it seem more clear and lifelike.

Over the years, the telecommunications and, subsequently, broadcast industries developed a great many EQ products to help solve this problem. Some, like the legendary Pultec passive EQ unit—which originated in the 1930s and remained in production, with modifications, until the 1970s—remain prized and much-emulated devices to this day.

EQ controls are tone controls that affect different frequencies of sound: in the most basic sense, the treble, mid, and bass controls you can find on everything from an electric guitar to a car stereo. Turn up the treble and it boosts the high frequencies. Turn up the bass and you'll boost the low frequencies. Originally, you needed tone controls on your car stereo to compensate for the environment in which you were listening to music. Nowadays, you might feel the need to use EQ so that your bass frequencies can be heard two blocks away! *Chacun à son goût.*

Similarly, when it comes to recording music, equalization lets you compensate for what you perceive as deficiencies in your original sound—an acoustic guitar that's too boomy, a hi-hat that's too thick, a snare drum that needs beefing up . . .

EQ is the adjustment of different frequencies or sound wavelengths, which are generally indicated and measured in hertz (Hz). Back in the day, we actually measured frequency in *cycles per second*. One cycle per second (1 c/s) equals 1 Hz. Ten kilocycles per second (10 Kc/s) equals 10 kHz.

Hertz is a unit measuring how many times the sound wave occurs or cycles each second. Low sound frequencies, which have a long wavelength, go through a "cycle" between thirty and a few hundred times a second, whereas the highest-frequency sound waves we can hear happen as often as several thousand times a second. Humans—well, young ones—can hear from approximately 20 Hz to 16 kHz or even higher. Sadly, as you get older, your ability to hear high frequencies drops off dramatically, even though you may still be able to sense or feel frequencies in the upper registers (see **figure 8.1**).

FIGURE 8.1. **The range of human hearing, which, sadly, decreases with age.**

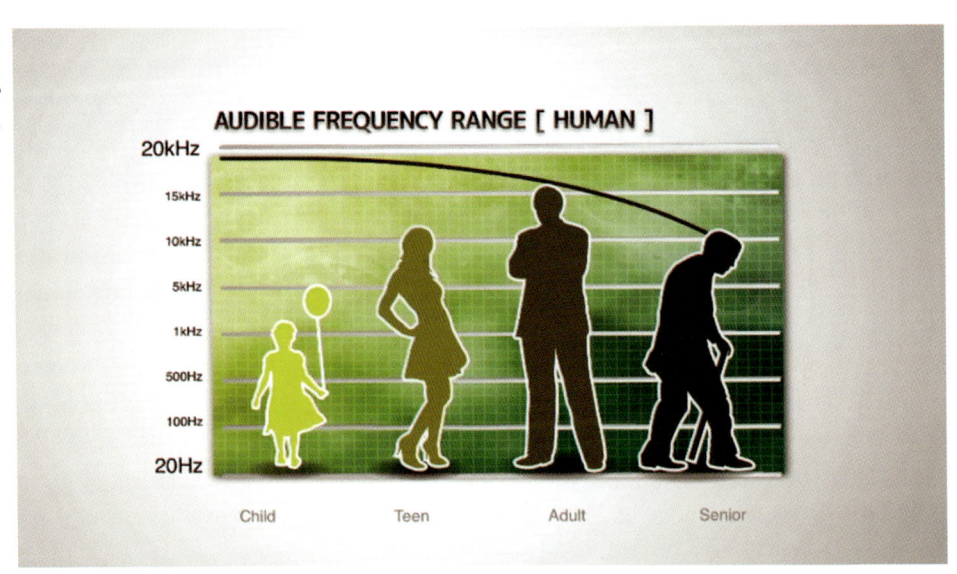

The same can happen if you listen to too much loud music, but that's another story. There are two things you can do to a frequency: you can boost it or you can cut it or, as we say, attenuate it. Different EQ processors and devices may offer different means to the same end, but this is the underlying principle behind all EQ adjustment.

EQ Types/Definitions

There are many instances in nature where certain frequencies can be enhanced or filtered, such as a sandbank or a wall of trees. For example, if we are on a beach behind a sandbank, we will find that the sound of the waves will be more of a rumble than a whoosh. In man-made structures, shape, size, and construction materials all combine to determine how a room will "sound."

So how do we deal with or make up for these phenomena in the studio?

All EQ devices employ some form of frequency selection by filtering. **Figure 8.2** shows a *graphic equalizer*, so named because as we boost and cut certain frequencies, the graph of the frequency response changes. And in this case, the sliders also actually draw their own graph, making it easy for us to see what is happening.

Figure 8.2 produces a graph of a totally flat or unchanged frequency response. The horizontal numbers represent frequency in hertz (Hz), and the vertical numbers represent volume in decibels (dB).

If we increase the level with EQ at, say, 2 kHz, the curve changes to show that levels in the area around 2 kHz will get louder (see **figure 8.3**). We call this a *bell curve*. **Figure 8.4** shows a cut at 200 Hz applying a negative bell curve. This will reduce the frequencies in that general vicinity. By making further adjustments, we can build the exact response curve we need.

Equalizers can also produce what we call *shelf curves*. This means that for a treble EQ, *all* the frequencies above a particular chosen frequency are boosted or cut. Likewise for bass EQ, all the frequencies below a certain value are altered. In other words, if we apply a boost to a 3 kHz shelf, then all frequencies above 3 kHz will be boosted by that amount.

There is another type of equalization called *filtering*. For example, we often want to totally remove all frequencies below, say, 100 Hz to get rid of low-frequency rumble or a pop on a vocal mic. To do this we apply a high-pass filter—so named because it "passes" the high frequencies and blocks the lows.

At the other end of the scale, a low-pass filter filters out information above a certain frequency. This might be used to get rid of hiss coming from a guitar amp, for example, but will still "pass" the low end of the sound.

It's a little confusing that high-pass is referring to a low-end filter and low-pass is a high-end filter. But that's how it is, and we've all mixed them up at some time or another.

Choosing the right frequency to equalize is crucial. Most graphic equalizers allow you to adjust a "center" or "base" frequency every one-third of an octave—in other words, the equivalent of between three and four notes on a chromatic musical scale.

FIGURE 8.2. **A stereo graphic equalizer with a "flat" frequency response, with all sliders/frequencies at 0 dB.**

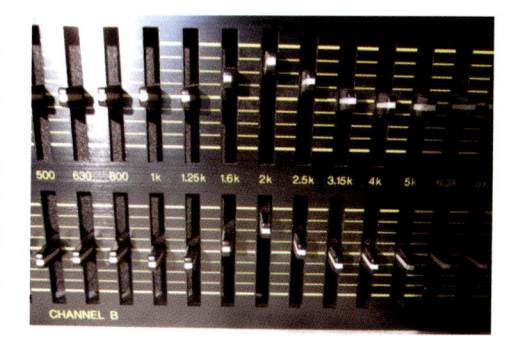

FIGURE 8.3. **A graphic equalizer showing a "bell curve" with a volume boost around 2 kHz.**

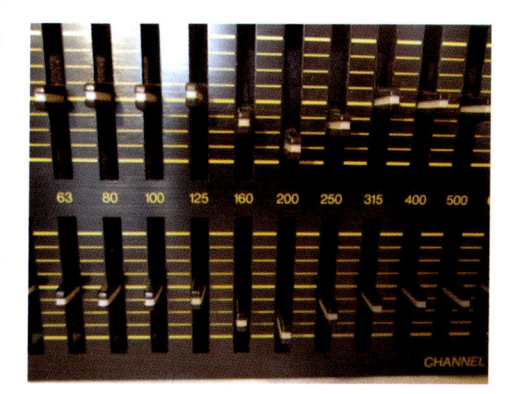

FIGURE 8.4. **A negative bell curve on a graphic equalizer showing reduced levels around 200 Hz.**

Equally crucial is the amount of adjustment you make. Making anything more than gentle adjustments on a graphic EQ has quite a dramatic and not necessarily pleasant effect on the sound. If you want a natural effect, EQ is best used subtly and smoothly. Yanking one particular frequency up or down too much tends to make things sound unnatural.

Back in the 1970s, one of the pioneers of modern music engineering, George Massenburg, developed what became known as the *parametric equalizer*. Instead of working with static frequencies, a parametric EQ device allows us to home in on a particular frequency using the frequency control. With another knob, we can also choose how sharp we'd like the focus to be—in other words, how many neighboring frequencies we want to include. This is referred to as the bandwidth or Q control, and was no doubt invented in a James Bond gadget lab, since we can't think of any other reason it's called Q!

A very low setting—represented graphically as a broad loop—gives you quite a wide range of control around the set frequency. A higher setting gives you a narrow, sharper range of control around the set frequency. Removing a very narrow band of frequencies is called *notch filtering*. For example, we might want to filter out a hum without affecting anything else.

Many modern consoles have full-blown parametric EQ built in, plus of course there are both stand-alone hardware devices and a thousand and one parametric EQ plug-ins.

FIGURE 8.5. "No low-lifers frequenting this neighborhood!"

EQ Devices

The earliest form of tone control was perhaps the touch of the player and the manner in which he or she made physical contact with the instrument. On a recording, "tone" can be drastically affected by where a microphone is placed. On electric instruments, artificial tone controls or EQ are normally included. In the case of the electric guitar, switches control which pickup is active, which has a similar effect to playing an acoustic guitar near the bridge or nearer the fingerboard. These are forms of EQ, just created and applied differently.

On electronic keyboards and synths you'll find a whole range of tone controls, from basic treble, mid, and bass to quite sophisticated graphic and even parametric EQ devices. With drums, tone is set not only by the drum itself, but also by the head or drum skin, and then of course by way the player hits it as well the implement he or she uses—a soft beater will produce a vastly different sound from a drumstick.

Alan:

> I've always felt that if it doesn't sound right to the human ear, it's not going to sound right to the microphone. So the first step is simply to listen to a sound acoustically, or unprocessed, and see what it needs.

During recording we may want to apply EQ to enhance or mask a certain characteristic, or we might want to leave it alone, EQ-wise. We call this recording "flat." There's a certain satisfaction in recording flat. It means the source sound is good and we've made the right microphone and placement choices. Of course, we can always EQ later if we want to. Many engineers prefer to record everything flat and not to commit to any EQ, or any other processing for that matter, until the final mix.

If we are using a mixing desk, the microphone's channel strip is bound to provide some form of EQ. **Figure 8.6** shows a fairly standard analog mixer, on which you can see that each channel

FIGURE 8.6. **Basic three-band EQ on an analog mixer.**

offers three frequency bands of EQ control. Often you will see a high-pass filter set at 80 Hz, under button control, that can simply be switched in, per channel, to eliminate low-frequency hums or rumbles that can so often invade an incoming signal.

On *digital* mixers you're more likely to find a single hands-on parametric EQ panel that can be used to set the EQ of each audio source individually. The settings can be stored away in the console's brain.

Higher up the ladder, classic recording and mixing consoles from companies like SSL, API, and Neve gained fame and favor due to their perceived distinctive sound, which at least in part was down to the EQ controls on their channel strips. Nowadays you don't need to mortgage your house to buy a complete console; you can simply buy a single channel strip or just use GarageBand!

There are also stand-alone hardware filter and EQ units. Vintage models, especially tube designs, are notoriously expensive, and even modern interpretations of the classics are hard to find under several hundred dollars.

Alan:

> If you can afford something like a Pultec or a Manley unit, then I strongly recommend you don't resist the temptation.

Luckily, there are other more cost-effective solutions today that can be had for a fraction of the cost. Today, the option that's definitely the most affordable—and to some extent, the most flexible—is software. Processing plug-ins that operate from within your DAW can come bundled in with the platform, or they can be "stand-alone"—i.e., purchased and installed separately. Another option is for a plug-in to come with a card-based processor that takes some of the load off your CPU. Processor specialists Universal Audio have had particular success with their "UAD" cards.

EQ is a very personal, almost emotional process, and there's wide debate amongst engineers and producers as to whether obviously "digital" EQ plug-ins—even emulations of classic analog EQ—can come close to sounding like their genuinely analog counterparts.

John McBride:

> I've always found that I can get a better end result from using analog gear. And I've had engineers come in to my studio and, as opposed to using the Pultecs that are in the rack, they ask for the Pultec plug-in, and I always thought, *What in the world are they doing?* But it's because when they go somewhere else to work on their record further, they want to be able to duplicate exactly what they had. And maybe the next studio, wherever they work next, may not have the Pultecs. So, you have to do what you have to do.

But not everyone thinks like this.

David Thoener:

> What I do love about plug-ins is the ability to use *ten* LA2s or *ten* Fairchilds or *ten* Pultecs. If there's a certain sound that I've gotten, and I've got twenty backing vocals, I can subgroup and just put the stereo subgroup through the Neve or a Pultec, or I could have twenty Pultecs—one for each track. I think Bob Clearmountain had twenty-four Pultecs in one of his rooms, but very few rooms have that much gear. So plug-ins allow me to have that freedom. It can be done totally with plug-ins. It's not the technology that dictates the sound of the record—it's the man working the technology.

Using EQ

What are we trying to achieve with EQ? Make an individual instrument sound better, or create a balanced, unified whole? Unfortunately, the answer is yes all round, and the thing to keep in mind with EQ is that it's really a matter of constant reassessment. Here are some common questions:

How do you EQ an instrument before you know what it's going to be combined with?

Try to EQ for the current state of the track and don't necessarily think too far ahead about how the overall sound is going to develop. We can always re-equalize an individual sound at a later stage if it's not sitting quite right in the mix. An advantage of DAWs is that you always have a permanent record of your EQ settings. So if something works well for you, you can use it again and again.

Should EQ always be printed—in other words, committed to on the recorded track?

In tape days, generally yes. Monitor EQ or EQ applied to the played-back sound, as opposed to the sound to be recorded, was not a widely adopted concept. In digital it really doesn't matter when you commit to EQ. But until you do, of course, you're adding one more set of spider legs to the decision process—something to bear in mind.

Do you ever need to EQ a whole mix, or is that the job of a mastering engineer?

You should always be aware that you can add EQ or other processing over the entire final mix, but on the final product, the mastering engineer—if you have the luxury of using one—really should be the judge. However, if your mastering engineer says, "I don't need to do anything to this"—which in ideal circumstances can happen—then give yourself a pat on the back.

At what point should you make the decision to EQ something rather than try to fix a problem on the instrument or with mic choice or mic positioning?

It's always good to get the source sounding its absolute best. Garbage in means garbage out. In a high-pressure recording session, changing or moving the mic more than once might try the patience of the artist or interrupt the flow of the session. It's the skill of the engineer to know which solution to any given problem is best.

How do you test your system or learn to trust it?

Knowing your own system is extremely important. Most engineers in their own environment should be able to make informed decisions. But in an unfamiliar environment, take along some music you know, and assess what compensation is necessary. Simply taking your own near-field monitors to a new environment can be helpful—provided the room itself is not having a significant adverse effect on the sound you hear.

Should you apply EQ only using your biggest monitors, or should you switch between systems as you adjust? Or even check on headphones?

It's good practice to keep checking your sound on a variety of speakers and locations, especially during mixing. Checking on headphones is especially important in the iPod and smartphone age.

Are there any pitfalls in boosting using one EQ, then cutting on another? Do you undo what you did originally or just continue making new adjustments?

If you're simply monitoring the EQ—in other words, EQing on playback—then you can take it off without having any effect on the recorded sound. It's quite acceptable to boost a broad range of frequencies on one device and then cut a very specific frequency in that band on another device, yes. If you have applied EQ and committed it to disk or tape, it'll be more difficult to get your original sound back.

Which is better, analog or digital EQ?

Digital has the reputation for not being as musical, but this is very much a subjective judgment and decision.

What makes a good EQ device?

Being able to reach for a knob or control and knowing what it's going to do. Part of that is familiarity, but another part of it is good design.

Applying EQ

If you can record "flat" with a good result, that's an ideal situation. But most of us end up applying a little EQ to everything, even if it doesn't happen until the final mix or in mastering. EQ is making up the difference—or equalizing—between what you want to hear and what you've got. So let's now look at some of the main instrument groups, and sounds, and discuss some common sonic deficiencies and how best to correct them with EQ.

Bass guitar

Start off by making the sound as good as possible by adjusting the controls on the instrument before applying any external EQ. You might think a bass only generates low frequencies, but in fact a lot of the energy comes from the mid-range, and even mid to high frequencies as well. Certainly, if you adjust anything around 12 kHz, you're not going to make any noticeable difference, because you can only adjust frequencies that actually exist in the sound itself. But if we look around any frequency up to 3 kHz on a bass, we will definitely hear a difference.

If we need to accentuate the attack, we can boost frequencies in the mids (1–2 kHz) and even high mid range up to 5 kHz. If the bass is a bit boomy, it can be thinned out by filtering some low end using a high-pass filter, or low frequency EQ in the 50–100 Hz area.

Drums

Drums are complex because they're a collection of related instruments recorded to feel like they operate as a whole. Even though you may apply EQ to one drum or cymbal at a time, it's important that the components fit together naturally. Simon Phillips, a man who has practically lived in the recording studio since he was a teenager, explains more about this:

> A drum kit is made out of many parts, but to me, I always look at it as one instrument, like the piano; because if I take my four toms away, the snare drum will sound different—it's just physics. The toms all have a sympathetic ring. Even though the microphone is only two inches from the head, if the source changes, then it's going to affect what it picks up.

For an example of a complete drum kit, see **figure 16.1, p. 153.**

Alan:

> The kick drum (or the bass drum, if you're as old as I am) is where most engineers will start on a kit. Kick drums operate mainly in the 40 Hz to 250 Hz area, although the "attack" of a kick drum you'll find up around 1–3 kHz. Once you're sure the instrument itself is the best it can be with respect to tuning, damping, heads, etc., look at around 50 Hz to reinforce or back off its density and thickness. If you need more attack, you'll find that at around 1 kHz. If your kick drum is a bit indistinct, try cutting around 200–400 Hz.
>
> The heartbeat sound on *Dark Side of the Moon*, you may be interested to hear, is simply a heavily EQed kick drum used in conjunction with a noise gate. The attack was minimized by reduction of mids and highs, and the "boom-boom" was achieved by increasing the low frequencies right down to 30 Hz.

When recording the snare drum, it's very important to get the natural sound right acoustically, with tuning and damping, before you start applying EQ. Having said that, rock and pop recording techniques normally include a mic an inch or two from the snare head. Please don't put your head this close to a snare drum in full flight unless you want to go deaf.

"Ring" on the snare is a common phenomenon, but here's the issue: we may want to get rid of ring on a snare, but we don't want to resort to heavy damping, which can destroy the overall sound of the drum.

Here is where parametric EQ comes into its own. The trick is to decide roughly where you think the problem area is. As often as not, it'll be in 600–700 Hz range, and one easy way to locate the culprit is to apply a dramatic boost and then "sweep" the general area using a fairly sharp Q or resonance setting. When we hit the right spot, the ring will then go into overdrive! At this point we can switch an equally dramatic "cut" to the signal at that frequency and the ring should be substantially reduced or disappear. To get as natural a sound as possible, we can fine-tune the Q and/or the amount of cut being applied until we have the best possible result.

Snare drums can inhabit quite a wide range of frequencies, from 100 Hz right up to 10 kHz or higher for the "crack" of a snare. If more depth is needed, try adding a little at 100 Hz. If the sound is a little muddy, take out a little in the mid-range, around 350–750 Hz.

Alan:

> I invariably end up adding quite a lot of top end to a snare drum.

Err on the side of caution, though. Don't paint yourself into a corner this early in the recording process.

Depending upon what size drums are being used, toms (once known as tom-toms to us geriatrics) can live in a frequency range from almost kick drum depth to beyond snare highs. What we're looking for in a recorded tom is, generally, definition and punch. Tom fills are played as punctuation, so we want them to speak and be heard clearly. That said, it's helpful to keep in mind the overall perspective of the toms and not focus too much on the individual sound of one drum. Most engineers will spread the toms across the stereo picture, leaving the kick and snare in the center.

Alan:

> I usually find that I record toms flat. If they don't sound good, I'm more likely to suggest a retune or physical damping on the drum.

Cymbals are the drummer's only sustaining instruments, and their tone is crucially important because their sound lives on beyond mere milliseconds. They would normally be captured by overhead mics placed two or three feet above the kit. Overhead mic placement will depend on the location and spread of the cymbals. They can be miked individually, but it's not a very common practice these days, although sometimes the ride cymbal is lacking on the overheads and might need its own mic. Remember that if we apply EQ to overhead mics, we are effectively EQing the whole kit, but by applying EQ at high frequencies only—say, 8–12 kHz—we can change the perceived balance between the cymbals and the rest of the kit.

That said, cymbals should be trusted to speak for themselves and shouldn't need a lot of EQ. When recording either very old, dirty, or somehow dull cymbals, they might need brightening up a little—a lot of people call this giving them a little "air"—at around 8–10 kHz. Do not overdo this, though, especially on recording, as overly or unnaturally bright cymbals will get very wearing on the ears, and they will be very difficult to get to "sit" in the track.

Alan:

> Ribbon mics work particularly well with cymbals, and I almost always use them as overheads. They need to have top end added because they are "darker" than condenser mics, but I prefer that result over the brighter, non-EQed sound of condensers as overheads.

Hi-hat can pose several challenges—especially its relationship with the snare drum, to which it is both aurally and physically close.

Alan:

> Level is what I've found to be the most important adjustment. Personally, I'll very rarely EQ the hi-hat. Because of its proximity, it's often the snare EQ that will define the sound of the hi-hat.
>
> I'll usually pan the hi-hat hard right but adjust its level so it appears to be halfway between center and right. The snare mic will have some hi-hat on it, especially with a lot of top EQ, so the snare mic will tend to pull the hi-hat toward the center.

A hi-hat shares the same "shimmer" as an acoustic guitar, so you can look at the 8–10 kHz region if you want to add or subtract in that area. A thick or clangy hi-hat not only devours space in a track, it also just doesn't sound good. Depending on the player, their flexibility, the hi-hat they're using, and of course the material being recorded, a shelving filter—rolling off everything below, say, 600–700 Hz—can be effective. The "clang" of hi-hat is in the mid-range—anywhere between 1 and 3 kHz—so if this is a problem cut at around these frequencies.

Electric guitar

The basic tone is best left to the guitar, the player, and the amplifier. The idea, then, is to capture that tone as faithfully as we can, using the best combination of close and room mics, or in some cases the direct sound right out of the instrument or preamp.

EQing electric guitar is more a matter of bracketing—in other words, encapsulating the sound the engineer or the guitarist wants to capture and not clouding it with unnecessary top or bottom (which can be done using high- and low-pass filters), and then making very gentle adjustments to refine or perfect the sound.

An interesting side note is that the popular wah-wah guitar stomp-box effect is actually an EQ boost at variable frequencies according to the position of the pedal. Here's how to do it on a parametric equalizer: set something like a 12 dB boost and then sweep the center frequency with a narrow Q setting.

Acoustic guitar

Acoustic guitars generally have their own individual character, and we want to capture that character as faithfully as possible. Boominess can be a problem area, as it will tend to cloud the rest of the track if not addressed. Boominess can be minimized by appropriate mic positioning (the closer the mic, the more boomy it will tend to be). You can also do it with EQ.

Alan:

> I usually use a high-pass shelving filter around 250 Hz. This should reduce the bottom end without losing too much richness.

To add sparkle or presence to an acoustic guitar, try adding a little around 10–12 kHz using a broad Q.

Brass, horns, reeds, and woodwinds

Brass, horns, reeds, and woodwinds shouldn't require too much by way of EQ on recording. When recording a section, you obviously rely on the tonality of the players and the blend of instruments you're working with to produce a unified "section" sound. Trumpets and trombones tend to cut through everything like a laser! Conversely, French horns can sound muffled. If you want a bit more "rasp," rather than apply EQ to solve the problem, ask the performer (diplomatically!) to blow harder, and then reduce your level. A close-miked sax that is sounding honky might need some brightening up and removal of mid-range at around 700–800 Hz.

For some strange reason, French horns have a tendency to throw the mix out of phase. Ask any classical engineer. It's probably something to do with the fact that the bell of the horn faces backwards. This can be averted by not panning them to extreme edges of the stereo picture. There are endless arguments about whether they should be miked from in front or behind.

Alan:

> A personal point I'd like to make about saxophone and other reed instruments: the sound does not just come from the bell. It also comes from the mouthpiece and along the entire length of the instrument. You often see saxes recorded only through the bell on TV, but I prefer to record them from a distance of three to four feet.

Flutes, oboes, clarinets, and bassoons can sometimes be given a more airy sound by adding brightness around 8 kHz. Bottom-end EQ is unlikely to be needed, unless there are boominess or rumble problems, which can usually be fixed with a high-pass filter.

Percussion

Percussion covers an enormous range of sounds, from everything that shakes, rattles, and rolls to tuned percussion like marimba, xylophone, and glockenspiel. It's impossible to generalize about EQ with such a wide range of tonalities. An orchestral percussion section might go through hundreds of instrument changes.

A good solution to brightening up tuned percussion, rather than EQing them, is asking the player to use harder sticks. Pro session players will usually be able to accommodate that request. This also applies to vibraphone, which is a notoriously difficult instrument to record.

Alan:

> In fact, the only thing harder to record than a vibraphone is a steel drum—for which, in my experience, no form of EQ ever seems to work!

Strings

A lot will depend on the miking technique being used on strings. For an ensemble of string players, we can mike each pair of players; or we can use a more distant mic to cover the entire string section. Close-miked violins might tend to get a little "hard," and an EQ cut around 1–3 kHz can help. Violas and cellos might cut through better with some EQ boost around 6–8 kHz. Double basses can occasionally get boomy and can benefit from a cut in the low frequencies or the application of a high-pass filter. If you've got a lot of mics going, you might not have the inclination to activate say, twenty equalizers. With the luxury of unlimited tracks on DAWs, it's probably best to get the balance right and think about EQ later, maybe section by section, rather than mic by mic.

Acoustic piano

Acoustic piano, especially a grand piano, is a complete orchestra in a box, and it occupies a frequency range from bass and kick drum depth at around 30 Hz to competing with the highest of the high in the upper registers at 15 kHz or above. Ideally, tonal adjustment is best left to the player, microphones, and mic placement, unless we are going for a very specific type of effect. In a nonclassical or jazz setting, acoustic piano frequently needs to fit into an arrangement of other instruments with competing frequencies. The player's left hand might, for example, compete with the bass guitar. This can be tackled with EQ, but a better solution may be to work on the arrangement so clashes don't occur in the first place. For rock recordings we might need to brighten up the average piano between 4 and 6 dB with an 8 kHz shelf. But some studio pianos are very bright to start with, having had their hammers "doped" to make them so.

Sampled pianos should need little EQ, as it may have been applied during the sampling process. Upright pianos sound very different from grands, but a lot of the same general rules apply.

Electric piano

Electric piano—in particular, the Fender Rhodes—is another notoriously difficult instrument to record. The bass runs to extreme bouts of boominess, the middle can be extremely muddy, and the top end teeters between shrill and annoying or light and insubstantial.

Although EQ can be used to offset these, it's really best to adjust the balance of the instrument internally and then use some compression to even up the overall sound.

Vocals

Vocal EQ is another sensitive area. Over-EQing a vocal, unless we're going for a particular effect like a telephone voice or space-alien sound, can easily result in a vocal sound that is tiring and harsh.

Microphones play a huge role in the tone of a vocal. A good approach is just to apply a high-pass shelving filter to lose any potential rumbles and reduce pops, but check that it is not affecting the vocal sound in any way. Wait until the mix for final adjustments to make the vocal cut, sit, or have some air around it. As with snare drums, 1–2 kHz is often a problem area where vocals can get a bit honky and nasal. Of course limiting, compression, and reverb are all going to affect the vocal sound.

To make a vocal stand out better, try boosting the vocals at around 4 kHz and at the same time *cutting* that frequency on instruments playing at the same time. This way, the vocals get a bit of space by themselves. But be careful not to over-EQ vocals so that they become harsh. To add a bit more fizz to vocals, boost the frequency range starting at about 10 kHz. Alternately, if there's a sibilance problem—the S sound—back off the same frequency or use a de-esser, which is looked at more closely in the next chapter.

If a vocal is sounding hard, look at frequencies around 2.5–3 kHz and apply a gentle cut. A parametric EQ or notch filter can be useful here so as to focus in on the optimum frequencies and not disturb the balance of neighboring material.

Problems

Unwanted hum (OK, hum is very rarely wanted!) is usually low-frequency and often at the frequency of the AC electricity supply—50 or 60 Hz. Depending upon the circumstances, a simple high-pass filter can be applied, so long as there's no other information around the hum frequency we want to retain. For all kinds of consistent hums, buzzes, and whines, parametric EQ can dial very specifically into the frequency

Frequency	Instrument	Results
30–60 Hz	Kick drum / sub-bass	Boost to reinforce or thicken.
	Vocals	Cut to get rid of rumble or pops.
70–100 Hz	Bass, kick drum	
200–400 Hz	Guitars, vocals, keys	Boost to add thickening. Cut to add clarity.
	Snare drums	Useful range for tonal adjustment.
400–800 Hz	Toms, guitars, keys	Boost to add warmth. Cut to gain clarity.
	Bass	Boost to make it pop out more. Or cut other instruments.
800 Hz–1 kHz	Vocals, edge of kick drum	
1–3 kHz	Piano mid-range	Boost to add grit.
	Guitar	Boost to add bite. Cut to reduce harshness.
3–6 kHz	Vocals and guitars	Boost to add bite. Cut to reduce harshness.
6–10 kHz	Vocal	Boost to add edge.
	Acoustic guitar	Boost to add crispness.
	Percussion and cymbals	Boost to add crispness.
	Snare	Boost to add crack.
10–16 kHz	Vocals	Boost to add airiness.
	Drums and percussion	Boost to add sizzle.

FIGURE 8.7. **Instant guide to frequencies.**

of the noise without affecting too much else around it. So, the sharper your Q the better. This is an ideal application for notch filtering.

We look at mixing in its own chapter, but here are some helpful guidelines to EQ solutions during the mixing process. If a track lacks punch, try boosting the upper frequencies of the drums or the rhythm section, or even the whole mix. If the track seems boomy or thick, try applying EQ cut over individual sounds or even the entire track at around 200 Hz. Be careful, though—if backed off too much, the track will start sounding thin.

Afterthoughts

EQ has become one of the most used—and sadly, often overused—forms of sound manipulation. Nothing is more subjective or more defining of the skills of an engineer than his or her use of EQ. An entire production style can be defined by how EQ is used.

Finally, some wise words on EQ from Jack Joseph Puig, an engineer and producer who's worked with John Mayer, Green Day, U2, Fergie, No Doubt, and countless others:

> The mid-range has always been the most important to me, because the mid-range is where the soul, the cry, the heart, the life, the love, the laughter, the real perspective lives; it doesn't live in the highs, and it doesn't live in the lows. That's what really speaks to the heart. It's also in the frequency that's the most common to every system in the world. A sound system might have five woofers, and one might not have any, one might have ten tweeters—but all of them have mid-range, so that has got to be right.

Like all things artistic, there is no "magic formula" for achieving a great sound. Develop your own set of skills. Experience through listening is the key.

COMPRESSORS AND LIMITERS

The difference in level between the loudest and the quietest sounds in any piece of audio is called its *dynamic range*.

In a recording, a vocal or instrumental part with too much variation in level, or a high dynamic range, is both hard to fit into a mix and also quite uncomfortable to listen to. This is where compressors and limiters come into the picture. Virtually every vocal track in rock or pop music has involved a limiter or compressor to control its dynamics.

You could argue that your own hands are the cheapest or the most expensive compressors you can get. Physically moving levels up and down with a fader is a very effective way of controlling dynamic range. However, you have to have your wits about you to do it effectively, and it's much easier to use electronic means.

Son of the legendary engineer Bill Putnam, Universal Audio's CEO, Bill Putnam Jr., explains a bit of the history:

> Compressors came out of the world of radio to solve a very practical problem, and that problem was to deal with sound sources at different levels. What typically used to be done was, the engineer would be riding a volume knob, and if the sound came in loud or the soloist was a little closer to the microphone, you'd have to turn that person down quickly. If the soloist was further back, you'd have to turn that person up to achieve an overall balance. Compressors do just that—they take loud sounds and they reduce the volume, or they'll take softer sounds and bring them up.

The Difference Between Compression and Limiting

Compression and limiting are two related processes that are frequently offered on the same piece of equipment. Compression, as its name suggests, squashes or "compresses" the dynamics of a sound to reduce the differential in volume between its loudest and quietest moments. A compressor both amplifies quiet sounds and softens loud ones (see **figure 9.1**).

Limiting puts a firm lid on any excessively loud parts to prevent a signal from overloading. Pitfalls of compression and limiting include increased noise and a tendency to increase sibilance on vocals.

A compressor is a more complex device that allows us to smooth out dynamics so that large changes in volume become small changes in volume. In practice, the effects of limiting and compression can be similar, and the differences between them quite subtle.

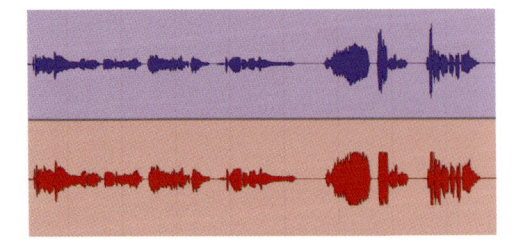

FIGURE 9.1. Two versions of a waveform. The blue waveform (*top*) is uncompressed. The red waveform below it is the same clip but heavily compressed. Note how the level is generally higher on the compressed waveform and it still has sharp peaks. It doesn't hit a "brick wall" until toward the end of the clip.

Compressors

The huge number of compression and limiting products available can make the choice difficult. There are hardware devices from manufacturers like Universal Audio, Fairchild, and DBX. Dynamic range controls can be built into a console or channel strip, and there are now countless software plug-ins—some new, some emulations of classic compressors of the past.

Analog devices can employ solid-state circuitry or tube ("valve," as they say in Britain) electronics, which can play an important part in terms of the "sound" of the compression. But it's important to remember that dynamic control can be done in either the analog or the digital domain. Highly prized units like the Fairchild 660 and Universal Audio 1176 are analog devices, so you would definitely want to use these direct from your mic or instrument, rather than coming out of the digital domain just to use a vintage analog unit—that would entail two conversion processes, which, it could be argued, might be not worth the potential degradation.

Once you are in the digital domain, there's a good argument for staying "in the box" as we say, for limiting and compression—i.e., remaining resolutely digital. It's certainly the most economic choice. But some engineers like to come out of the digital domain and process their dynamics with analog gear, particularly for mixing, even across the whole mix.

Alan:

> NOT ME! I absolutely detest limiting or compression on a mix.

Compressor Controls

Before we look at the knobs that control the functions of a limiter or compressor, it's important to understand that meters on a limiter and compressor can show input and output levels in a conventional way, but can also be switched to show the amount of *gain reduction* taking place. When in gain reduction mode, the meter reads zero when nothing is happening and dips to minus values—say, −5 dB or −10 dB—when the device is actually affecting the gain of the signal.

Threshold. One of the key settings of a compressor is the *threshold*, which governs how aggressively it operates. The threshold knob determines the level at which the device will kick in. Below a certain level, sound will pass through unaffected.

Alan:

> When I first started engineering, it took me awhile to grasp that the threshold level was directly related to the input level. At a certain threshold setting, increasing the input level will make the device work harder, effectively lowering the threshold. In other words, threshold and input are interactive.

In fact, Universal Audio's classic 1176 doesn't even have a threshold control, because its input level is governing the threshold. On a unit like the LA-610, where the T4 optical compressor side of the unit has been taken from the equally classic LA-2A, the "Peak Reduction" control adjusts the threshold.

If we increase the input or lower the threshold, more gain reduction is being applied and this will show as a greater minus value on the meter.

Compression ratio. The "formula" used to squash up the sound is governed by the ratio controls. At 2:1, for every 2 dB increase in volume going into the compressor above the threshold, only 1 dB increase in volume is going to come out. At a ratio of 10:1, an increase in input volume would have to be 10 dB to produce the same 1 dB increase in output volume.

So the higher the ratio, the more severe the compression. And although a standard ratio of compression would be anywhere between 2:1 and 10:1, the choice is really yours, depending on the effect you want. In practice, most of us regard compression of 10:1 and above as limiting, although in theory we would need an "∞:1" ratio to produce no gain increase no matter how loud the input is above the threshold (see **figure 9.2**). You can see that with no compression (1:1), there is no effect on the output level; but as the threshold (in this case 0 dB) is reached, the gain reduction kicks in—by different amounts according to the compression ratio.

On the classic Universal Audio 1176 there are four ratio buttons, each preset to a particular ratio. Each setting will produce a different amount of dynamic processing, although in practice the differences might be quite subtle. One popular trick on this unit is the "all buttons in" mode. What compression ratio that actually gives you is open to discussion!

Some devices offer what we call a "soft knee" characteristic, which offers a gentle ramp-up to the set compression ratio. This is considered by many to be easier on the ear. If you don't see a soft knee control, don't panic. This is a relatively recent option, and your unit will otherwise be hard knee by default.

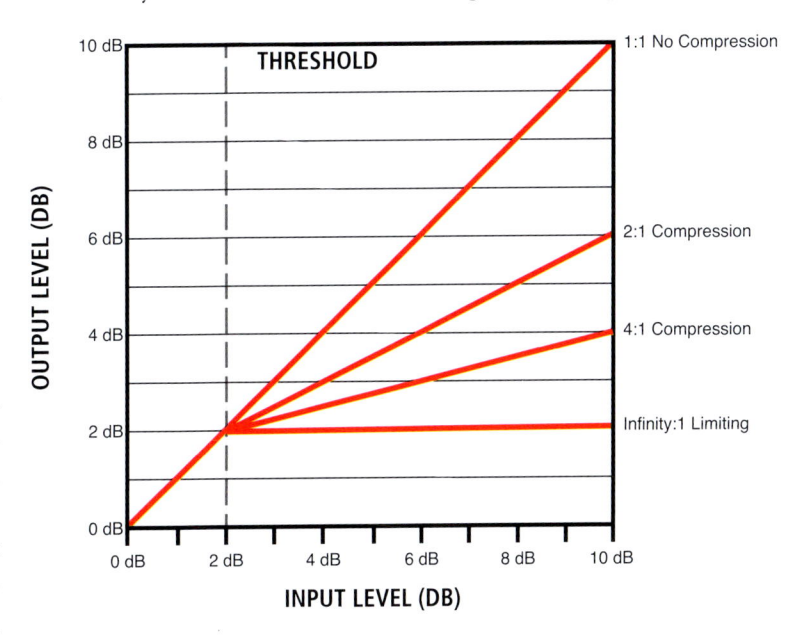

FIGURE 9.2. **Compression ratios.**

Compression, as well as controlling the dynamic range, can also affect the sound in other appealing ways, which is one of the reasons vintage compressors are so sought after.

A good, quality compressor will be extremely forgiving to the ear, still producing a natural effect even when working hard. Generally, you don't want to hear a compressor working unless you're after a deliberately squashed sound. Extreme settings will cause you to hear wide variations in level, which engineers call "pumping." Having said this, though, that might be the exact effect you're looking for.

The remaining controls fine-tune the effect.

Attack. This governs how quickly compression actually kicks in. For most sounds (drums, vocals, guitars), you want a pretty fast attack. Sometimes, though, you might want to compress, say, a bass guitar but keep the click or edge at the front of the note, in which case you'd go for a slightly slower attack. A slow attack time means the compressor will wait a little while before it applies compression.

Release. This governs the time the compressor takes to return to a normal state once it senses the input has fallen below the threshold. Longer release times tend to give a more natural result, whereas short releases tend to accentuate pumping (see above).

Output. If the device has an output control (not all do), this governs the overall output of the device so you can record at a comfortable level. But its function is also to compensate for the reduction of gain caused by the compression or limiting process. This is sometimes referred to as "gain make-up" or "make-up gain." If there is no gain reduction and you are outputting a comfortable level, that's fine. But if you're mostly seeing a gain reduction of 5 dB, you'll want to make up the output gain by that amount.

Compression and Frequencies

Compressors and limiters are not only used for the simple reduction of dynamics, to make a sound more manageable. They can also be applied to specific frequencies in the audio spectrum. On some units, you can set up different amounts of compression for a number of frequencies contained in a song or sound. This is called multiband compression. Multiband compression in the wrong hands can completely ruin a recording. The most common uses are in mastering and also in broadcast to increase the geographical footprint of a radio station.

Alan:

> There are now many multiband compressor plug-ins that offer these advanced facilities for little cost, and it's obviously very tempting to use them. However, I never have. I prefer to leave mastering to a mastering engineer.

There's another form of frequency-dependent compression that's extremely useful, and this involves the use of what's called a *side chain* or *key input*. What happens is that the compressor acts upon the information it sees from a separate input fed into the device's side chain, but it applies the action to the program received at its *main* input. For instance, you can reshape what's received at the side chain input with EQ, so that compression only kicks in, say, on zingy trebly sounds and leaves the rest of the signal unaffected.

One application for this is making a compressor only respond to the "S" sounds in a voice, which we call "sibilants," so that a vocal with harsh S sounds can be smoothed out. We do this by feeding in a heavily EQed or deliberately harsh "essy" version of the sound into the side chain. There are also various custom boxes and plug-ins to achieve the *de-essing* effect without having to set up the process on a side chain.

It's an interesting and not often realized fact that if a vocalist has a quiet voice, there are likely to be more problems with sibilance than with a singer who deafens you. The sound from the vocal cords can be loud or quiet according to the singer, but different singers do not necessarily have louder or quieter S sounds, or other consonants for that matter. Singers cannot easily turn their consonant sounds up or down. So a quiet singer is most likely to give sibilance problems.

Alan says:

> I recorded three albums with Al Stewart in the late 1970s, who is notoriously hard on sibilants or S sounds, with a unit made by a company called Orban, which has literally one knob on it per channel—simply controlling more or less de-essing.

Be careful not to overdo de-essing—otherwise, S sounds turn into F sounds and can make even the *butch-etht vocalitht thound thomewhat lithpy*.

Compression and tonal adjustments often need to be worked on together, which makes a channel strip such as the Aphex Channel or the LA-610 a very useful solution. You've got a mic pre, EQ, and compressor all linked together, which saves a lot of patching because one connection sends the signal to all the facilities. The Aphex unit also has dedicated de-essing on board.

Software Compressors

If you want to use an analog hardware unit, you should apply compression before you enter the digital domain, of course, or else you'd need to go through two more digital conversion processes.

Software compressors are no different from their hardware counterparts in function, but they do have one very important advantage when you're using DAWs. If you're already in the digital domain, with a plug-in sitting inside your computer, everything can stay digital. Plug-ins come in all shapes and sizes in an ever-increasing number of formats for an ever-increasing number of host platforms. Some are based around a card you need to install in your computer. The card then takes on some of the processing power required without placing any additional strain on your computer. At the time of this writing, the leading exponent of this type of this type of system is Universal Audio with its UAD Powered Plug-Ins.

In addition to being able to "stay digital," plug-ins make it very simple to change the order of where a compressor sits in the audio chain. In other words: do you want to EQ a sound and then compress it, or vice versa? You can do a quick experiment to see how much impact changing the order of processors will have on a sound. As with so many things in audio, there are decisions to be made and trade-offs between using one type of device or process or another.

Using Compression

Approaches

Jack Joseph Puig:

> We all know that if someone said they really wanted to get the sound that sounded like Ringo and Paul, you're not going to get it from the DBX 165. You can try all day; you won't. As soon as you plug in the Fairchild and you run anything through it, you'll have that sound.

Niko Bolas:

> I went through my phase of compressing everything, because I own a Fairchild and it was like, "Oh, my God, this thing is amazing—it sounds great." And then I finally got to the point where I said, "No, it's not, and no, it doesn't." [*Laughs*] It just looks really cool.

Compression can be applied on playback without committing to anything. On the other hand, it can be printed at the time of recording—in other words, in that case, it will be applied permanently. It's sometimes appropriate to apply compression while recording, especially if the dynamics are out of control. But it's important not to overdo it.

Niko Bolas:

> I err on the cautious side, because you can't undo compression; you can always add more.

With compressors and limiters, there's always a delicate balance between too much and too little, and also between making an improvement to one aspect of your sound without it creating a problem somewhere else. For example, it's best to make sure you don't solve your level issues at the expense of tone or performance.

Alan:

> Personally, and as a general rule, I prefer limiting over compressing. I would always have a limiter in circuit for a vocal, or a bass guitar. Otherwise, I would only use a limiter if I was specifically looking for a squashed effect. I prefer a natural dynamic. But this is definitely down to ears and individual taste.

Vocals

Over the years, dynamic control of vocals has had a huge effect on how records sound.

Bill Putnam Jr.:

> People would yell into big horns with a little needle that was etching in wax. They would have hand signals to tell a performer to get closer or further back.

Without limiting and compression, we would be deafened one minute and straining to hear the words the next. Before electronic limiting and compression came into being, engineers were forced to place the vocalist incredibly loud in the mix to make sure no words got buried. Artists had to control their own dynamics.

Good singers still do—watch Streisand or Michael McDonald at work, and they will move the mic away when they're loud and closer when they're quiet and everything in between. Good vocal mic technique on an artist's part is an engineer's dream.

Michael McDonald:

> I have to work so much harder than singing live, you know, because of what I have to work through just to get to that place where the compressor setting is right and I've sung the song enough to where I'm not trying to kill it like a golf swing.

Alan:

> I would normally apply around 7–10 dB of gain reduction to a vocal. I set my attack and release times so that it's not imposing any artifacts. The harder I limit, the more risk I'll have with sibilance. If the vocal sound is good but has become sibilant, you can use a de-esser later or on the mix. I'm especially careful not to overdo any kind of limiting on a vocal. I can always ride the vocal or apply more limiting on the mix.

Jack Joseph Puig:

> A lot of people comment in particular about the way I make vocals sound, and it's interesting, because I continually have people come into sessions, and the first comment will always be like, "Oh, my gosh, the voice is just fabulous." A humorous aspect of that is that I've used every possible compressor, always looking for something different to better my art and to better the job I'm doing.

Bass guitar

One of the functions of bass is to provide a solid foundation to your music. You'll probably want to put on a limiter for safety to catch unexpected peaks, especially on a slap bass part, which can be very unpredictable. It's best not to overdo any limiting or compression or make the attack too short, or else you'll lose the initial click at the front of each note, which will take away a lot of character. Alan likes to set the release fairly fast—but not so fast that it pumps. If you take away the attack of every sound you record, everything will sound like an organ.

If you're recording the bass direct, through a DI box—in other words, not going through an amp—the "tube-like" properties of a vintage compressor can help provide some warmth you might find missing otherwise. An inferior instrument, with old strings, played by an enthusiastic headbanger on their first recording session, is always going to pose a dynamics problem. But a well-set-up instrument with new strings, played by a professional, is always a joy to record and will not need the same degree of compression.

Alan:

> I've had the very good fortune to record some truly excellent players, of course, such as Paul McCartney, Roger Waters, and David Paton. I always wanted to work with Carol Kaye, the amazing bass player who was featured on so many classic Motown records, to see for myself what she did to achieve that great sound.

During the making of the *Art & Science of Sound Recording* video series, Alan finally did get to meet and interview Carol. Along with other gems such as "The engineers didn't do anything," she also revealed:

> Muting, picks . . . it's a lot of different things. It's the strings, it's the dark wood on your neck . . .

More of which you can read in Chapter 18, on bass guitar.

Drums

Compression on drums is very much a style thing. If you want the drum sound to be as natural as possible—for example, on a jazz recording—you would probably not want to apply any artificial dynamic control. However, compressed drum sounds have been used on countless successful rock and pop recordings. You might want to limit and compress to make all the hits of a particular drum sound consistent, level-wise, or you might want the compressor to change the character of the drum entirely by modifying its attack and release times. On toms, for example, compression will make the toms sustain more. On a kick drum, a compressor with a fairly fast attack produces a bit more weight, while a slower attack lets more transients through, allowing you to hear more edge or the sound of the beater.

Alan:

> On most of the records I've made, I've gone for a fairly natural drum sound. For instance, on *Dark Side of the Moon*, Chris Thomas, who was brought in for the mixing sessions, asked to apply compression to the entire mix. However, I managed to persuade him that it sounded better when the drums were excluded! So generally, we ended up with everything being compressed except the drums on the final mix.

Hard compression on the overhead mics will most likely produce a swishing, pumping effect on the cymbals, which was a feature heard on many Beatles records. You love it or you hate it!

Electric guitar

Compression can be used to increase sustain, as it will effectively "lift" a sound that would otherwise be fading away. This can be particularly effective on a rhythm guitar playing power chords. If the program can take it, use a slow release time. On solos, particularly with clean sounds, compression can help reduce peaks and bring up quieter moments. There are guitarists, particularly amongst session players, who have a rack full of their own equipment that may well include all necessary processing—including dynamics—before it reaches you. But be aware that their processing might be taking place in relatively low-cost pedals or stomp boxes, and that "studio" processing might well give you a better result.

What you should look for is controlled dynamics without increased noise and hums, or unwanted pumping effects. All-in-one amp modelers like the Line 6 Pod or the SansAmp both offer quite sophisticated dynamics control. Others prefer an all-analog signal path to a real speaker cabinet.

Acoustic guitar

Acoustic guitar has a very wide dynamic range, especially on a part where single notes are combined with strumming. It may be necessary to rein this in a bit by manual fader control, if you don't want the louder sounds to dominate your track. If you want an open, natural sound, you're best leaving acoustic guitar uncompressed. An acoustic guitar solo can benefit from quite a lot of compression as an effect, but it will sound less natural.

Alan:

> I recorded a song by Cockney Rebel called "Come Up and See Me," where I did apply heavy compression on Jim Cregan's acoustic solo using the onboard compression on the EMI desk in Studio 2 at Abbey Road. I've read online that this solo was recorded at a TV show and somehow inserted into the song at a later date. As the person who spent many hours recording it in the studio, I have to report that this is simply not true!

Brass, reeds, horns, woodwinds, and strings

Common practice would probably tend to leave all these instruments alone in terms of compression and let the players control their own dynamics. A sax or brass solo on a rock track might benefit from compression just to tame the peaks and troughs, so that no notes get lost.

Alan:

> Most of the beauty of strings is inherently in their natural dynamics. In fact, if you want to make beautiful real strings sound like they're sampled or coming out of an old synthesizer, put them through a compressor!

Piano

The more compression you apply to a piano, the more unnatural it will sound. But if you are looking for that tight, squashed, "Lady Madonna" type of effect, then by all means compress it into oblivion.

Compression on a Mix

In the same way that limiting and compression smooths out the peaks and troughs of a single sound, the process can also be applied to an entire mix. Applying compression to a mix—in other words, across the stereo bus—is a common practice, but a subject of continual debate: should you do it at all—and if so, how much?

A compressed mix will tend to seem more "in your face." Is that a good thing or a bad thing? As with most aspects of limiting and compression, it's not a simple good-or-bad/do-or-don't situation. There are arguments and counterarguments, as well as musical and commercial considerations.

On a mix, limiting and compression don't only have the effect of reining in and smoothing. When applied aggressively, these processes can also make a final mix sound louder, more powerful, more like a song sounds on the radio.

Dynamics processing can take place in both analog and digital domains. Hardware units exist for both analog and digital compression. You may like to use "soft" digital limiting available on some hardware, notably from Apogee, which is designed to totally transparently raise the volume of a mix—or any sound sent through it, for that matter.

However, heavy compression produces a certain type of sound, and it's become a hot debate as to whether this enhances or destroys the music on a mix. People argue strongly for it or against it, while others say there's simply no reason to do it in the first place when radio is going to compress it anyway. But to counter that, you have to ask yourself how important "radio" is as a listening medium, compared with direct digital media such as iTunes or Spotify.

So let's look at some of the basic pros and cons:

- My record will sound as loud as the next person's. Or preferably louder.
- Loud is good.
- Loud sells more records.
- I don't want to have listeners turn their volume up or down during the course of a song.
- Labels will usually apply pressure so that their record will stand out in the crowd.

And here's the other viewpoint:

- There comes a point at which increased loudness becomes distortion.
- Light and shade are good.
- Constant high level is fatiguing.
- Our brains filter out sounds that are repetitive or monotonous, like a ticking clock or traffic noise. In other words, we respond emotionally to variation.

Eventually, digital audio reaches a point where the levels can't go any higher and the sound goes into what is called "clipping." The irony is that the CD format gave us the opportunity to record music with a much wider dynamic range than vinyl. Below –50 dB on vinyl you're into clicks, pops, and general surface noise. On CD, the dynamic range was effectively doubled. The loudest fortissimo could be juxtaposed against the quietest whisper.

Pop music has always been about energy and the power of the beat, and given the option to make a song at least seem more powerful, with an attendant effect on its popularity, it's unrealistic not to expect pressure from record companies, managers, agents, distributors, and many producers to make a final mix as commercially viable as it possibly can be. However, many musicians, engineers, and producers subscribe to the opposite school of thought—not in order to reduce sales, of course, but to preserve the music. And so . . .

Welcome to the Loudness Wars.

John Fields:

> When you listen to current rock songs on the radio—or not even on the radio, just current rock songs—there's a certain kind of power involved in the drums and the guitar. Everything is the loudest thing in the mix, I like to say.

Niko Bolas:

> I hate it. I more than hate it—I'm disgusted with it. Because the guys that have pummeled music into the brains of the people that make the choices for what goes out with level have cleared away any semblance of what we fought so hard to get with digital recording. Digital recording was designed, and we refined it, and we fought for 96k, 192k so that we can have unbelievable dynamics, which is what an instrument does. You know, I want what an instrument does to be in front of me, and what it does is go from

really quiet to really loud. And now that we have a noise floor that's nonexistent, or minimal, they've lost it, because they can make it loud; just because everyone's too lazy to turn it up or you're competing against the last hit single.

Grammy Award–winning engineer Richard Dodd:

Engineers are faced with having to convince somebody that the thing is finished and as good as everybody else's record, which is all about volume. So, they not only send the version that is peak-limited and maximized to the max, but they actually print the mixes like that, too, because they're mixed that way. This is this whole thing of no one makes a decision anymore because they don't have to. Shrink-wrap never gets around it. It's always "update the download" or whatever. It's a terrible thing, because the poor engineer is faced with five or six different people, some of them relevant, most of them not, telling him to just raise this, just raise that, and now that you've done that, just turn that up. And the only way they can do that, having given them the max, is to just overdo it. I just say sure, I've got that limiter there. Volume wins any contest—except for audiophiles, of course—unless somebody actually cares what it sounds like.

Top Nashville recording engineer Steve Marcantonio:

I guess that's the way kids like it, because that's who we're making records for. And I really hate it. And we are going through that process with labels. When they put a mix in their stereo, if it's not as loud as the demo, they think it's a problem. And I just recently worked with an artist who went through that. She wanted her record to sound like everyone else, and we mastered it that way, and I was very honest with her. I said you know, ten years from now, you might regret this, and she went with my recommendation, and I love the way it sounds now. And I do make records for years to come.

John Fields:

I don't get making records that aren't competitive-sounding. I guess it's like, look, there's compressors. We've always had compressors, and we can put them on the entire drum mix and we can, you know, excite those drums to a certain point. I guess I am into loud and proud and power sounds, so maybe I'm part of the problem, I don't know.

However these wise words might have affected your overall opinion, we'll conclude with some guidelines about applying limiting or compression to a final mix.

It's futile to try to replicate a mastered recording on a mix. Try to preserve the integrity of your production and your artistic ideas. If you apply compression to your mix so that it seems to sound like a mastered record on radio (if you're lucky enough to get the track played on radio), the sound will actually be smaller. Radio inherently applies substantial amounts of compression, so compressing an already heavily compressed mix is actually going to make the music sound distorted and small.

Allen Sides:

> When it hits the radio, there's no difference. The end volume is exactly the same, because the radio compressor already does it. So, the fact is, the mix that is less compressed actually sounds punchier on the radio and just as loud. It doesn't sound any louder. To some degree, I almost say that the compression is to satisfy the A&R guy at the record company, not because it sounds better on the radio.

There's a big difference between peak limiting, which will curb occasional peaks or musical highs in a track that can be smoothed out without any noticeable adverse effect on the bulk of the track, and heavy compression. If the compressor is working flat-out at every moment of the track, sucking and pumping every subtlety out of the mix to keep the needle glued to the end stop or hovering between zero and minus one-half, then you might want to question whether you've overdone it a bit.

Mixing is not only about adjusting levels, it's about adjusting perceived levels. Compressors can clearly help create the feeling of loudness, but they're not the only way of doing this. Here's an interesting compromise from Allen Sides:

> Years ago, I remember I was with Jim Keltner and Ry Cooder. We were doing a mix, and Cooder says to me, "You know, it sounds pretty good, but can you jam it up and make it nuclear?" We used to have this kind of a boom box thing, like a cheap little cassette machine that had a compressor in it that had a certain sound. And we put up a couple little mics, and I'd record it, and I would put it in the headphones when they recorded, because it would give you all this roar and sustain, and Keltner would play around it. And so, we ended up needing some of that floor.
>
> Sometimes I take mults of my stereo bus [duplicates of what is being received at the stereo bus —*Ed.*] and I compress the mults and add them back in again, so that I get the floor, but all my peaked transients are untouched.

Alan:

> It's pretty much a universal view that vocals in rock and pop always have a need for compression and/or limiting. Some producers will try to make compression sound completely natural, while others will want a deliberately squashed-up sound. Some will insist on compressing their entire mix to get their mixes louder than anyone else's, while I for one like to preserve any natural dynamics as much as possible. It's a question of whether you want to just keep dynamics under control so that a particular sound isn't drowning everything one moment and becoming inaudible the next. So the use of compression can be a style issue. It can set trends in recording, as well as being a tool of the trade.

10

NOISE GATES

Noise gates started to appear in studios in the early 1970s. Allison Research, which later became Valley People, produced the first commercial noise gate, called the Kepex, in the USA in 1969. (See **figure 10.1.**)

Allison's Paul Buff owned Pal Recording Studio, one of the earliest multitrack studios in California, and he developed the Kepex to combat the resulting noise buildups caused by the use of multiple tape tracks and overdubs. Buff recorded the classic surf instrumental "Wipeout."

A British company, Drawmer, became the industry standard for rack-mounted noise gates in the 1980s. Many console manufacturers, notably SSL, incorporated gates into the dynamics sections of their consoles, and in fact continue to do so today on their channel strips and software emulations.

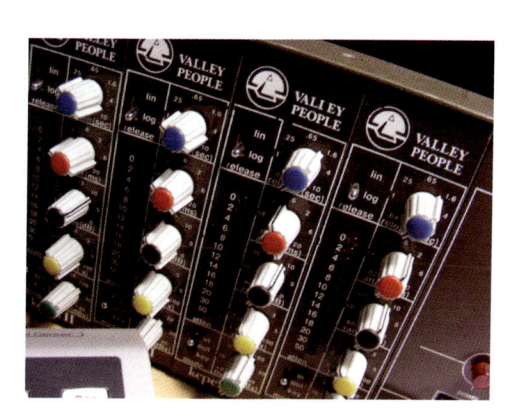

FIGURE 10.1. **Kepex noise gate. Photo by John M. Athayde.**

What Is a Noise Gate?

As the name implies, one of the main functions of a noise gate is just that: to gate out or remove sounds below a certain level threshold. They can also be used as *expanders* to just reduce the level of sounds below a certain threshold, rather than cut them off completely. Expanders actually increase dynamic range and can therefore be thought of as the opposite of compressors.

Typical applications for gates include removing hiss on a guitar amp when the guitar isn't being played—spill from the hi-hat chattering away on the track reserved for a snare drum—or breathing or mouth noises from a singer.

However, noise gates—both the original hardware units and their modern software equivalents—have applications beyond getting rid of unwanted noise. These include altering both the timing and envelope of a sound to produce specific effects, which we'll look at shortly.

Main Controls and Features

A clear understanding of the workings of a noise gate is important because its controls and parameters are to a certain extent interactive and interrelational. The main controls are:

Threshold. This sets the level at the input (in dB) below which the gate will be activated. Information above this level will pass through. As a general rule, and dependant upon the attack and decay settings, lowering the threshold will progressively allow more and more of the quieter elements of a sound to come through.

Ratio (or Range). A low ratio will result in a small amount of expansion, whereas a high ratio or range will cause sounds below the threshold to disappear or be gated completely. The result you hear will also be affected by the attack and decay settings. We normally associate a ratio of 10 or higher as gating, and below 10 as expanding.

FIGURE 10.2. **Front panel of a typical noise gate, showing range, release, and threshold controls.**

Attack. This shapes the speed at which the gate recovers, or returns to a normal output level after expansion or gating has taken place. A fast attack will result in an immediate recognition of an incoming signal if it's above the threshold, allowing it to pass through. A slow attack will cause the sound to fade in more slowly.

Decay. This control is sometimes known as "Release" and it governs how fast the sound fades to zero or to the chosen expanded level. A fast decay will mean the signal will "gate out" or drop immediately to the lower end of the selected range. A slow decay will mean the level will slowly sink down to the lower level. However, if a sound above the threshold is sensed by the device, it will, as we say, "open up" and let the sound through—as fast as the attack setting allows.

Hold. This governs how long the gate remains "open" before being closed at the chosen decay speed—once sound dips below the threshold. This can be invaluable if your sound fluctuates a lot in level, because it will stop the gate from continually opening and closing, which will both drive you mad and sound pretty awful. Generally, you would set the hold quite short. Hold is also the key parameter when setting up what we call gated reverb. Here it governs how long the gate is going to be open—allowing the reverb to be heard—before the gate closes and takes it out. More about this later.

Side Chain/Key Input. This is an additional input provided on most gates, also known sometimes as a "trigger input." This allows you to control the gating effect of one sound using the level characteristics of another. More about that later, too.

A more sophisticated device is a "frequency-dependent" noise gate/expander, which allows you to not only expand the overall *level* characteristics of a sound, but also to affect certain frequencies more than others. For example, we might have a guitar part with lots of high-frequency hiss, which may respond very favorably to having high frequencies removed when being played quietly, giving the impression that we have reduced the level of the hiss. This was essentially the principle used by Dolby (a pioneering audio encoding company) in their early noise reduction systems.

Using a Noise Gate

If we are using a noise gate to remove some unwanted characteristic or aspect of a sound, we might connect the gate to an individual track or channel, as an insert. Unless we're totally sure we're getting the desired result, it's best to avoid only recording the output of the noise gate—in other words, the processed signal—because you can't "un-gate" it after the event. It's best to record both the clean and gated signals separately, or leave the gate in-line as a monitored rather than a recorded effect.

Even though DAWs allow you to examine waveforms in microscopic detail, and physically cut out unwanted material, using a noise gate can in some cases be both quicker and more customizable.

Alan:

> I used a Kepex noise gate on the "heartbeat" kick drum sound on *Dark Side of the Moon* to get rid of tape hiss and to give the sound more isolated definition.

More commonly, noise gates are used to help isolate individual drum sounds on a kit—for instance, reducing the amount of hi-hat or cymbals that will be picked up by a snare drum mic. Although this technique is nowhere near as commonly practiced as it used to be in the recording studio, in *live* applications it remains as popular as ever. Here are seven different applications of a noise gate.

1. Removing cymbal/hi-hat spill on a snare drum track

Apply the noise gate to the recorded snare drum track and set the threshold so that the snare hits are just "opening" the gate. Now adjust the ratio or range control until you are only hearing the snare. All sound below the set threshold—such as the cymbal spill—will now disappear, because its volume is below your set threshold, and so the gate "closes" and none of that sound will be heard.

Initially, the snare might sound a bit unnatural because the gate is closing very fast and chopping off some of its natural decay. Increase the decay or release time. A final tiny adjustment of the threshold may now be necessary to catch all of the unwanted signal but keep the snare sounding natural. If the noise gate has an attack parameter, keep it fast.

2. Masking noises, hums, and buzzes on a guitar amp

Ideally, we'd want to record a guitar part without any extraneous noise to begin with. Tim Pierce, whom we worked with on the *Art & Science of Sound Recording* video series, employs a wonderfully simple but effective device. It's called—tada!—a volume pedal.

Tim Pierce:

> There's always noise, as a guitar player; it's just how *much* noise? And so, for me, it's always about disguising noise. I have something that's an appendage at this point, which is a volume pedal under my right foot. And the minute I stop playing, I draw that thing back. Because if I put a pedal in front of this, it's going to be so noisy. So I'll play the sound, draw the pedal back, and the noise disappears.

But if you're dealing with material that is already recorded with noise and "dirty," as they say, here is how you can clean it up.

Adjust the threshold until you are catching the sound you want to keep. On a melodic line you will probably want a fairly fast release, so that the gate closes as soon as the part finishes. Unless there are some unwanted noises at the beginning of the part, you will probably want to keep the attack fast.

3. Changing the envelope of a sound

Noise gates don't always have to be fixit devices. They also have tons of creative uses and applications. One interesting application is to use the envelope parameters to change the nature of a sound, making it different from when the part was originally recorded. For instance, we can soften the attack of a piano chord and make it "fade in" at any rate we choose. This will dramatically alter the sound while still preserving the part. Combine a soft attack with, say, a fast release, and we can create a brand-new sound.

4. Gated reverb

Gated reverb—which now would almost be better named "dated reverb"—was dramatically used on Phil Collins' drums by engineer/producer Hugh Padgham for the track "In the Air Tonight," which went on to spawn a thousand and one imitations. Today, gated reverb can be found as a preset on most reverb units, but let's see what the advantage might be of rolling one ourselves.

Apply reverb to your chosen sound/part and then feed the output of the reverb into your noise gate. Additionally, feed the raw sound into the key input of the gate and then adjust the hold time to create the desired "length" of reverbed sound before the gate closes, thus killing the reverb. A short release creates the classic "dead stop" effect. Increasing or lengthening the decay or release time will proportionally add a little tail to the reverb effect.

5. Keying a bass line to a kick drum to solve timing issues

In the digital age, we can achieve the same result by moving problem notes on the grid. However, if there are timing problems throughout a song, this method might still be the quickest way to a fix.

Feed the part whose timing you want to use as the "master" into the key input. The gate will then open only at those times, thus revealing the part whose timing was less than perfect. In the case of linking a bass guitar part with a kick drum, if the original bass part is rushing all the time, you will probably lose some of the attack portion of the bass, but the combined kick drum and bass line sound should still—indeed, somewhat magically—appear to be playing perfectly in time with each other.

6. Tremolo

Tremolo, which is smooth, repetitive volume modulation, was a standard effect on guitar amps back in the day. But what happens if we'd like to add some tremolo to a recorded guitar part when the guitarist has left the building? You can lazily reach for a plug-in that everyone else uses . . . or you can create a custom tremolo using a noise gate!

This effect once again employs an additional sound source—in this instance, a constant, rhythmic pattern like a simple drum or percussion loop will work well—that we feed into the noise gate's key input. The rhythm of the loop will dictate the rhythm of the tremolo. The gate's attack control will either smooth out the effect or, if set to a shorter attack, give it a somewhat harder, sharper sound.

A note for fans of *Dark Side of the Moon*: Alan used a Kepex driven by a low-frequency sine wave signal for the tremolo on Dave Gilmour's downbeat chords on the track "Money."

7. Gate effects

Another gate effect is a time-honored process that again uses a noise gate's key input. Similar to the tremolo experiment above, a drum pattern is fed into the key input, whose "rhythm" is used to "play" (typically) a sustained synth pad sound playing smooth chords. What makes the effect so compelling for dance music is that no matter what the raw, "ungated" synth part is actually doing, the gate creates a bouncing, stuttering effect lock-tight with the rest of the track.

The attack control is normally kept as short as possible (softening the attack will simply make the effect less dramatic). Shortening the decay or release will make the result more staccato.

Most commonly, a simple sixteenth-beat feel pattern creates a very natural groove, but this is a golden opportunity to be creative: experiment with triplet feels, polyrhythms, different grooves, and beats until you produce something special and unique for the track.

Tips, Tricks, and Observations

One of the benefits of applying a gate after recording on a DAW is that you can commit to each section of the song via automation—in other words, tailoring the gating to each individual instance where it's needed.

A very fast decay setting makes a gate act as an "instant switch," which can produce audible clicks. For this reason, we tend to use a fast but not instantaneous decay time.

Although in most recording studios we no longer have to deal with tape hiss, tape noise could still be an issue if you're remixing older, analog material that you'd like to fit into a comparatively noiseless digital environment. Great performances or great material can often be recorded under less than perfect circumstances.

Using Gates Live

One area where hardware noise gates are still used extensively is live shows. Most digital consoles offer extensive dynamics facilities, so the need for separate hardware is sometimes not necessary.

In live applications, we are generally more concerned with getting better separation between mics. You might want to EQ in additional bottom end onto a kick drum mic, for example. In doing so you might be getting dangerously close to feedback, so a gate can offer you added protection here. In a live situation you can create cleaner, more controllable tracks by using gates.

Vocals might seem to be the most obvious candidate for a noise gate, so that extraneous stage noise isn't being picked up and sent through the PA. That may be true, but you still need to be very careful, because the low threshold setting you'd need to catch every vocal inflection could easily be crossed by the onstage sound or even nearby screaming fans. Gating out a vocal mic when the singer is not singing might cause a noticeable sound change on everything else—you might want to consider a level reduction when using the gate rather than gating it all the way out. You might be better off accepting some extraneous noise as part of the sound. As ever, on a live lead vocal, keep your fingers on the faders!

A specialized product called an Optogate senses the physical position of a vocalist to a mic and gates the output except when he or she's right at the mic. The only adjustment on it is a knob that increases or decreases the level threshold where the gate kicks in, adjusting for the required distance of the singer from the mic.

Once you understand its capabilities and functions, a noise gate is quite a straightforward piece of studio equipment. Armed with that understanding, it's "what you do with it" that counts, of course. And it's worth spending time with this surprisingly powerful studio tool.

Let's raise a glass to Paul Buff.

11

REVERB

Shouting at mountains and hearing our voice bounce back was man's first recording/replay medium. It was also our first form of signal processing. Echoes are sound waves bouncing back off hard surfaces. The time it takes to hear the echo—in other words, the delay between shouting "Hello!" and the mountain sending it back—is governed by the distance. On a sunny afternoon in California, sound would be traveling at about 775 miles per hour or 1140 feet per second. What in sound recording we have come to call reverberation, or "reverb" for short, is a series of multiple echoes that are so close together, so dense, that our ears can no longer distinguish them as separate slices of sound.

Nonetheless, that's what they are, and that's why echoes, reverbs, and delays are all referred to as "time-based" effects. They are often confused with each other.

Acoustic instruments all have some sort of resonating chamber built in to their design—for instance, the hollow wooden body of a guitar or a violin, or the soundboard of a piano. Size, shape, and construction materials all play a part in how the sound moves about inside the chamber, thus affecting the eventual sound we hear.

Similarly, sound in the natural world bounces off neighboring surfaces. Rarely do we hear a sound that's completely flat and devoid of reflections.

Artificial Reverb Devices

Early recordings used the acoustics of the room in which the recording was being made to create natural-sounding reverberation. Classical recordings continue to do so, but as pop music recording became more sophisticated, it became necessary to re-create room acoustics artificially to give the impression of a recording in an entirely different space. Bill Putnam Sr. is credited with the first use of artificial reverb on a pop record, back in the 1940s.

Bill Putnam Jr.:

> Essentially, what he did was use a bathroom at the Opera House. His recording studio was in Chicago at the time, and he just put a microphone

> and a speaker in there—a kind of forerunner of echo chambers—and captured the reverb from that.

The concept might have been sound (pun intended), but the presence of plumbing and flushing made such an idea somewhat impractical. Soon, dedicated echo chambers became popular features in recording studios.

EMI Studios in Abbey Road, London, constructed one of the first purpose-built echo chambers. Up until the 1980s, when digital media leveled so many of the audio playing fields, studios like Abbey Road and Capitol Records in Los Angeles (whose chamber was designed by Les Paul) were not only sought after because of the sound of their actual rooms, but also because of the sound of their virtual rooms—echo chambers housed deep in the foundations.

Alan:

> Echo chambers like to be driven hard and loud. The one at the back of Studio 2 at Abbey Road is not particularly soundproof and sometimes causes complaints from the residential neighbors late at night.

What exactly is an echo chamber? Or should it be called a reverb chamber?

Typically, they are highly reverberant rooms, either by design or by accident, that produce lots of reflections of sound. They're like big freezers with concrete, plaster, or tile walls, with a speaker or maybe multiple speakers receiving the sound to be echoed and a couple of microphones around the room pick up the result. A carefully placed pair of mics will produce a very pleasing stereo reverb. The highly reverberated sound is mixed back with the original dry sound to simulate the instrument or vocal actually being produced in the chamber itself.

Another way of creating reverb artificially is to send the audio signal via a vibrating transducer into a sealed box containing metal plates or springs, which respond and resonate as the sound swirls and bounces around. Somewhat less intrusive than a live chamber, so-named *plate echo* units, originally made by EMT in Germany in the 1950s, manage to produce a very smooth and natural reverb sound. Plates and digitally re-created versions of them remain classic reverb effects to this day.

Also in the 1950s, "echo" started to be created electronically with the use of tape machines. Tape echo, as it was called, was distinctively if not deliberately unnatural. Pioneers like Sam Phillips at Sun Studios in Memphis and, later, Charlie Watkins in the U.K. made use of the time it took for magnetic tape to pass between the record head and the replay head on a tape recorder to reproduce a delayed version of the recording. In other words, it was a delayed version or an "echo" of the input signal. Different delay times could be achieved by changing the speed of the tape travel across the heads, or by mechanically moving the replay head nearer or further from the record head.

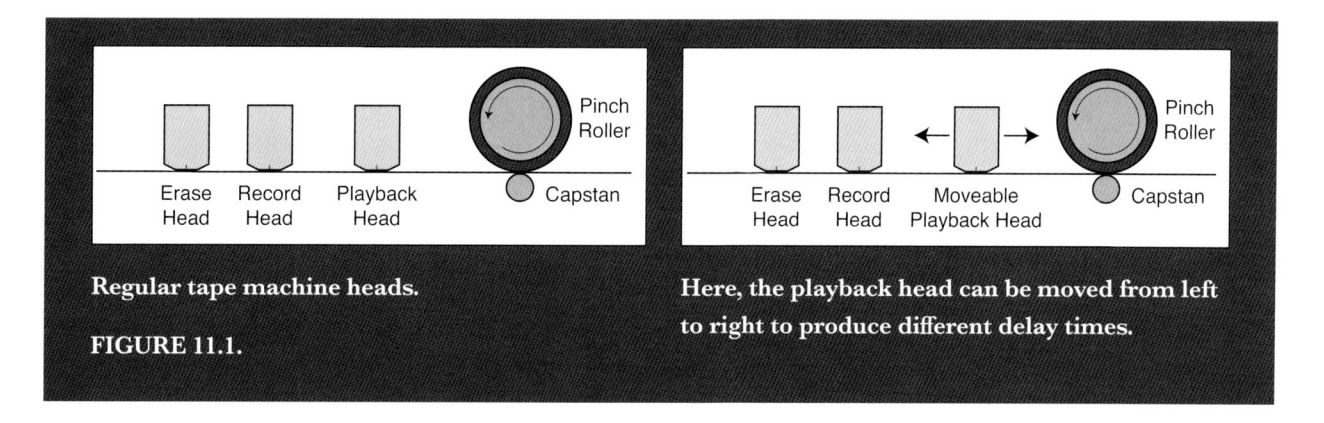

Regular tape machine heads.

FIGURE 11.1.

Here, the playback head can be moved from left to right to produce different delay times.

If the echo signal was fed back to the record head again, multiple repeats could be produced. Tape echo using just one or two repeats also became known as slap or slapback echo—a sound that came to define an entire era of popular music. Further developments produced multiple echoes with different timings by using several replay heads, as on purpose-built tape echo units such as the Watkins Copicat and the Binson Echorec, which used a magnetic revolving drum instead of tape.

So-called *spring reverbs* were most commonly seen on instruments—notably, the Hammond organ in the fifties, and on instrument amplifiers by Fender, for example, in the sixties and seventies. Spring reverbs generate reverb by passing the audio signal through encased metal springs, causing them to vibrate. Basic and understandably metallic-sounding, spring reverb units were a sort of dedicated poor man's portable echo chamber.

In the 1960s, Philips Research Labs (no relation to Sam) came up with an intriguing way to shift sound along a line of capacitors, each causing a fixed time delay. This classically analog device, somewhat reminiscent of the process of moving water by passing buckets along a line of people, was named "the bucket brigade."

When microprocessors started to be used in musical equipment in the late 1970s, everything changed once again. A whole range of reverb and delay types could be created and stored in microprocessor memory. Some of the first companies to do this were Eventide with their groundbreaking Harmonizer, and Lexicon, whose Dr. David Griesinger helped the company unveil one of the landmark products in signal processing, the Lexicon 224, at AES in 1978.

Bill Putnam Jr.:

> What artificial reverb has done is decouple the reality of the performance space for a number of different ends. One is to re-create something that sounds realistic but may be different than the environment that it was recorded in, but another is to create abstract spaces that aren't necessarily based in reality, and which are used purely as an interesting musical effect.

Digital Reverb

Although chambers, plates, and tape echo units all survive to this day, as do naturally reverberant studios, what we're going to look at now is how you can create these and other types of reverb using digital signal processing.

The first thing to keep in mind is that no matter how many fancy parameter names you've got in front of you, digital reverb devices all boil down how a sound bounces around an imaginary room and will offer control over the size of the space, the number of reflective surfaces in that space, and the acoustic properties of the construction materials.

Unless you have the money to spend on the construction of an echo chamber, reverb devices are going to fall into one of four categories: mechanical ones—like spring or plate reverbs; dedicated digital hardware units; vintage tape-based units; or software effects that can be called up in your DAW or mobile device.

Reverb Types

Presets and parameters on a digital reverb unit will relate to spaces and artifacts in the natural world. Although an empty cathedral or mosque whose acoustics, emanating from a vast amount of stonework, might be useful on some modern music recordings, realistically the largest musically sympathetic space you'd want to place a recorded sound would be the concert hall. Moving down in scale might be a smaller hall, and then spaces that can loosely just be called "rooms."

Each type of space has its own set of characteristics that identify its size and construction. A concert hall, for instance, has very low initial reflection density because of the room's size, and because most concert halls are constructed using musically sympathetic materials such as wood and natural fibers, with a great many surfaces that break up any immediately obvious echoes. These are large spaces, so reverberation time is appropriately long; plus, the lower frequencies tend to reverberate longer than higher frequencies. It all adds up to a pleasingly warm effect.

So-named "rooms" are just that: places of infinite tonal and reflective variety. Here we can see and hear a wide range of different rooms, each with their own unique sonic characteristics.

Halls, rooms, chambers, and the like are the initial starting-off points manufacturers use—each based on a specific algorithm or model—so that you know the general tonality of the reverb. Within each broad category you will generally find a number of parameters that let you customize the reverb to the exact size, tone, or density that you need. So let's look at what these are and what they do.

The Main Reverb Parameters

Setting the reverb time or reverb length is probably the easiest to understand. If we have a very short reverb time, it will sound like we're in a very small room. If we increase the reverb time, we can go to a hall, a church or to the Grand Canyon.

Density and diffusion are ways to control what we call *early reflections*. These are the first echoes bouncing off the walls in our imaginary room. Some units give you minute examination of these parameters, and others maybe offer you a range of room types. These reflections help define the character, altering the feel and shape of the room by changing how distinctly and how intensely you hear these first repeats. On a very dense setting, you can actually hear individual repeats. On a less dense setting they are more blurred, or diffused.

An often overlooked parameter is *pre-delay*. This governs the length of time it takes for your dry sound to bounce back off any wall. This short period of non-reverb is extremely useful for giving a sound some clarity and definition in a reverb setting. It can have a dramatic affect on the performance of a reverb. Increasing pre-delay time will always result in enlarging the apparent space.

When sound is reflected, it rarely comes zinging back at you with quite the same crispness as when it left, because the walls progressively absorb or dampen the sound. In fact, the most common reason for reverbs sounding cheap is that you're not shaving off enough of these high frequencies. The *damping* or *high-frequency decay* controls allow us to soften the higher frequencies for a warmer and more natural effect.

Applying Reverb

You might well want to hear some reverb on a sound as you're playing, or singing, but to commit to any type of reverb during tracking makes no sense unless it has a unique character you can't later re-create. So most of the time we will just use reverb that is not printed—in other words not applied to the recording. We call this monitor echo.

Alan:

> I've done some of my best work with just one single reverb unit—one plate, for example. In my early days of recording, the only machines we had at our disposal were tape machines. There were no digital delays, nothing like that. All processing had to be done either with live echo chamber plates or tape machines. On most of the *Dark Side of the Moon* album, for example, there was just one echo plate in use with a tape-generated pre-delay. I still think a lot of the very best records use effects sparingly. After all, what's really important is the song and the performance.

On a full-blown console, most engineers prefer to apply delays and reverbs through a traditional routing procedure we call send and return. The send control is an individual knob on each track or channel that governs the level going to the effects processor, and the return can be in a dedicated area on the console or brought back to console faders patched to the reverb device's output. Each track can then make use of the effect in various amounts by using its own auxiliary control. (These are usually called Aux sends or effect sends.) Each track or sound source can thus be added to the mix complete with its own specifically tailored amount of processing. All the various sends to the device are mixed or combined together at their various levels by the Aux send knobs and fed to the reverb unit's input. The processed result—i.e., the reverb device's output—is brought back as the return, usually in stereo.

By this means we have the option of sending nothing to the device, leaving the source dry, or sending a precise amount of the signal into the device.

An option of the send and return procedure is whether we apply it pre- or post-fader. On post-fade, the send level will increase in direct proportion to the fader level. On pre-fade, the send level is the same no matter where the fader is.

On a DAW we can also set up sends and returns, but adding reverb as an *insert* is also popular as a quick and easy method of applying a reverb or other effect to a particular track. Inserted effects use the full processing power of the device each time they are used, so we can sometimes run out of computer power by using too many inserts. So the send and return technique can be thought of as a shared resource, whereas inserts apply individually to each source they are applied to.

A signal that is not being processed at all, we call *dry*. We say the processed signal is *wet* even if it contains only a small amount of reverb. On DAWs we might see a wet/dry control in the effect software. Dry is 100 percent unprocessed; 100 percent wet is all processed with no dry signal.

The skill, as with any good chef de studio, comes down to blending the amount of wet and dry signal to achieve the exact sound you want. On both analog and digital consoles, it's quite easy to see the amounts of reverb applied by looking at the Aux send level settings. On DAWs it can be more difficult to see at a glance how much effect is being applied to each channel.

Reverb Settings

Drums
Slapping reverb over your entire drum track might be something to consider—certainly Phil Spector made a career out of that type of effect—but mostly, rock and pop drums benefit from reverb being applied in different amounts to different drums. If you have a huge reverberant snare, we may not want to apply anything like as much—if any—to the kick drum. You'd also probably not want to give the impression that the snare drum was being played in one room and the toms in another. So it's best to find the appropriate reverb type for your track and then apply different amounts of it to each individual drum.

Bass
Except for fretless parts, which do respond well to some moody reverb, bass doesn't normally require much in the reverb department. Sometimes some gated reverb can help out, not only to tighten the feel of a part, but also help it tie in with the drums.

Alan:

> On "Psychobabble" by the Alan Parsons Project, I did put a little reverb on the bass, as it was a featured part.

Guitar

Guitar effects are now very much part of the guitar sound, as opposed to being something applied to the sound. Both electric and acoustic guitars can benefit from reverb and delay effects. Even though a guitarist may well come armed with their own effects, when recording in a pro studio it still might be worth considering replacing the *reverb element* of their effects with something you generate in the studio.

John Shanks:

> I print all my effects with guitars. I mean, if it's a stereo thing, where there's reverb, I'll print it. If there's ping-pong delay, I print it, because that's part of the feel, that's part of the sound that I'm going for.

Keyboards

Keyboards cover a wide range of sounds and instrument types, from acoustic pianos that absolutely depend upon some kind of reverberation to sound real, to those that can happily sound very close and intimate, to pads, beds, and effects, whose reverb requirement should be judged very much case by case.

Vocals

Reverb on vocals tend to be very much a fashion statement and a style consideration. Very few singers like to record totally dry—it simply sounds very naked and uncomfortable, which is why singing in the shower is so satisfying—but that doesn't mean the final vocal necessarily needs reverb. Reverb creates a sense of distance, and a bone-dry vocal can show every wave or a crack in the voice. That could be the effect you're after, and certainly even a small overdose of pure reverb can make vocals sound very distant and indistinct.

Michael McDonald:

> I don't like a lot of reverb ever usually, and I like the dry feeling of my voice when I'm singing. And a lot of times, I like it on the dry side these days when I'm mixing it.
>
> When I was doing the Motown remakes, I learned in listening to those old recordings, many times the voice was way out there, you know. And that was really what was so wonderful about Marvin Gaye's records. You really got that feeling of when he went a little hoarse, or whatever he did; it was always evident, always really crystal clear, and kind of above the track.

Multiple Grammy-winning engineer Elliot Scheiner says:

> For me, it's still hearing the instruments as they were designed to be heard and not necessarily covering up with reverb . . . I think I always yield a little bit to the vocal, end up putting the slightest bit of maybe a delayed 'verb or a delay itself, or maybe just a delay.

Using pure reverb settings, here are some points to bear in mind. More reverb will take the vocal back into the track. Less reverb will make it sound close and up-front. If your reverb setting makes the vocal too sibilant, use some high-frequency damping. That will help cure it.

Afterthoughts

The reverb on a record can be a defining element. Imagine the Righteous Brothers' "You've Lost That Lovin' Feelin'" without reverb—it might have sounded like a high school demo. And it's probably fair to say U2 or Coldplay would sound considerably less epic sans reverb. Conversely, Kanye West with a huge, cathedral-like reverb on him would sound horribly syrupy. Use reverb not because it's there, but because it can be the character-defining feature of your recording.

12

DELAYS

Causes and Effects

The words "delay," "echo," and "reverb" often get confused with each other. All are time-based phenomena. An echo represents a single reflection or repeat of a sound. Reverb consists of a large number of interrelated echoes or reflections.

Delay, meanwhile, is just that: a sound heard slightly later than its source.

To add to the confusion, an effect called "tape echo" or "slap echo" was the first form of man-made "delay." This was what Sam Phillips and Charlie Watkins did when they took advantage of the time it took for magnetic tape to pass from the record head to the replay head on a recorder, as discussed in the previous chapter. (See **figure 11.1, p. 107.**)

Tape echo is normally associated with short delay times and is an effect that came to define an entire era of popular music. Think "Be-Bop-A-Lula" by Gene Vincent or "Heartbreak Hotel" by Elvis (Elvis who? —*Ed.*), and virtually everything by John Lennon as a solo artist.

Further developments produced hardware devices that could create multiple echoes. Different timings could be created by using several replay heads, as with purpose-built tape echo units like the Watkins Copicat and the Binson Echorec, which used a magnetic revolving drum instead of tape. The Binson unit was heavily employed by Pink Floyd, both live and in the studio (e.g., the single-note guitar on "Time," from *Dark Side of the Moon*). Once digital got in on the act, the sky was the limit. Now, a whole range of complex effects could be generated, in stereo, with precision timing and even under MIDI control.

Delay effects come in all shapes and sizes. The simplest is a single repeat like this—ONE one, TWO two. If we delay the delay by feeding it back into the system, we get multiple repeats: One, one, one, one, Two, two, two, two. The length, intensity, feedback, and stereo positioning of the delays are adjusted to produce the final effect.

As with reverb, delays add life and character to what might otherwise be dull and inanimate sound sources. Similarly, delays—providing the illusion of a natural, live sound—can inspire or give confidence to a performer, especially a singer imprisoned in the rather unnatural world of a studio vocal booth.

Delay Devices

In the early days of digital, "digital delay line" units did nothing but generate delays. What made them so useful was that you could adjust the delay time—something far more difficult to do on a tape-based device. As digital delay units became more complex, we could instantly achieve effects like phasing, pitch manipulation, and artificial double tracking (or ADT). The Eventide Harmonizer, an industry-standard device for many years, could produce all these effects in various combinations.

Nowadays, dedicated outboard digital delay units have become less evident. Plug-ins and on-screen time-shifting have made delay effects very easy to achieve on a DAW. But there are still a number of favored outboard digital reverb units made by such companies as the legendary Lexicon, as well as by Yamaha and TC Electronics, for example.

One area where hardware delays have actually blossomed in recent years is dedicated guitar processors and pedals, or "stomp boxes." We look at these in detail in Chapter 19.

Tim Pierce:

> Reverbs and delays have gotten easier with Pro Tools, because delays are an addiction to a guitar player. I mean, you just want to use them all the time, because it just makes everything flow, and it just feels so good.

It has also become common to see "delay" as part of a suite of processing effects "built in" to a digital console. As well as being convenient, this could ease the burden of processing—including the matter of latency on your computer.

Tape Delay

Back in the days when taped-based delays were popular, we would normally send a signal from the console to the input of a tape machine dedicated to this purpose. The tape machine would always be in record mode, and the time taken for the tape to travel from the record head to the replay head represented a fixed time value. The machine's now "delayed" output would be returned to a channel on the desk. One job for "tape ops" (or "button pushers," as Abbey Road used to call them) was to make sure the echo tape never ran out during a take. The tape would be reused over and over again, and sometimes a continuous loop would be used to save rewinding (and blushes), but it wasn't long before a loop would wear out.

Tape loops were also used extensively in the sixties and seventies on dedicated portable devices like the Echoplex and the Watkins Copicat, which got delay effects out of the studio for the first time. The Roland Space Echo, from the mid-seventies, was another much revered tape loop device for the live stage or home studio.

With tape-based devices, the only way to alter the delay time was to alter the tape speed, or in the case of the Echoplex, move the positioning of the playback head. Today, with digital delays, it's a piece of cake to get any delay time we want, from microseconds up to two, three, four seconds, or even hours if we so desire!

Alan:

> A total tangent here: I remember on a session in the mid-seventies with Roy Harper, we managed to produce a tape delay lasting five seconds or so using two machines side by side. Roy was wearing headphones, and everything he said or sang would come back at him in his ears after those five seconds, and then again as a slightly quieter fed-back signal five seconds after that. After a while, there were hundreds of voices in his head. He would either laugh hysterically—the laughter also coming back at him—or start screaming. I recommend trying this as a sanity test!

The Main Delay Device/Plug-in Controls

Delay time: Normally measured in milliseconds (ms) or thousandths of a second, and the most crucial parameter, since it establishes the basic style of the effect. A short delay time can produce effects like phasing and chorus, where you don't actually "hear" an echo as such. Delay times longer than, say, 50 ms will produce a discernable "repeat."

Feedback: Soon after the invention of tape echo, it was discovered that feeding the delayed signal back into the tape machine would cause a multiple repeat effect. Feedback level determines how many repeats are audible.

EQ: With tape, because each repeat is a rerecording of the signal, there is a degradation in quality on each repeat, which gives it a certain character. The process works essentially the same in the digital domain, where the delayed output is fed back into the input, but because of the nature of digital electronics, the quality loss on each repeat is minimal. So if we want to emulate tape delay effects with plug-ins, we might need to introduce some sort of degradation artificially. EQ controls on a delay device are often offered simply as "high" and "low."

Setting Up Delays

In its simplest form, a delay is the source signal reproduced after a certain amount of time. Although we often add a delay to an original source to create an echo effect, we might simply delay a sound just to make it come later—for example, to improve timing. DAWs also allow us to put an "echo" *before* the original sound—something we could only have dreamed of using tape machines.

For the *Art & Science of Sound Recording* video series we conducted a series of delay experiments simply using a Yamaha 01V96 (a fairly modest digital console that has effects built in).

We fed a vocal into a delay and brought up the feedback control (i.e., going back into the delay) on a separate fader. By pushing the fader up, we increased the number of repeats that were being heard, right up to the point of "actual" feedback.

EQing the delay channel produced some interesting results, because with each subsequent repeat whatever EQ is being applied will be more and more accentuated. With a high-frequency boost, the sound becomes progressively sharper and harder on each repeat. Demonstrating a mid- to low-frequency EQ boost, we would make the sound progressively lo-fi; while when applying a low-frequency boost, the effect progressively disintegrates into distortion.

Applying EQ cuts produces similar "building upon itself" effects—i.e., sounds that progressively become thinner or duller over time. If the feedback level is lower than the first delay, then each repeat will be progressively quieter, which is actually how natural echoes and reflections work in the real world.

If the feedback level is *higher* in volume than the first delay, each successive repeat gets louder and louder, resulting in a classic though artificial delay effect that has become very popular in styles of music such as dubstep. Ultimately, because each repeat is getting louder and louder, the effect eventually hits distortion level and can go no further.

Sometimes we only want a fixed number of repeats on certain words or phrases. In a DAW, this is best achieved by copying them to new tracks and moving the copies on the grid—especially if you only want a repeat at very specific points in the song, for instance, a repeat simply on a last word or phrase.

Delay-Based Effects

Flanging

Flanging got its name from the effect produced by altering the speed of a tape machine by physically and expressively taking your hand on and off the "flange" of one of the tape spools. What makes flanging distinctive is the temporary pitch change caused by the manipulation of the tape speed. For genuine flanging we need to be able to both pre-delay and post-delay the source and travel across the point where there is zero delay. You can find ways to do this on the Internet, but the genuine sound of tape flanging is quite difficult to emulate in the digital world.

Phasing

Phasing and flanging are similar-sounding and often mixed up. Phasing is achieved by a phenomenon called comb filtering, which happens when a signal is applied to itself with a very short delay time. The same applies with a very short pre-delay time. As we increase or decrease the delay time, we hear a variance in the comb filtering, giving us a distinctive whooshing sound. When we cross over the point where a "pre-delay" crosses zero into a "post-delay," the effect is greatly enhanced. For both flanging and phasing, both the delayed and original signals have to be in the same place in the stereo picture. If they are on opposite sides, we will end up with an out-of-phase program, which in most cases will be problematic. Phasing is simply phase shifting, which, unlike flanging, does not cause any change in pitch.

Chorus

Chorusing is produced by combining two similar signals—one of which is, at any given moment, higher or lower in pitch. The pitch change can be constant or modulated by a low-frequency oscillator (LFO for short). To achieve a pitch change in a digital processor in real time, an inherent delay is a requirement, and the scientific principles needed to achieve real-time pitch change tend to cause glitches or unwanted clicks at the output.

Tempo-synced delays

Sometimes we want to base our delay time around the tempo of a song. We start by finding out how long one beat lasts at our chosen tempo. We'll want to know this value in milliseconds. Our tempo is measured in beats per minute, or BPM. To get the time for one beat—or, in musical terms, a quarter note or crotchet—we take the number 60,000, which is the number of milliseconds in a minute—and divide it by our tempo in BPM.

At 120 BPM, for example, we divide 60,000 by 120 and we get a value of 500 milliseconds per quarter note. So we set our delay device at 500 milliseconds. For eighth notes—in other words, notes lasting half as long as a quarter note—we would divide this value by two, giving us 250 milliseconds. For sixteenth notes—half as long again—we'd divide the value by two again, giving us 125 milliseconds.

If mathematical formulae are not your forte, you can find countless delay calculators on the Internet, which will also give you dotted note and triplet delay times. It can be useful to see all the common delay times listed together at a particular tempo. Or you can just work by trial and error, which can sometimes give better results. There's no rule decreeing that your delays have to be exactly in time with your music.

You can also use MIDI to synchronize not only delays but also the speed of LFO modulation and other time-based effects within your DAW. (We looked at this in Chapter 7.) Delays have blossomed from fairly basic emulations of real-world phenomena into almost an art form in themselves. And nowhere has this been more evident than for guitarists, for whom "delay lines" have frequently become lifelines.

Tricks and Tips

A crucial parameter of delays is the volume of the repeat. We shouldn't confuse that with the volume of the effect, because this we can control on the DAW. What we're talking about here is the relative level of the repeats, and it's important because in real life, echoes do get progressively quieter as they go.

Even mono delays help create a feeling of space. Stereo delays, multi-tap, and other ping-pong delays create more of a rhythmic picture, almost like electronic percussion. And the big question here is how much control you need or want in terms of timing these delays to the tempo of your track.

Delays have become crucial ingredients in a number of musical genres, as well as standard rock and pop. Electronic music, hip-hop, and dubstep all use delays in a big way. In general, it's best to preserve enough space between words, notes, or hits for the delay to "speak" but neither clutter nor undermine a performance.

John Shanks:

> I don't print delay. I'll print delays with guitars. I print all my effects with guitars. I mean, if it's a stereo thing, where there's reverb, I'll print it. If there's a ping-pong delay, I print it, because that's part of the feel, that's part of the sound that I'm going for.

Tim Pierce:

> The great thing about Pro Tools is you can put up [the plug-in] EchoBoy or any other delay, and then the delay is negotiable all the way down the line. You can get your fix while you're recording, and you can dry it up later. Most of the people I work with want me to print delays so they don't have to think about it later. But I try and get them to use a plug-in in certain situations, just so they can make it sound the way they want it later, so there are no regrets, basically.

Echoes, reverb, and delays can make or break a recording if used tastefully and effectively. But as Billy Bob Thornton said in the video version of this book, "Bad engineers, producers, and Santas tend to overdo these effects and ruin everything." YOU HAVE BEEN WARNED!

13

A BAND TRACKING SESSION

As computers have become more powerful, both the raw processing capability of desktops and the sheer portability of laptops have freed us from having to pack up our instruments and equipment and trudge off to a dedicated recording studio whenever inspiration strikes. Unlike real estate, "location, location, location" is only part of the story for sound recording.

Professional studios come in all shapes and sizes, and some of them are capable of recording anything from a singer-songwriter to a full-blown symphony orchestra and chorus. The best studios will have a series of acoustically treated and isolated rooms, a substantial-size console, and a good collection of vintage and modern microphones and outboard equipment.

Even if its dimensions are quite modest, a proper studio is a place designed so that musicians can hear and see each other and where ideas can be generated, discussed, and developed. (See **figure 13.1.**)

It's all too easy for modern recording to be a very lonely sport. Even if multiple musicians are being used, each player can record their own parts separately in their own home studio and simply upload their performances for the great Producer or Artist in the Sky to assemble at some later date. This is a very efficient

FIGURE 13.1. **Alan listening to players and talking to them out in the studio on a tracking session.**

and cost-effective way to make a record, but arguably it might also be missing one of the key points—namely, placing a bunch of musicians in a room together, letting them hear what they and their fellow musicians are playing, giving them a chance to interact, and capturing it!

Planning a Session

We booked some of L.A.'s finest musicians for our tracking session for the *ASSR* video series: Nathan East on bass, Rami Jaffee on keyboards, Tim Pierce on guitar, and fellow Brit Simon Phillips on drums.

Simon runs a beautiful, spacious state-of-the-art commercial studio in L.A.'s San Fernando Valley called Phantom Recordings, and we jumped at the chance to record there. Simon has a drum kit permanently set up there, and he's a talented engineer too, so we knew we would get a great drum sound.

For any session involving more than a couple of mics, it's important to plan ahead and decide where each of the players are going to be placed on the studio floor.

Any decent-size studio should have a layout sheet (see **figure 13.2**) with space to write in the mic choices, approximate placements, and the studio lines they are plugged into.

For reasons of timing tightness, bass players normally like to be physically near the drummer in a studio environment. We decided Nathan wouldn't be using a bass cabinet on this occasion (saving us several hundred dollars in cartage fees), so we didn't have to worry about isolating it—we used a DI box. (We discuss DI boxes more in Chapter 18, when we talk about recording bass guitar.) Simon's studio has the luxury of two isolation booths, and we used one for the grand piano—always a separation challenge when recording with live drums in the same room—so we knew that wouldn't be a problem.

We anticipated before the session that, like many guitarists, Tim would want to play in the control room. It's not really practical to have a guitar amp and cabinet blasting away in the control room, so we placed his amp in the second, smaller, vocal *iso* (isolation) booth. Another advantage of a pro studio is having tie lines to connect to Tim's guitar and pedal board in the control room. Using a tie line, which was part of the studio's hidden wiring, meant we didn't have to run a cable across doorways and over the studio floor.

Alan:

> A guide vocal can be extremely helpful if the singer and song are defined at this point. But it's not essential. What these guys were going to get was me, singing some unfinished lyrics to them in the control room. I just had to hope that would work!

Simon's console was a Digidesign "Pro Control" specifically designed for use with Pro Tools. We recorded in Pro Tools HD at 88.2 kHz with a bit rate of 24 bits. Simon's drums alone took twenty tracks—but that's a reflection of the fact that it's the drummer's studio! Mics should normally be plugged in and checked at the console long before anyone's arrived at the studio.

Alan:

> If I'm really familiar with the console and the mics I'm using, I'll have a pretty good idea of what input level I'll set them at before anyone arrives. There were legendary engineers at Abbey Road who would set all their mic levels, even set EQ and reverb for a full rhythm section and orchestra, push up the faders and the main groups, turn on the red light, and be ready to record without hearing a note—and the balance would be near perfect. And many of these sessions were recorded live—direct to stereo—no multitrack.

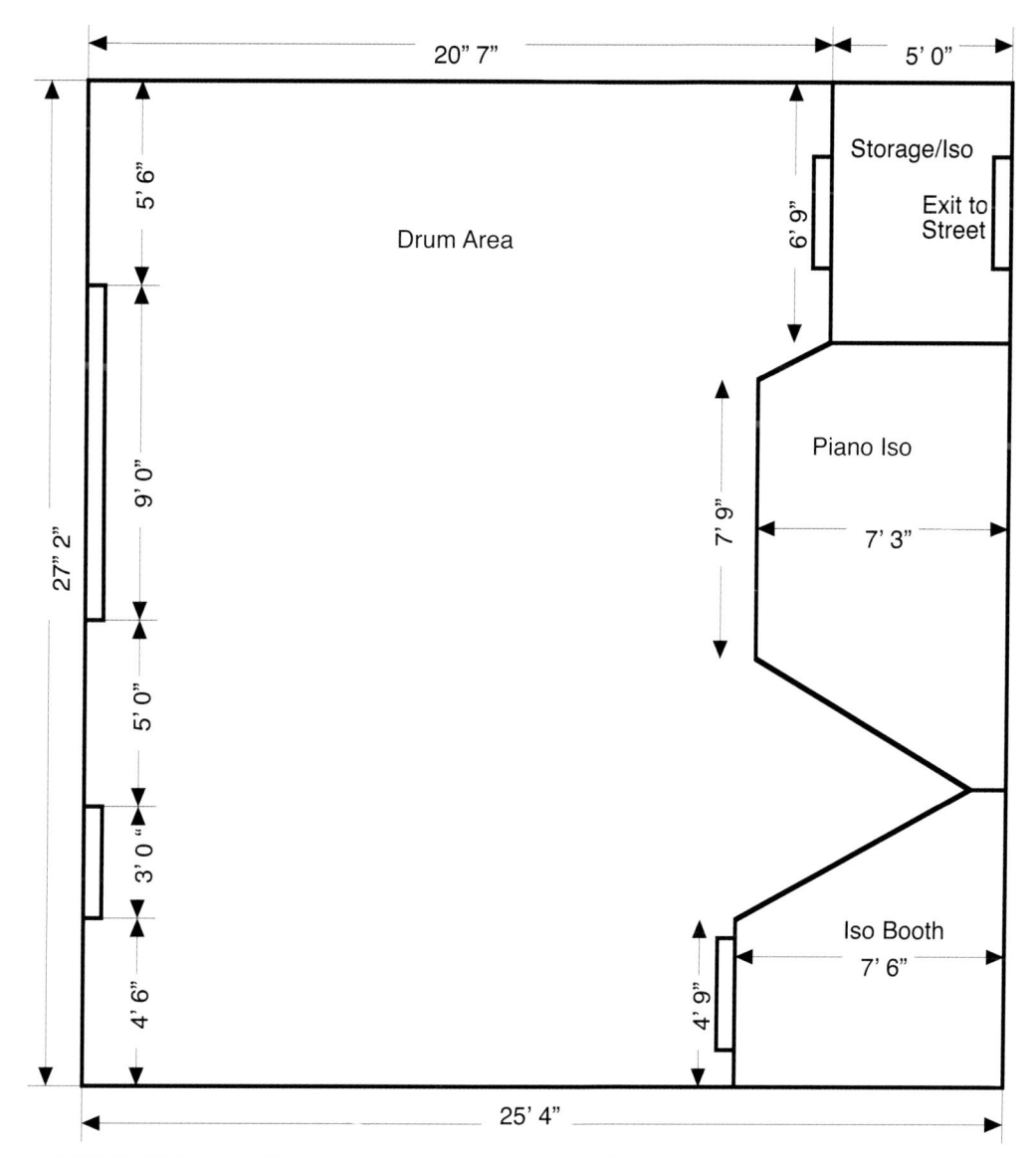

FIGURE 13.2. A studio layout sheet is vital so that instruments can be drawn in and mic types and patching identified.

Setting Up the Band

Before the musicians come in, you should try and have everything ready to go: mics plugged in, outboard gear set up and ready to go, the DAW session created and tracks assigned, possibly even named at this point, headphones ready . . . There's nothing worse than eager musicians waiting for an engineer to get his act together or to find the right plug.

The old-school way to start a session was that as soon as mics had been positioned, everybody in the band played together, and all the various monitoring and headphone balances came together over the course of a few minutes of playing.

We were lucky because Simon's studio had everything ready to go, and we were able to avoid the normal amount of time spent placing and angling the mulitiplicity of mics on the drums and in the room.

These days, it's normal to spend a little time initially with the drummer on his own to balance up all the various mics to a good overall balance that can not only be monitored in the control room but also fed to the other players in their headphones. Rather than reading a written part in music notation, rock musicians are usually more comfortable hearing a demo—no matter how rough.

Chord and bar charts are always a help, no matter how versed the players are in musical notation. Even a chart saying "intro, verse, chorus, verse, chorus, bridge, etc." is better than nothing—unless it's an established band that's been playing the tune to be recorded for months on end.

Click Tracks

More often than not, click tracks are just used to keep the tempo even and to act as a reference for timing. It's important to have a tempo reference for synchronized sequencing with MIDI. Another reason is to have a bar count on a DAW screen to identify where we are in the song, and to be able to edit between takes. Most modern recordings use clicks—sometimes only because of insecurity: "What if we speed up?" "How will I know when to come in after a break?"

There are a lot of opinions about clicks.

Producer and Dire Straits engineer Chuck Ainlay:

> I like tracks that aren't cut to click, and certainly the great musicians in Nashville can do it without any problem—you know—just feeding off of each other.

Jack Joseph Puig:

> A real experienced musician understands the click track is his friend, and he knows how to play around it, and he knows how to play ball with it. The inexperienced musician hears a click track and goes, "Oh, my gosh. That's Hitler, and if I make a mistake I'll be shot in the head," and so they're focused just on making sure that they're nailing the click, nailing the click, nailing the click, which means that the creative part of the brain is turned off.

For our session, the band played to a drum loop, so no click track was needed. it's common practice for a band to play to some kind of rhythmic loop rather than a click—whether or not it's going to be heard on the finished record . . .

After hearing the demo, Simon suggested that the loop on the demo could be improved upon to make it easier to play to. So he went into the studio and recorded a simple pattern which we looped and then had the band, including Simon, play to it.

The Structure

We also discussed the key, tempo, and the verse-chorus-bridge-solo, "structure"—often these days called the "arrangement."

Alan:

> The arrangement, in old-school circles, represents what parts are going to be played by what instruments and when. An *arranger* would have been the one who writes parts in musical notation for each player, including any orchestral score that might be needed—he or she would most likely conduct any orchestral parts as well. In the modern DAW world, arranging has come to mean the order that verses, choruses, solos, bridges, and so on occur. That's because in the nonlinear world of DAWs, the song can be rearranged or restructured via cutting and pasting with a few mouse clicks. Younger musicians refer to the term—arrangement—meaning who plays what part and when—as *production*. Confused? I certainly am!

FIGURE 13.3. Communication is key. Alan talking to the players in the control room during a tracking session.

The Band Plays a Run-Through/Headphone Mixes

The drums are effectively in their own space—the bass doesn't affect them because Nathan is DI'ed. The guitar is isolated because the amp is in the iso booth. Likewise, the piano is totally isolated. So we have no problems with separation.

The first moments of any band playing together in the studio can be chaotic, because they're not hearing a pleasing balance between themselves and the other players. This is where an engineer's skills *really* come into play. Mic levels have to be set with lightning speed, and a rough headphone mix assembled within a matter of seconds after the band starts to play. The band can't play if they can't hear—and the engineer can't balance unless the band is playing. A real conundrum.

Some of the pressure was off here in Simon's studio because each player had a little audio mixer in front of them, so they could each set up their own ideal mix.

Chuck Ainlay:

> With [guitarist and Dire Straits frontman Mark] Knopfler, when we first started working together, you know, the musicians all said, "Oh, Chuck gets the greatest headphone mix." And so, Mark kind of took that on. You know, he had been used to having the multichannel mixer and having a fader for everything, and he said, "Well, let me hear your mix." And, from that point on, he basically insisted, even though we had these multichannel mixers, he said, "Everybody's listening to the same mix. I want everybody to play off of each other." And, I think that's really important. So, what I do is I tell the guys, you know, here's a stereo mix; the vocal is going to be low in it, so, you know, adjust your amount of vocal, but just add to it rather than, you know, build your own mix. If you need to hear a bit more of yourself, you can tweak that fader, but try and use this stereo cue mix, so that everybody plays together. The musicians can only play as good as what they hear, and the singer wants to know what's going on. I really spend a lot of attention on getting a great headphone mix.

David Thoener:

> In Nashville, and lately in other studios, they do have the ability to make their own mixes. And a lot of times, I don't necessarily like that approach, because when we're doing playbacks, I'll sometimes go out into the studio and check and see what the players are listening to and, unfortunately, a lot of times it's click and themselves, and the remaining instrumentation has gotten ignored.

Jack Joseph Puig:

> I always make the record sound the best it can in the control room, as well as the headphones. Firstly, so that you have the inspiration of all the people involved, and secondly, so you're making the right decisions about what you're putting on the record. If the record feels empty, you may be adding a bunch of instruments that you don't need, because the instruments that do exist are not in their right relationship. So therefore, you are not making a proper record, because you're not making proper decisions.

We had no idea what kind of headphone mix Nathan, Simon, and Rami were listening to, because they were controlling it themselves on their own little consoles. But it's a safe bet they were all hearing each other. As Chuck said, there's little point in recording as a *band* unless everybody is hearing each other to some degree and there is interaction. Tim heard the same mix as us over the speakers in the control room.

Recording in Earnest

Modern thinking is that everything can be fixed later—which, of course, it can. But a live tracking session like this is all about trying to capture the magic. We don't want to lose that magic by making excessive repairs and doing retakes of a great take when it happens.

Alan:

> I felt that Tim's guitar and Rami's piano parts were not really establishing the chord structure adequately—and, nice though their parts were, we needed a basic foundation to play the chords all the way through the song. So we got Rami to lay down a synth pad on a Yamaha Motif keyboard as a separate pass. One of the sounds we found after going through a few presets on the Motif struck me as being right because it didn't take up too much space in the audio spectrum. We all felt that we now had a good bed that the band could comfortably play their parts over. I wasn't sure at this point if this pad would be replaced at a later stage, but in the end we did use it on the final mix—although, as you'll see in the mixing section of the program, we did have to do some work on it.
>
> I've done as many as fifty takes with artists in the past, but that was generally because we had to deal with wrong notes, technical problems, and artistic temperaments—none of which we had here. Once we had established the arrangement and structure for this song, it took only a few minutes for the band to get the right feel. One of the key roles of a producer is to make the decision about when the perfect take has been recorded. I gave the thumbs up after four takes.

It is of course easy to just keep recording over and over again ad nauseam, but there comes a point when a plateau is reached and everything just starts to sound tired. Alan says he's happy with the last take. Everybody seems to agree, but Simon wants to go for another. He was actually happier with what he played on the previous take.

A solution is found because the technology allows it: the piano, bass, and guitar parts will use the last take, but Simon's previous favorite take will be combined with them. A few clicks of the mouse and Simon's previous take has been inserted in place of the last performance and added to everyone else's last take. This would have been impossible without playing to the loop, and a mere fantasy if it had been recorded on analog tape.

FIGURE 13.4. More scenes from the tracking session.

Alan:

> Computer-based recording lets you get everything perfectly in time, perfectly in tune. Quantized. That may be appropriate in some styles of music, but on a live tracking session for a rock song, we should really be going for feel not perfection—or else why use human beings? Actually, I've never been the kind of producer who insists every note is metronomically correct. To me, feel is in fact *defined* by slight imperfections.

Housekeeping and Recorded Levels

Unlike analog tape, computer files can simply disappear in the blink of a save, crash, or conflict. Backups at every key stage, as we have said so often throughout this book, are nothing short of essential. And back up the backup and store it in a completely different location.

Ideally, all the sounds in a track will come over in a good balance when all the track output faders are in a straight line. That's important when a DAW session is played on an analog console—we don't want the faders to all be at radically different levels. Having a straight line of faders doesn't necessarily mean all the tracks will all be recorded at an equal level on the meters. Sometimes, even though a sound is recorded at a strong level on the meters, it still can't be heard properly.

Alan:

> "Value for Money," an expression that I learnt at Abbey Road, describes how loud an instrument or vocal actually sounds with reference to its level on the meter. Thick, muffled, boomy sounds would be considered bad Value for Money, whereas a bright percussive sound will be considered good Value for Money. A very good Value for Money sound might seem ridiculously loud against other tracks recorded at the same metered level.

A case in point was Simon's percussion overdubs on this track, where the tambourine was recorded with the meters barely moving. Featuring a sound that is bad Value for Money has the potential to send your mix into the red, which means the overall level of the mix will have to be decreased, which is not generally going to be considered a good thing.

Afterthoughts

So is everyone happy with what they've achieved? Did it work recording the track as a band, as opposed to assembling a jigsaw of individual performances? With Alan tucked away in the control room, Julian, our video producer, snuck in a quick interview with each player to talk about the experience—particularly the now all-too-rare experience of being in the studio, playing as a *live band*.

Simon Phillips:

> At the end of the day, it's so much quicker. You get four tracks down in one take. And the energy you get from the interaction with three other human beings really shows in the music.

Nathan East:

> There's nothing better than playing with the guys at the same time.

Rami Jaffee:

> It's pretty unusual these days to be tracking as a band. It's also unusual to be playing the way I'm playing on this song. The track seemed to be looking for a lot of flourishes, whereas usually it's more like "Try not to use both hands" or "Try not to use all your fingers."

Tim Pierce:

> Alan is great. He gets out of the way when he should and he gets in the way when he needs to. That's the mark of a great producer.

Here's more from other engineers and producers about their approaches to live tracking.
Chuck Ainlay:

> On a Mark Knopfler album that I worked on, half of it was kind of built from click track, and half was built around tracking with the musicians. Each approach has a different outcome, and they're both good. I think there's a more immediate impressiveness about a track that's built up piece by piece, where you can make things really happen in different moments and it's all constructed and it's just like "Wow" the first time you hear it. Whereas a band track, to me, is something that goes a little deeper to the soul and maybe you can listen to it more times.

Tony Brown:

> I like to know what a song is going to sound like—plus, a lot of magic happens on the floor. I mean, my best records I've made that I'm really proud of, the guitar solo happened on the fly. That's the thing about Nashville—it really happens on the floor. When I cast a rhythm section for an artist, I really study who should be on that session, because the dynamic of the musicians and the artists here in Nashville is really an important thing.

Sylvia Massy:

> Well, I would always prefer having a band play together. And in fact, part of the reason why I have set up a studio in an old theater is because it has a brilliant stage, and when the artists come to work in this studio, they set up onstage and it's like a live show. So they're playing to a house, and there is a different energy when artists are onstage. Sometimes when musicians think too much, they sound stiff. So, when you put them onstage, they're really much more natural, and I think there's a great energy that can be captured there.

14

VOCALS

On almost any pop, rock, country, R&B, or hip-hop record, the singer is the track's shop window, the performance that defines its appeal.

If you listen to records from the 1950s, the singer is not only the most important feature of the record, but virtually the only thing you can hear. Nowadays, where the vocal needs to sit in the final mix remains an often hotly contested debate between the singer, the engineer, the producer, and, ultimately, the record company.

Nashville vocal coach Kim Copeland says:

> Labels are looking for uniqueness. And if there's a groove that allows you to do your unique vocal style over, write it. Once you find someone to help you identify your uniqueness, do not apologize for it. That's the only chance you have of being discovered and being unique.

There have been few more unique voices in pop music than Michael McDonald, who sang background on countless hit records back in the seventies, and later recorded hit after hit with the Doobie Brothers and more as a solo artist. More recently, he has become a peerless interpreter of classic songs from the Motown years.

You'd think that after a lifetime's experience of singing in the studio, it'd be like falling off a log for Michael. And you'd be dead wrong.

Michael McDonald:

> It's a love/hate thing. It's the pinnacle of doing any recording for me, and if I finally get a vocal I'm happy with, I'm thrilled, but getting there is just . . . it's like a bloodbath.

The human voice is the most basic and yet the most complex instrument we have. Just ask Siri! Almost any other instrument can be replicated, mimicked, reproduced, and repeated. Recording the voice remains both the trickiest and also the most crucial component of any modern record.

Preparation

As with most things in life, being prepared is half the battle. When it comes to recording a vocal, leaving as little as possible to chance is a good place to start.

It's always good to be able to walk into a session with equipment you feel confident with and at least have an idea of what to expect from the equipment—whether the voice itself is loud, medium, or quiet, whether the singer is going to hit the limiter hard or soft. Vocalists have an enormous range of levels.

Alan:

> I have recorded countless singers over the years, and each one poses a unique challenge. If I compare, say, Colin Blunstone with Allan Clarke: Allan could be heard singing the song in the control room over a surprisingly loud backing track, whereas conversely, poor old Colin's breathy voice could barely be heard above even a whisper of a playback in the control room.

Another crucial thing you should discuss before you record the backing is the *key* the song is in. Even today, in the forgiving world of seemingly limitless digital manipulation, transposing an entire track's worth of instruments to a different key remains a hassle best avoided.

Alan:

> On Alan Parsons Project records, Eric [Woolfson] and I would always just record in a key that suited us, because at that time we'd never know who the singer was going to be!

Kim Copeland:

> I always test the keys. I'll always make them go at least a step to a step and a half up and down, so we find the sweet spot.

Michael McDonald:

> I like to put it up a half step above what I think I can do comfortably, because then I'm going to give it something that I won't give it, if it's just that much more comfortable. And again, that's a changing thing, not so much because I'm getting older, but I've learned that on some things, there's a timbre when I sing lower that I haven't really gone to much in my career that works for certain songs.

Preparation is also crucial for the singer. This includes being healthy (singing for long periods is an aerobic workout), eating and drinking appropriately (dairy is generally best avoided as it is a mucus stimulant). Warm drinks are thought better than cold, and alcohol, let's just say, comes with baggage. Warming up—i.e., doing some vocal exercises, or just singing for a few minutes, at least—is good. Imagine a runner hitting the blocks without stretching out and warming up!

Michael McDonald:

> If I stay down in the lower registers for a good twenty minutes, it'll take care of itself up there. But early in the day for me is anybody's guess, you know. I don't go there until I have to, because I'll be better off staying low, and I learned that from some singers over

the years, and it does really work. You'll wear yourself out trying to get your high range back. All you're doing is making it harder for yourself.

Alan:

If I'm with a first-time vocalist, I would probably start trying to make them feel as relaxed as possible. The main thing is that the singer feels comfortable with what they're hearing, because that's everything. If you're not comfortable with what you're hearing while you're trying to give a performance, then it's never going to work. I encourage singers to tell me if they want more of their own voice, more reverb, less reverb—anything. That's the singer's prerogative.

Kim Copeland works a lot with young singers, and she'll go through a range of sessions and techniques to get them feeling comfortable:

One of the sessions would be us reading through the lyrics, and we're not only looking for emotion—I want them to say the lyric to me, so that we can sing that lyric the same way you would say it in a normal conversational tone, because that's what's going to make me believe it. If you tell me I lost my dog today, I lost my job, and my mother is dying of cancer, and you go in and sing it and say, [*sings in a happy voice*] "I lost my job today, my dog died, my mom's dying of cancer," I'm not very well going to believe it, you know. So I want you to read me that lyric. I want the right accents falling on the right syllables. I want the right emotion delivered at the right time. I want the voice inflection correct.

Another session would be for me just to get to know them vocally, for me to get to know what tricks, what natural tricks, they have, and which ones they've copied from Reba McEntire, Winona, or whoever, get them to try some new ones or to morph the ones they have into something that makes them unique for their style.

The Recording Environment

Professional recording studios offer isolated rooms or vocal booths that normally offer flat or neutral acoustics. (See **figure 14.1.**) Some singers prefer the less claustrophobic environment of the main performing area, or even the control room. In a domestic recording situation, just avoid a space that adds a "sound" to the voice—unless you want that "old church vibe," in which case, head out to your local neighborhood old church, of course.

FIGURE 14.1. **Vocal booth at MCS Recording, Toronto. Photo courtesy of Mike Rocha.**

Alan:

> I've made very good recordings in totally dead rooms, sometimes hanging drapes even. I once had John Miles completely surrounded by blankets six inches from his mouth . . . that gives you one effect. If you want a little bit of air, that's fine. From mouth to the mic, I'd generally give between six and nine inches for large diaphragm, and for a dynamic mic a bit closer. It's all down to what feels good at the time. Every song is different and should be treated on its own merits.

Grammy-winning singer-songwriter Erykah Badu says:

> *Baduizm* [her debut] would be the only album I recorded in the sound booth. Every other song I've recorded has been in the control room, on the couch, situated mathematically, strategically between two speakers so I didn't get feedback . . . it was a more fulfilling experience, like I was performing.

Choosing a Vocal Mic

If you were to hear Frank Sinatra on your iPod recorded on a lapel mic, as opposed to a U 47, you'd probably say there's not much in it really! But if you were listening on a highly specified system, then you'd hear the difference. The aesthetics are just as important as technicalities. To say a mic will contribute to how a record sells is arguable; but you can say that the right mic for a singer will help you capture the spirit you're after. A certain mic can be perfect for one singer and disappointing for another. Condenser mics are usually a favorite choice, but that's not a hard-and-fast rule.

During the making of the *Art & Science of Sound Recording* video series, we visited John McBride, engineer and husband of Martina McBride, and keeper of one of the world's greatest mic collections at Blackbird Studios in Nashville. He let us in on some of his secrets:

> The Telefunken 251 is famous for female vocals. I think a lot of the great female vocalists—Streisand, Céline Dion—will use about, seven times out of ten, a Telefunken 251. This microphone was built for Martina, and, in particular, serial number 584, there's no question about it. She sounds perfect on this microphone. That mic going through a V76 Telefunken Mic Pre and using the channel strip on the console, a Neve 31105. It's four bands of EQ. I may engage the top band and possibly the low mid. Compression-wise, a UA 1176 black face.
>
> I love to put the windscreen about one inch, an inch and a half in front of the microphone. And, the closer the windscreen is to the mic, the better I like it, generally. There's a proximity effect—if you want the beautiful low end, the closer you get, the nicer it gets. There's another mic, an RFT. It's an old company that's been out of business for fifty years. They built a mic that's called a 7151. It's a big bottle mic, and it uses an M7 capsule, same as a U 47. It's got an extra gain stage in it to where you don't even use a mic pre. We used that mic for probably two, two and a half records on Martina, and it was fantastic. It's very warm. It doesn't have quite the top end that the 251 has.

Everyone has an opinion about mics, vocal mics in particular. But before we get too carried away, here's some very sound advice.

Niko Bolas, talking sense about mics and moments:

> I did an interview for a magazine once where they asked me, "What's your secret to drum sounds?" and I said, "You put a mic over a good drummer." And, the truth is, if you have some guy that really is having a great day, and he's slamming, it's going to be a grooving drum sound. Everybody else is going to want to know the dimensions in my closet, they're going to want to know the serial number of the microphone. They're missing the point. Those moments just happen, and then they're gone.

Some decisions may be based simply on what mics you have available—not everyone can afford a vintage Neumann—and also on what has worked for you in the past. A friendly singer who doesn't mind being a guinea pig for a few hours could be very helpful. But it's probably best not to subject a professional singer on a commercial session to your experiments! The need for a speedy setup is rarely more crucial than when working with singers.

John Shanks:

> I try to find what works quickly. With certain people you can hear in their voices that they suit certain types of mics. I mean, I'm doing an album with guys right now, and a U 47 sounds great on one guy, and a 67 sounds great on the other guy, and a FET sounds great when we're trying to go for just a different sound with one of the other guys.

Patrick Leonard:

> I have a U 47 that I love that I've had for years, and a [AKG] C24 that has a magic capsule, the top capsule of it. It is just the best vocal mic that I've ever heard and has outshone everything in a line-up of 50 mics, blindfold. Everybody goes, "What's that? Why does that sound that way?" I go, "I think it was dropped," honestly. But whatever it is, there it is.

Erykah Badu:

> I use a 67 and . . . just little handheld mics. I like those because they allow my voice to do most of the work.

Michael McDonald:

> I like the Manley Reference Capsule. That seems to be the mic that works for me—that with Neve mic pres. I change around, but that's the one combination I like. Either the Neve compressor—a tube compressor—or Manley makes kind of a compressor combination limiter that I like very much. It reminds me of the old Fairchilds.

Multiple Grammy-winning engineer Jimmy Douglass:

> A nice mic pre. And then, I'll use an 1176. And, that's pretty much it. And the reason I ended up with the 87, by the way, is there are different mics that sound different on different people. And back in the day, I would spend the time with the artist to try all the different mics and hear them, and you'd go, "Oh, that's better for you; oh, that's better for you." But now, what happens is somebody just says, "Put it down before the vibe goes away." And it's like, OK, well here's a mic. And then they go, "Oh, in the middle of my vocal, I'm doing my verse one, he's going to do a part." Hey, go do a part. So, now everything I got lined up doesn't mean anything anymore. So, now it's like, alright—so I'm going to get a different mic for this guy, who I don't know either, and you're talking about, "Hurry up before we lose it." So, you know what, I found the 87 to be a pretty versatile mic for pretty much everything. You know, that's the only reason I really use it. Why I say that, because people go, "Oh, that's not a great mic" . . . It works.

Alan:

> I've had a lot of luck with the Audio-Technica AT 4033 on vocals ever since its introduction in the early 1990s. I find it rarely needs EQ—it has an enhanced high end, which is usually good for vocals, and it's why I chose it for my vocal on our special *ASSR* track, "All Our Yesterdays." There are so many mics out there, and new ones appear almost weekly, and I really wonder why the designers and manufacturers bother, when everyone knows that the classics always win. Having said that, my latest discovery is the Miktek CV4, which is an amazingly good mic. It stands up well against even a classic like the Neumann U 67.

Nowadays you hear the phrase "vocal chain" a lot. This refers to the series of devices the signal from a microphone will go through before it reaches your DAW: a pre-amp, probably a compressor, an equalizer, and certainly an A-to-D converter. Each of these can exert some influence over the initial tone of your recording. Some people swear by a very carefully chosen chain of command from one device to another.

Jack Joseph Puig:

> We are in a service-oriented business, and we get handed songs, which are a very precious thing for an artist, and you want that song to be to its fullest and to be alive, and I'll do whatever it takes to make that song come alive. And yet, even though I use all these different pieces of recording equipment, the comment is still about the vocal.

Controlling Dynamics

Some singers belt, some whisper, and some do both in the same song. While we don't want to kill dynamics, we need to have them under control to make a final performance sound even and dynamically balanced. To do this, we use compressors and limiters—devices that help us manage dynamics. The compressor/limiter is the engineer's friend. It's almost impossible to imagine modern recording without them.

Alan:

> I always plug in a limiter for a vocal session. It's an absolute certainty that I'm going to need it. In the initial stages of getting a vocal level and listening to the singer—without the track—I'll let the limiter sit most of the time with an average gain reduction of about 5 dB, but being careful not to go much more than about 10 dB except on really hard peaks.

Michael McDonald:

> On so many of the great vocals on the old R&B records, a lot of what you're hearing was that little bit of distortion hitting the compressor. Some of those great Ray Charles screams and James Brown screams, it was kind of like it was just starting to mess up the compressor. And I always thought it was that great tone in their voice, but it actually . . . so much of it, it all goes so hand in hand, and the chain is so much more important to me now.

For a more detailed look at how to apply compressors and limiters to vocals, see Chapter 9.

Experienced singers tend to know how to use mic technique to make the engineer's job easier. Michael McDonald is the perfect example. If he hits a note hard, he'll look away from the mic. You can see that when he performs live. A little bit of self-limiting is always going to be helpful. Some singers are really good at it. You can watch them on TV, and the mic will go anywhere from three inches away from the singer's mouth to maybe even as much as eighteen inches away, and it will still sound consistent. Mariah Carey is a great example of someone who really knows how her voice behaves and how to control it. That level of understanding can only be a plus when you're recording because you won't have to use an unnatural amount of limiting or compression.

Michael McDonald:

> In the studio, the whole thing is, I have to sing enough so that I'm relaxed; I'm actually singing the song now. That's usually about somewhere like fifteen takes later, where I'm actually starting to get takes that I like, that the pitch is better, and I'm relaxing more and I don't sound like I'm trying to sing too hard. To this day, I still go through that.

If you had a song where the verses were very quiet and the choruses were very loud, it might be best to suggest, "Could you please move into the mic so we could get a more close, intimate, breathy sound on the verses and then just back off on the chorus?" If the singer's vocal range is, say, as much as 20 dB, you're unlikely to want to do any gain reduction over 10 dB without it sounding squashed. A good general rule if we're going for a natural vocal sound would be not to gain-reduce more than 10–12 dB.

Headphone Mixes and Pitching

A good overall headphone mix for a singer is extremely important. There are two issues: the overall level of what they are hearing, and then the *relative* level of their voice against the backing. Getting both "right"—i.e., to where the singer is comfortable and performing at their best—is crucial.

Alan:

> If they're getting too little of themselves, they'll probably over-sing and therefore go out of tune. And if they're getting too much, they'll under-sing and probably go out of tune! The overall volume is also an issue. Ideally, they should have it at a level where they can hear their voice acoustically inside their head as well as from the cans.

Michael McDonald:

> Wearing headphones in the studio . . . It's a torture. I hate it, when I'm singing. I don't mind it when I'm playing and I get a good mix of the band, I'm fine with that. When I'm singing, it plays so much havoc with my pitch. And as I get older, I find I'm either more concerned than I used to be or it's just harder to hear pitch. And the level of headphones, you know, singers kind of want to get it loud so they can sing their hearts out, and basically it's like that Doppler effect: You get it a little louder, the pitch starts to get a little ambiguous.

Everyone is different, and it's good to experiment with what works in terms of how loud singers like the relationship and volume between their own voice and the track in the headphones. If a singer is singing in tune, then the ideal balance and volume has probably been found.

Michael McDonald:

> I spend a lot of time in that first two hours of doing any one vocal, just singing it out, getting it out of my system, not trying to sing too hard, and also getting the level right and getting the compressor setting right. And then, when I realize I'm singing more relaxed because the compression is where it needs to be, it's allowing me to kind of not push too hard. A lot of times I'll play with taking one ear off, or barely off, so I'm still hearing stereo, but I can hear the room and I can hear my pitch.

The one-ear technique suits a lot of singers. (See **figure 14.2.**) Some singers also like to put one finger in their ear to increase the in-the-head volume and resonant sound of their voices. (Irish songwriter and poet Dominic Behan, when asked why he did this, is said to have replied: "I don't like half the stuff I'm singing.")

In a headphone mix it's generally a good idea to favor instruments with fixed tuning, like keyboards. Sometimes too much bass can confuse a singer. Sometimes you need to monitor a vocal at an artificially high level against the track, so that it can be analyzed in greater detail. It's an interesting subject, whether the balance heard by the singer should also be heard by the producer or engineer.

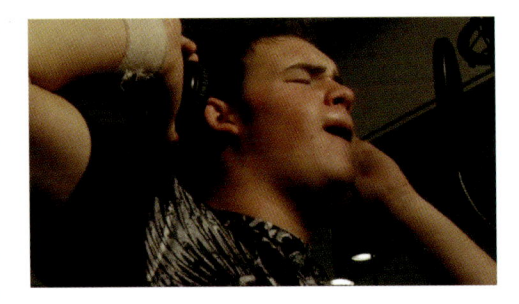

FIGURE 14.2. James Durbin recording with Alan in 2009. Some singers like to remove one side of their headphones as they record to help with pitching.

Jimmy Douglass:

> I basically give them the stereo mix I'm listening to. That way, if something's wrong, I can hear it right there with them. The only thing about that is that sometimes their headphones are not relating the way your speakers are, in terms of the level you're feeding them.

Most singers, particularly inexperienced ones, do find it difficult to sing in tune when wearing headphones. The usual tendency is to sing flat. There are a number of things to try if this is becomes a problem:

- Turn the overall headphone level up or down.
- Turn the vocal up or down against the track.
- Suggest the singer take one earphone off the ear, so that he or she hears the voice acoustically in the room in one ear.
- Deliberately tell the singer to pitch up or sing sharp.
- Adjust the mic position so the singer physically looks up. This can be very effective in helping them "pitch" up.
- Telling the singer to smile sometimes works. This might not work too well for a death metal outfit, of course.
- Use artificial pitch correction, the best-known examples of which are Auto-Tune and Melodyne. But don't overdo it, as so many do—please!!!

Sometimes a singer just cannot get on pitch with headphones. In such cases, it can be worth trying a single speaker or a pair of speakers. A vocal mic with a good cardioid polar pattern will pick up remarkably little of the track on the speaker(s), provided it's not at an earth-shattering level. It's also worth experimenting with the speakers out of phase and angled, so that in theory at least, there is no sound at the mic. Another technique is to record another take without the performer singing, reverse its phase, and combine it with the vocal performance at exactly the same level. That substantially reduces or eliminates the track. Spill is usually not a problem, and Alan has even recorded vocals with the singer facing the control room main monitors at surprisingly high levels.

John Shanks:

> It's interesting, when you look at a great singer on a pitch correction screen and you can see the wave of their vocal, and see where they are to the note. A great singer is like a great violinist. It's the micro tones. Sometimes the thing with Auto-Tuning is what feels good is not what is perfectly in tune. When you're tuning a diva, you know, you want to make sure it still has her character and it doesn't sound like you're just putting her through a box.

Perhaps what John is also saying about using pitch correction software is: Having looked, stop looking, and start listening.

There are lots of ways to deal with pitching, but we'd like to give the final words on the subject to Ms. Erykah Badu.

Erykah Badu:

> If you squeeze your ass cheeks together, the pitching is usually good. And if you do it on Wednesdays it's even better. And eat Lay's potato chips . . . it's that oily, salty thing . . . helps it slide . . . the vocal cords.

Vocal Recording Approaches

Experienced singers generally know which basic approach to vocal recording works for them. No matter how you end up getting the finished vocal, it's best is to have the singer perform the song all the way through at least once. That way, you can get a feel for the type of performance you are looking for, and where any problems might lie.

You can then decide whether to record a series of complete takes or, for example, tackle just the verses, just the choruses, or do the whole song line by line. We can record several takes and choose the best verse, chorus, lines, or even individual words. These can then be assembled and compiled into a master take you feel sells the song best. The industry calls this *comping*.

> *Comping is the technique of recording multiple takes of a performance and then assembling one "master performance" out of the best bits later on. (See also "Comping" later in this chapter.)*

Alan:

> One-take wonders are rare, but always welcome! The line-by-line approach is often the way to go, so everyone can take a close look at each phrase for pitching, timing, strength, and overall performance. But be aware that some singers will get tired sooner than others. Once you have a tired vocalist, you might as well go home.

Michael McDonald:

> I don't like to tune things, but I'll do a hundred comps if you want and pick. But I have to sing it all the way through to get anything that will feel natural even as a comp later. So, basically, I have about ten vocals after I've sung it maybe thirty times, you know.

Punching in (sometimes called *dropping in*, particularly in the U.K.)—the practice of replacing a word or line in a section of a song by letting the singer hear, typically, the preceding line and then going into record over the offending part—is a time-honored process that works well, although some singers find it difficult to maintain the flow of their performance if it's been recorded in too many slices and dices.

Michael McDonald:

> I don't like punching in. I'd rather comp and get where things are actually kind of coming from that place that I think they need to come from to be a vocal.

John Fields:

> I'll sometimes set up a singer in another room and just say, cut eight takes of vocals or do it at home and just send me those vocals, because I know he's going to sing differently alone than with me or with five band guys watching. So, no rules.

Alan:

> Great attitude. I'd like to try that. I'd like to try sending a singer home, saying, "Come back in the morning. I want a vocal on my desk by nine sharp!"

Michael McDonald:

> We'll listen to, like, the ten vocals we're going to comp, we'll listen to the same line, and it sounds exactly the same to most people—you know, there's nothing unusual about any of them. But I can hear a little bit of pitch or a little bit of something I don't like, and I want to make sure I get the right phrase.

Erykah Badu:

> There have been songs when I sing it line by line if I'm not comfortable singing it all the way through. Like, sometimes I write songs and I don't know how to sing it yet. I can just hear it in my mind. I have to train myself how to sing it. But for the most part, we either pick take one, two, or three. There's not a lot of comping and stuff . . . it's just—that's the take, that's the one, the performance.

It's pretty unnerving to walk into a studio all on your own with complete silence all around and have a pair of cans strapped onto your ears. And because of this feeling of isolation, it's very important that the talkback remains active. Always press the button between takes, even to say, "Just one more time." On the other hand, as Jack Douglas, who teaches a course for engineers at Expression College in California, observed:

> Don't go on the talkback right after a vocalist has done, you know, has sunk everything they have into this vocal, and say, "What do you think?" You know, they don't think at this point; they're looking for help. It's etiquette and psychology, the psychology of the recording studio, and the etiquette of the session.

Finally, adding reverb to the singer's voice in their headphones—this can help, in terms of helping them feel good and "perform" better, or it can be bad in terms of flattering to deceive. If the singer wants reverb and it makes them sing better, fine. But it's best to monitor (as well as record!) the performance "dry," so that you know what is actually being captured.

Getting the Performance

If anybody really knew how to get a hit performance out of a singer, the last thing they'd do is tell anyone. The best you can do is create an environment where the magic can be created by the person standing in front of the mic. So much of recording—and producing—is down to psychology, and this is never truer than when you are recording a singer. Comments and suggestions made to a vocalist about his or her performance need to be handled with a great deal of sensitivity. But there is no "trick." All you can do is have a range of options and ideas to call upon and, hopefully, the intuition to know which to present which performer.

During the making of the *Art & Science of Sound Recording* video series, we spoke with countless artists, engineers, and producers. The following range of thoughts should give you some ideas, plus some idea of the subtlety you need to employ when it comes to coaxing out a great vocal performance.

Kim Copeland:

> My first job working with any artist or songwriter is, check your ego at the door. What happens in this room, stays in this room, but we're going to explore. We're not here to sing, we're not here to play—we're here to explore, because that's the only way you get to the good stuff.

Erykah Badu:

> It's the take, it's the performance. When everybody becomes one living, breathing organism, together. And we all listen, and sometimes the drama is like, well, it's too bad. We all like this one. We all sound good.

Chuck Ainlay:

> That's one of the things I really love about Tony Brown. On a Lee Ann Womack album we did, he once said, "OK, I'm going to give you like four vocal takes," and that's pretty much all he gave her. And so, each time she sang, it was like each time was a performance and really feeling the song and putting it out. Whereas, you know, you tell somebody, well, let's just record and once you get warmed up, we'll start taking, and then whenever you're tired, maybe we'll move on to the next song—I don't think they ever really rise to the moment like that.

Here's John Shanks talking about his experience with Kelly Clarkson:

> She came in, and for, I guess it was about three and a half hours, maybe four, never left the booth, never . . . barely went to the bathroom. I mean, it was the lead vocal and all the backgrounds in one sitting, because she didn't want her voice to cool down. And I've noticed that certain singers . . . like, Céline is like that, where once she gets going and she's warmed up, she'll just keep going. And, what happens when you get somebody on a roll, you get to a better performance. As long as you're not blowing out their voice and . . . you know, that way if it's a really hard song or a rangey song, you know, I'll do verses first and then the choruses, and if there's the big third chorus, we'll kind of wait for that.

Recording a singer is a delicate and sensitive process, riddled with unspoken thought processes, insecurities, and issues. Something quite innocent going on in the control room can unnerve a singer or get them frustrated or anxious. A producer always needs to be on the lookout for a potential spanner in the works.

Jack Joseph Puig:

> So even though you might be trying different microphones, a quick funny story, a funny thing, a "Let's grab a coffee for a second," a wink to the second engineer. There's a

million ways to cause distractions so they have no idea that man behind the curtain is doing what he's doing. And that is why, you know, a really, really great record producer, the focus is not on the record business. No one actually knows what he's doing. His job is to empower the artist and empower the song without them knowing that that's what he's doing.

John Shanks:

Everybody's got their process. Sometimes you see a singer hit the wall—they start blaming the gear, or they start saying that it's the headphones and, you know, "If you put some more EQ on me or more compression . . ." And sometimes that's valid, but sometimes that's bullshit. You know, that's their bullshit, and you have to kind of try to not lose your patience and be supportive of that until they find what works for them.

Alan:

You can't say to a singer: "That was hopeless. You were flat all the way through." Or, "Maybe we should try someone else?" Diplomacy would dictate saying things like, "I think we should try it again, and let's concentrate on the pitching."

Patrick Leonard:

Some people really just want to sing it all the way down, some people need a shot of tequila and to be laid on the floor and sing it one line at a time. It's that thing of whatever they need, whatever they need to get there, until you start to believe them. Because in most cases, if I can possibly help it, people are pushed beyond their threshold, beyond what they're actually capable of, so they're at the edge of their ability, and then you start to get some vitality from their work, you know. And in that state, people are often times just like, "I can't do this," and you go, "Great. We're there then." If you really believe you can't, we're there. Because what's greater than being the consummate novice, to always feel like it's something you don't know anything about?

Niko Bolas:

I can always apologize for not having a limiter, but I can add one—but I can't get the vocal back. If I plug in a piece of outboard gear, or I think I've got the brilliant idea for, you know, if we use the Neve and we go through the API and we go sideways through the satellite dish and we bring it back through here and then cross-flange it, put it in Dolby, it's gonna be amazing, and somewhere in those five things, something doesn't like something else and it doesn't work, yank the whole hornet's nest of cables out of the wall and get the mic plugged in. Just get it.

No matter how you recorded your vocal, these days a DAW environment gives you incredible flexibility after the event. This can range from basic comping—mixing and matching different takes and lines and even words into one unified performance—to extreme processes such as the almost ubiquitous Auto-Tune. Although there's almost no problem you can't fix these days, artifacts such as popping—whose various cures we looked at in Chapter 3—and sibilance, which we discussed in both Chapter 8 and Chapter 9—are best tackled at the source, rather than fixed later.

Niko Bolas:

> I did a record with country singer Lorrie Morgan. There were forty people in a room, and we did fourteen songs in three days. And on about six of them, we had to use the first take, because at the end of it she was in tears, because she lived the lyric for three and a half minutes. And she had to leave the room and go fix her makeup. I mean, she brought it. I was just proud to be in the room.

Comping

Comping, as we have already mentioned, is the practice of taking multiple performances of a part that have been recorded on individual tracks and then choosing between the different takes of each individual line, phrase, even a word if you want, in order to compile a master performance. Comping is an age-old practice that was done even back in the days of recording onto analog tape. Provided you had enough spare tracks, of course.

Spare tracks are not the issue today, and all DAWs offer one, if not two ways to facilitate the assembly and dissembling of repeated performances. Comping is by no means exclusive to vocals, it should be said. Instrumental solos—anything where you want the ultimate performance that you may not have the time, energy, nor possibly the skills to create "for real," can be comped.

Comping is a skill because you obviously want to end up with a final performance that sounds like it was genuinely one single performance. Aside from obvious considerations like pitch and basic sound, we need to think about tone, intensity, and energy to create a finished track that really does sound like it could have been performed. Removing all the breaths or having every phrase on "11" does not sound especially "real." But there again, real might not be what you're going for. As Michael McDonald said, someone walking into the room would say that every take sounds the same—but it's our job to make magic out of what we have at our disposal.

Sometimes it might be best for the producer/engineer to do the comp without the singer. The singer can always comment on a comp once they hear it, but it's usually best to spare them the agonies of listening to every line over and over again, which is a necessary part of the process.

Effects

We look at reverbs and delays in their own chapters of the book, but sometimes you might want to apply other quite extreme processing to a vocal: chorus, flanging, even distortion.

Few vocals sound great totally "dry" or unprocessed. Applying some reverb, delay, or other processing can give both the singer and the listener something to get excited about. Too much in the way of effects can give the impression that the vocal is better than it actually is—which may not be a wise thing to do during the recording process, but ultimately isn't a bad thing, of course.

Alan:

> I remember in my early days at Abbey Road Studios, I just had to ask Geoff Emerick, "How did you get the amazing vocal sound on the Beatles' 'Tomorrow Never Knows'?" "Oh, it was just through a Leslie," he says. End of story—the ultimate John Lennon vocal sound ever—just "through a Leslie." Wow!

As we said at the beginning of this chapter, the lead vocal is a song's shop window, and it's OK to do pretty much whatever it takes to make it memorable either using effects, or possibly recording the vocal onto tape to get that much-in-favor-now "tape compression" density.

David Thoener recorded the monster hit "Smooth" by Carlos Santana, produced by Matt Serletic. Singer Rob Thomas has a very distinctive vocal sound on the track.

David Thoener:

> That was Matt's idea, and that was interesting. Clive Davis wasn't quite sure we should go with that vocal sound, so when we mixed the record, that was the master mix, and then Clive asked for another additional mix without the telephone filtering sound. It was filters, set properly. Matt is a genius when it comes to Pro Tools and getting things that he wants quickly. He came up with that idea and just went over to Pro Tools and went *tap-tap-tap-tap-tap*—and there it was! I was like wow, that sounds really cool. We did one mix with and one mix without, but Matt was confident that the one we had originally done was the right one, and that's the one that came out.

Jack Douglas:

> Back in the day, we made our reverb—you know, all of the reverb that went on the vocals, and the repeats, and all the effects, those decisions were made on the spot. And I kind of like the sound of those records. There's something about it being all captured right on its track, individually, that made it stand out.

Jimmy Douglass:

> Talking about distortion and how, you know, like a Justin Timberlake thing—I put distortion on the vocal, like that's a really cool thing, and I used modern technology to do that with plug-ins. But I was also remembering that when I used to record Aretha, and you know, being the kid that I was and I didn't know a lot about the gear around me. It was just there, and there she'd be, and it was like, well, you're doing it. And there she is, and she's singing, and you got to do it, and everything's happening. And like the only clue I had about her was that, you know, I think I would get kind of a level that kind of would be whatever it was, and it would be pretty much right, and then she would do this thing and she would hit that high note—*Waaaahhhhh!!!* And that's the only clue I had, because she would do this every time, and I'd go oh, shit, here it comes. And I didn't know what to do about it, so I would actually just lower the fader coming into the tape machine, because I had to stop it from doing it somehow. That's what I was doing. So, I'd be sitting there with her going, *Waaaahhhhh!!!*

> But, I'd listen to a lot of those records later, and I'd hear on some of those notes, she would sing, it would hit it so hard. I guess it was tape distortion is what it was, because it sounded like . . . the sound that I described was like a burning iron, but it was sweet. It was sweet distortion, you know what I mean, where everything was just rounded and melted, and nobody minded. It made her even sound even mightier when she hit up there, you know.

Double-Tracking and Harmonies

Double-tracking—somewhat obviously—is the technique of recording a vocalist singing each line of a song twice. This doubling-up obviously "thickens" the sound of a voice, because now there are two of you. But it also creates a pleasing shimmering type of effect due to the continual microscopic changes in pitch and timing. The science is simply to record the same vocal performance as soon after the original as you can, using the same mic and recording chain. The "art" lies in achieving a recording that's accurate but not so accurate as to lose the effect you're trying to create—something that can be relatively easy to do nowadays, using copy and paste in your DAW or using plug-ins that emulate so-named ADT effects. (See **figure 14.3**.) "Real" double-tracking actually relies upon human variations (even with the most laboratory-accurate of artists, like the Carpenters, back in the 1970s). So unless you're going for a deliberately artificial sound, the best double-tracking effects are always going to be achieved the old-fashioned way.

One of the most difficult things about double-tracking is that you hear your first voice in the headphones and you think it's the one you're doing now, and you make an adjustment and nothing happens! Generally speaking, it's best to have the first track at a lower level.

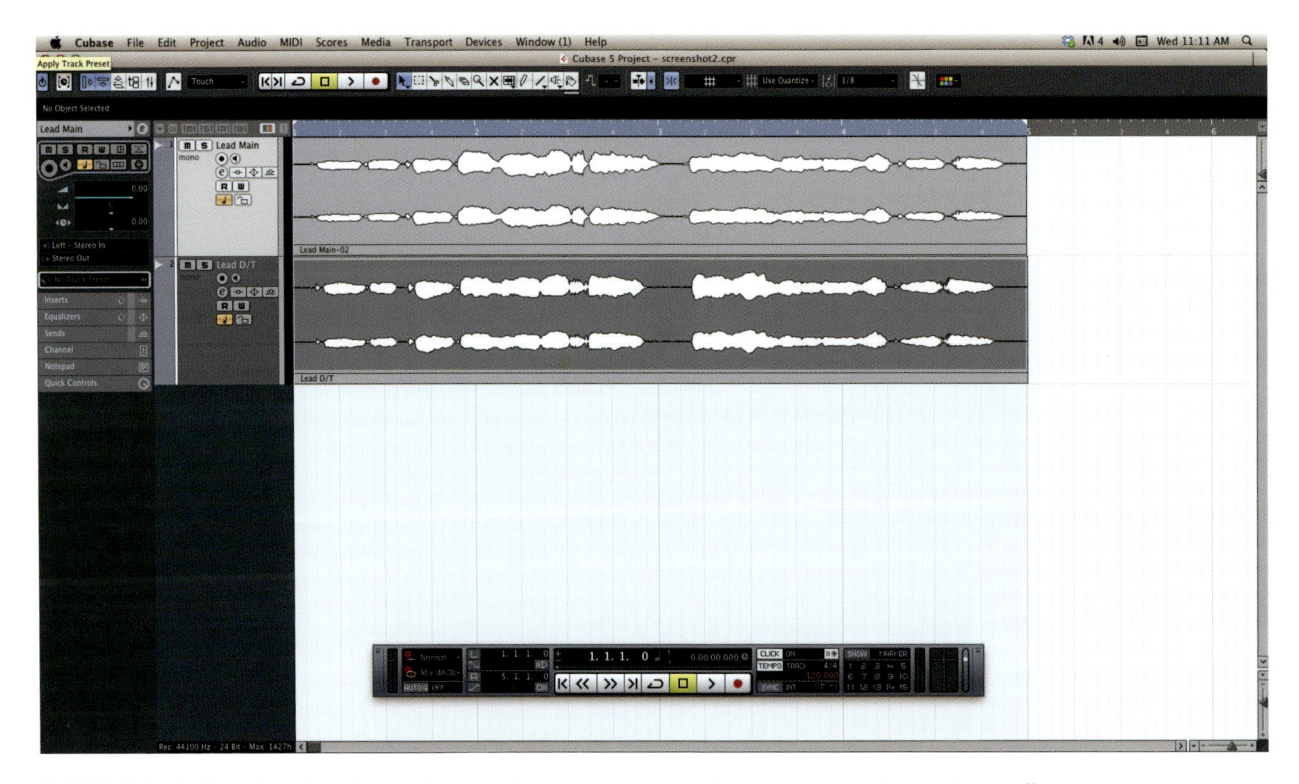

FIGURE 14.3. Genuine double-tracked audio: a separate performance, not just a time-offset copy.

For a lead vocal, you'd normally sit the double-track straight on top of the original track, keeping effects and relative volumes as similar as possible. But sometimes the double-track works better a little quieter than the original, especially when the doubling is less than perfect.

Alan:

> I remember suggesting to Hollies producer Ron Richards that we would get a better stereo effect by triple-tracking the harmony parts—the main vocal in the center and the double-track on the left and the triple-track on the right. So right through my time with them, that's what we did. Another effect is to record the lead vocal in octaves. You might even want to double each part, to create a four-vocal performance.

In most rock and pop recordings (artists like Crosby, Stills & Nash aside) harmony vocals normally appear in choruses. Working out harmonies can be anyone's job—the writer, the singer, the artist, the producer, or a professional arranger. And the style of recording can range from multiple tracking, one voice at a time, to having a group of singers clustered around a single mic. If you're doing the last, make sure you have the mic on an omni pattern, of course. In terms of relative balance, professional backing singers will almost invariably balance themselves. With less experienced singers, you may need to get one of them to move closer or further away from the mic.

Erykah Badu:

> When I do background vocals, I do the layer effect. It helps me make sure the pitch is good all the way through. The pitch has to be really good for background vocals. What I do is, on track 1, I'll sing the background vocal. And then on track 2, I'll layer it, the double. And the first one is loud when I do it; then I turn it down a little to do the second. Then I turn off the first one and only triple the double. Then I use those three until I keep going around and around in a layer. Then on the third one, I do the first one again. Usually the pitch gets better and better, and I get comfortable with the phrasing and the timing, and by the time we're gone around about sixteen times or so, it's tight. The triple is tight, and then I'll go to the next note.

Alan:

> For backing vocals, I tend to add a little high end: 2 or 3 dB at 10k. I am never afraid of spreading sounds in stereo. Most things that are double-tracked other than lead vocals get placed hard left and hard right.

Final Thoughts

A great performance, a good vocal sound, the right amount of limiting and compression, EQ, and so on will all contribute to making the vocal feel right in the track. Deficiencies in any of those areas, however, can come back to haunt you when you come to the final mix.

Niko Bolas:

> The big lesson that I wish we could just put on a billboard in front of a recording school is: You're only as good as what's in front of the microphone—end of story.

15

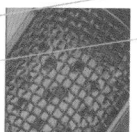

INTERNET RECORDING

There's very little you can't do online or over a network, and at time of writing, recording certainly isn't one of them. It's a small but crucial leap of faith, however, to go from recording a performance right there on the other side of the glass in a recording studio right in front of you, to recording a performer *in real time* who is several thousand miles away.

Ever since DAWs came along, there's been a trend for contributing musicians to record their own parts or individual elements of a song in their own studio.

Alan:

> A few years back, I asked Pink Floyd's David Gilmour to play guitar on a track I had originally recorded in my own studio in California. He would record at his U.K.-based studio (on a boat!). We corresponded by email to communicate what parts were needed, and sent each other WAV files on CD backward and forwards by FedEx. At the time, it was quite a test of going "cross-platform," as David was using Pro Tools on a Mac and I was using Nuendo on a PC.

With more powerful online storage systems and faster data transfer speeds, uploading and downloading files is far quicker and easier than it was in 2003, when Alan and David worked on "Return to Tunguska."

Tracks or stems can even be transferred by instant message, Skype, and iChat, or by FTP or dedicated file transfer services like Hightail and MediaFire. Online services also have the additional benefit of providing us with a backup. File sharing or linking via the Dropbox app is also very popular.

For some years it's been possible to beam an audio performance in high quality by satellite or high-speed ISDN telephone lines. The hugely successful Frank Sinatra *Duets* album was largely recorded this way. Frank actually specified to his producer, Phil Ramone, that his duet partners should not be around when he himself was singing!

Online Issues

Even though "remote" recording (another word for recording at a distance from home base) has been with us for several years now, genuine collaborative Internet recording is still in its infancy.

Sending audio over the Internet does take time. This is a problem we often encounter in digital audio, and it's called "latency." It's the equivalent of the frustrating delay or "dead air" we see every day on TV news when the anchor is talking to a correspondent in a foreign country.

Recording in *real time* is the Holy Grail, of course—being able to interact with the performer as if they were in the next room, not thousands of miles away. The trick is letting the "remote" performers hear themselves in sync with the backing track as they perform, and for the engineer or producer to hear everything in sync at their end—the master station—when the performance comes back to them.

The obstacle to this is basic physics.

Assuming electricity travels at the speed of light, 186,000 miles per second, our audio could travel 186,000 miles and would arrive one second later. To go halfway round the equator, about 12,500 miles, it would take about 67 milliseconds—enough to sound substantially late or out of sync. But it's not just the geographical distances at work here, it's also the processing times in the equipment at both ends, and the Internet itself, which transmits data not only by cables on land and sea but also by satellite. Fly me to the moon!

So it's perfectly possible for one performer to perform to the track they hear and send their performance back to the producer's end so that it synchronizes with the track being heard at the master station. But it's entirely unrealistic to have two or more performers playing together with the long delays brought about by physical distance, computer processing capacity, and the Internet. It would end up as a comedy of errors. Each time one player heard the collaborator's contribution, he or she might be several seconds out, in a sort of never-ending audio "house of mirrors" experience.

To some degree, you can "jam" across relatively short geographical distances using landline telephones (mobile phone technology has its own inbuilt latency, of course). Various manufacturers offer so-called "Internet jamming software." These manufacturers say you will learn to play with a little latency—so what happens at the live gig after practicing with latency? These systems may be OK for writing and entertainment or simple practicing, but they can't be considered professional products.

One application that seems to be leading the way (at the time of writing), with perhaps the most advanced program of its kind, is Source-Connect, a program from Chicago-based technology innovators Source Elements. It can be used as either a stand-alone app or a plug-in for a DAW program on both Windows and Mac.

A simpler version by the same manufacturer is called Source-Live and allows just the monitoring of a distant session on virtually any device, including—dare we say it?—the iPhone!

Setting Up an Internet Recording Session

For the making of the *Art & Science of Sound Recording* video series, we chose Source-Connect to examine the issues and processes surrounding Internet recording.

The specifics of the process have developed since the filming, so while we recount our experiences in this chapter, we also look at improvements and refinements that have been made in the interim. And improvements will surely continue to be made. However, even if you are reading this in the year 2053, we hope and trust that the human dimension, plus the "pure physics" of the process, will not be substantially different—even if the tools we describe below may soon go the way of the dodo.

The setup is for Source-Connect is fairly complex. Port forwarding functions on the Internet routers need to be specially configured, and various templates need to be set up on the DAWs at both ends for transferring the audio back and forth. It is important not to cause "loop backs" by feeding the performer his own signal. A good high-speed Internet connection is vital. The key issue that needs to be addressed is dealing with the extreme time delay that occurs sending audio over the Internet. Source-Connect deals with this by allowing the transport of the computers at both ends to be controlled by just one of the users.

The way Source-Connect works is that the application calculates the time taken to transmit the audio on the Web from one place to the other and delays the play or record commands by the right amount to compensate for the time taken to get to the other end. One end is nominated the "master" station. Both ends have a copy of the audio track that is being performed to. When we press the play button, the master transport starts when the correct delay time has been reached at the remote location, the track at the remote station starts at exactly the right moment to be in sync with the master station, and the performances synchronize perfectly. In real terms, however, they might be as much as three or four seconds apart.

The minimum setup a performer needs (as of this writing) is a subscription to the Source-Connect software, a DAW, a mic, and good Internet service. In a future version, Source Elements intends to remove the need for a DAW, eliminating the complexity of operations on the performers' side of the connection, thus making it sound more like they are in a studio with you. However, a performer will always need to add their own reverb and any other effects they want to hear locally. Care must be taken not to transmit that reverb to the recording side of the connection. See "Preparing for the Session" below.

The technology is still relatively in its infancy. Calls to HQ can still be necessary—Robert Marshall of Source Elements has always been very helpful troubleshooting for us.

Any tempo can be used as long as both workstations are set at the same tempo. If a tempo map is used, both workstations need the same tempo map.

Regardless of what you may need to do to achieve it, synchronization is vital, so that a performer can perform comfortably to the track at their end and the producer can record a faithful performance at the master station. One simple but fairly foolproof means of checking that everything is in sync is to do a test with the performer at the other end simply clapping in time with the music. Another way to check sync is to send the guide track back from the performer to see if it locks in with the tracks on the master workstation. But normally, only the performance itself would be sent back to the master station.

Communication on Source-Connect is easy, thanks to a talkback button that can be activated at the master station. It is assumed that at the performer's end, a live microphone is always on.

If the performer is singing and using headphones, they don't need a talkback switch. If the performer is using open speakers or has a mic set up far from themselves, or if you are recording an amped guitar and even shouting voices can't be heard, then Source-Connect has a dedicated Talkback plug-in available. The Talkback plug-in can be used anywhere talkback/listen back is needed—not just for remote sessions.

Preparing for the Session

Once everything is set up, running an Internet session shouldn't be vastly different from running any normal session. But there are some limitations and quirks. For example, singers like to hear some reverb on their voice. Because reverb is a real-time thing, it has to be applied where the performance is taking place. When we undertook the session for the *Art & Science of Sound Recording* video series, singer P. J. Olsson added his own (monitor) reverb at his studio. When his performance came back, it was dry—and we added our own reverb at our end. Care must be taken not to send a "wet" signal to the recording side of the connection.

The challenge in any recording session is to smooth out problems or issues as soon and easily as possible. If artist and producer are in the same building on a conventional face-to-face session, you might say, "Take five" or even, "Let's break for dinner" or, "Can I get you a glass of water?" That's not so easy when you're two thousand miles apart. Even so, it's all about *communication* and making sure the artist doesn't feel abandoned. On the session we conducted, P. J. had a terrible time singing "all *our* yesterdays." He kept on singing "all *your* yesterdays." When you have to continually correct someone, it's potentially damaging to the vibe.

The Session in Progress

Especially on vocal or solo sessions where notes or phrases often need to go under the microscope, we might want to punch in right in the middle of a verse or chorus of the song, or even halfway through a line.

With Internet recording, you'll invariably be making some adjustments to the way you work to allow for latency, and there can be additional hurdles. On our session, we naturally chose to make Alan's studio the master station. What this means, though, is that the "remote" performer won't automatically hear what he or she has just recorded on playback. A way around that is to have the performer(s) record a complete guide track—or better, everything they perform locally—to show where they are in the song. The guide track can be taken in and out as necessary. If the performer records locally, this also substantially simplifies punch-ins, which are otherwise complex or time-consuming if all the recording takes place only at the master station. The caveat to this is that the performer may then need an assistant to operate the DAW.

The nice thing for performers is that they are in their own environment. Some vocalists are very self-conscious when singing in front of other people.

It would have been considered impossible ten years ago . . . a high-quality microphone signal coming in from several thousand miles away. In Source-Connect, the performance we hear in real time—or rather almost real time—a few seconds later, is actually data compressed to a format something like MP3. But the program works in the background to update the file to a full-bandwidth uncompressed version. We don't have to go through a conversion process. If the program can play it full bandwidth, it does.

This unique feature of the Source-Connect software is called Q Manager. It takes care of recording on the performer's side, and the conversion of all the audio to full resolution at the master workstation happens automatically in the background, even cutting/conforming to existing edits. However, it's still a good idea to record the performance at both ends as backup.

It's very important that when sending out, you use the Source-Connect transport, not the DAW transport. Otherwise, it doesn't compensate for the latency at the performer's end.

Internet Recording Applications

- Voice-overs for commercials. Voice-over actors love to work from home and only need a one-mic setup and a simple DAW.
- Recording in a location where the instrument can't be recorded anywhere else—the pipe organ in the Royal Albert Hall, for instance, or simply a complex guitar rig at a session guitarist's home studio.
- Time and budget constraints—not enough time or money to fly the artist to the home base.

- Emotional reasons—"I'm not setting foot in the same room as that idiot guitar player."
- Quick replacements or repairs caused by technical problems, or just re-recording a line or two of an otherwise perfect performance.

The Future

Although Internet at-a-distance recording is technologically amazing, there's no real substitute for being there—interacting in the same location—so that the performer steps out of the studio and into the control room for playbacks. But improvements in videoconferencing and possibly "virtual" technologies can go a long way to bridging the long-distance communication gap. This session we undertook was still a very cost-effective and environmentally responsible exercise. Especially in hard economic times, it makes sense to record over the Internet instead of flying the artist halfway round the world. As we all gain experience with the technology and understand the setup requirements, we can do sessions like this at a moment's notice. We predict that within a few years, Internet recording will become an everyday practice.

16

DRUMS

An acoustic drum kit is an extremely complex piece of machinery. There are multiple components, a massive range of tone colors, a colossal dynamic range, and many different volumes that need balancing. There are resonances and rings and lots of mechanical parts that can squeak or generate unwanted noises. Above all, it's driven, in a very literal sense, by the raw, human power of a drummer.

FIGURE 16.1. A drum kit. *(1) Kick Drum:* The low frequency end of the kit. A pedal operates a beater normally played by the drummer's right foot. *(2) Snare:* Normally used for most of the offbeats. The most complex construction-wise, having a double thickness top head and the vibrating "snares" on the bottom skin or head. *(3) Hi-Hat:* Two cymbals opposing each other. The drummer opens and closes the gap between them with a pedal normally under the left foot. *(4) Toms:* These are drums either attached to the framework of the rest of the kit (rack toms) or freestanding floor toms with their own supports. They can have heads on the top and the bottom or only top heads (concert toms). *(5) Crash Cymbal:* Some drummers will have seemingly dozens of different shapes and sizes spread around from left to right. They are "crashed" usually only with a single hit at a time for dramatic effect. *(6) Ride Cymbal:* The cymbal that is played constantly and rhythmically to add an overall sizzle to a pattern or beat. The center of the cymbal is called the "bell," and hitting the cymbal here produces a distinctive "clangy" sound.

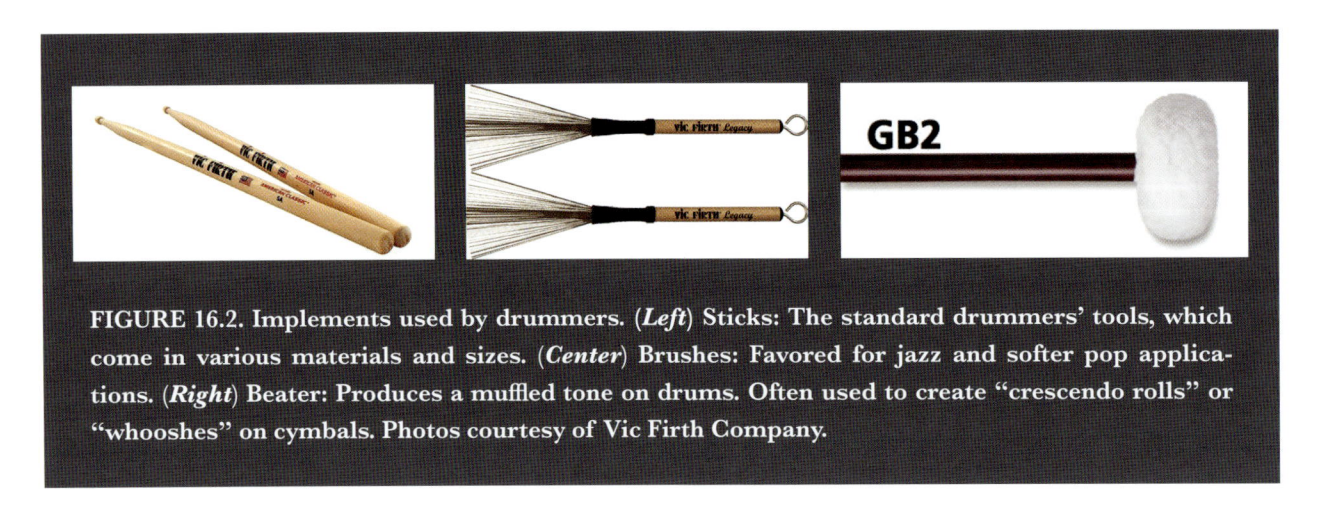

FIGURE 16.2. Implements used by drummers. (*Left*) Sticks: The standard drummers' tools, which come in various materials and sizes. (*Center*) Brushes: Favored for jazz and softer pop applications. (*Right*) Beater: Produces a muffled tone on drums. Often used to create "crescendo rolls" or "whooshes" on cymbals. Photos courtesy of Vic Firth Company.

You can be absolutely certain of hearing drums on just about every pop record made since rock 'n' roll started in the mid-fifties.

During the making of the *Art & Science of Sound Recording* video series, we were very fortunate to elicit the help of Simon Phillips, a British drummer who ruled the London session scene in the 1970s and '80s, and who has also toured with countless international artists, notably the Who and Toto.

Simon's unique and highly practical thoughts on everything from tuning, to miking, to recording drums, threads through both the video series and this chapter.

Simon Phillips:

> A drum kit is made out of many parts, but I always look at it as one instrument, like the piano. If I take the toms away, the snare drum will sound different. It's just physics. You're moving stuff away. Everything has a sympathetic ring, and that helps how it all works. Even though a microphone may be only two inches from the head, if the source changes, it's going to affect what that microphone picks up.

Overall Tuning Concepts

Simon Phillips:

> Whatever you're recording, the instrument has to sound great. Then you're starting out on the right foot. So, acoustically, the instrument has got to be tuned right. It's got to sound right. And there are certain things that, over time, you get to know what a microphone "likes."

Tuning drums is a matter of taste and should be a decision and a task laid at the drummer's door, as that is essentially "their sound." Having said that, it's helpful to have some understanding of the techniques that produce certain results. The tighter a drumhead is stretched, the higher the pitch. Sometimes it might be desirable to have a very constant "even" pitch across a series of toms, and sometimes you might prefer that "sinking" type of sound where the pitch noticeably drops. This effect can be achieved by detuning one or two of both top and bottom tension rods, which makes the sound more sustained. This will make the tension inconsistent over the surface of the drum, but it's a perfectly legitimate technique.

Ideally, a drum kit should tuned so that it appears to be part of a cohesive unit. Whatever style and methodology of tuning is adopted, it's best to try to take the same approach with the tuning of each drum—particularly the toms—so that they work well together. Simon uses his drum stool as a stand when tuning smaller and midsize toms. This lets him spin the drum around to adjust a particular area and also helps him develop a feel for a consistent amount of resistance, using the edge of the seat to push back against. Simple and neat!

Simon Phillips:

> I remember spending a lot of time at Trident Studios in London. At the time, they seemed to be London's real rock 'n' roll studio. They had recorded Elton John and Queen, for example, and they really had this signature bass drum sound, and they really wanted to get that. There was always a big issue with the snare drum. I always liked a fairly high-pitched jazzy live snare drum, and there was this fashion to really slacken it off and put loads of damping on it and really make it sound like a wodge of white noise. It didn't really sound like an instrument. And I also had a problem with the snare drum sounding twice as big as the bass drum. It didn't make sense to me in terms of audio perspective.

Foo Fighters drummer Taylor Hawkins:

> We all know that pretty much the best rock 'n' roll drum sound of all time was John Bonham, which is down to how he played as well, obviously. I mean, he knew how to tune, which is an art. I don't feel I have it necessarily, but another art to studio drumming is being aware of your surroundings and mixing yourself. Like, the hi-hats are going to be really crispy in here, so I need to lay off the hi-hat a little bit. I play drums 50 percent out of love for music and 50 percent out of anger management. And I have to fight that, because you really don't need to beat the shit out of them all the time.

The Kick Drum

There was a time when the kick or "bass drum" was almost considered unrecordable. It was loud and boomy and had lots of sustain.

In the big-band era of the 1950s, the kick drum was more of an ambient instrument, played relatively quietly. Invariably, both heads of the drum were kept on. To help minimize the booming, drummers frequently used some form of muffling. One common technique was a felt strip attached to the inside of the "batter head"—i.e., the drumhead that gets hit by the beater (activated by the pedal).

By the 1960s, with the advent of rock 'n' roll, bands were starting to generate a much thicker sound, often using distortion. The kick drum, as it had typically been played and recorded, simply couldn't compete.

Simon Phillips:

> I don't know who first took the front head off, but somebody did! By taking that front head off, you could get rid of that boom and sustain and get a much more instant sound that was more recordable and more useful. And that was before anyone figured out about putting stuff inside the bass drum—overcoats, piano covers, people used to tear up newspapers and put them in the bass drum . . .

One of the problems with taking the front head completely off is that all the hardware used to attach the head is left to rattle. The front head, as Simon points out, substantially changes how a kick drum sounds:

> With the front head completely off, as you play the drum, all of the air is coming straight out. So we've lost a lot of volume, a lot of low end, and a lot of high end. This will create a very undynamic, mid-sounding thump, which may well suit some types of music.

A solution Simon likes (as do many other drummers): Rather than removing the head completely, cut a small round hole in the front head about five inches in diameter. (To avoid any feedback problems, especially in a live performance, Simon advises keeping the front head fairly tight). He also likes to add another sound-enhancing device: a can of paint, placed inside the drum on some form of foam or padding.

Simon Phillips:

> It's just mass. It makes it microphone-friendly. It makes a very complex sound, with a lot of low end floating around. But it tightens up the low end and makes it easier for the microphone to understand. By putting the front head back on, you get a little more low end, definitely more high end, and more dynamics.

The Snare Drum

The pitch and tone of a snare drum is influenced by the size and construction of the drum itself, as well as tension of the heads.

Simon Phillips:

> A snare drum is made up from a very thick shell compared to the toms. The top head may be coated, but is a regular thickness. The bottom head is what we call a resonant head and is very thin. It is not designed to be hit with a stick. Its only purpose is to make the snares [the thin strands of wire that lie stretched across the resonant head] vibrate. The better the snare drum, the faster the response of these snares.

It's fair to say that the sound of the snare drum tends to define the style of a recording. For every era, there was a snare sound and technique that helped create that era. At one point, it became popular to minimize the snare drum's ever-present propensity to create a harsh ringing sound by deadening it with a cloth. Ringo Starr and Nick Mason (playing very lightly and with very dampened snare heads) would be two classic examples of drummers who did that. Simon feels this still a perfectly legitimate practice—especially with enough gain and EQ—but that a cloth-dampened drum may only speak properly when hit in the center. "Rimshots," hits on the rim at the same time as the head, tend to just become rather flat and dull. Alternate and more subtle damping can be achieved by attaching pieces of tape, rubber, paper, or (a current popular solution) blobs of self-adhesive gel that you simply plop onto the drumhead.

Part of a snare's sound may not, of course, come from the snare itself, but from surrounding drums. In particular, the toms may produce a ringing sound every time the snare is hit. How much of a problem is this? Simon takes the view that you're always going to have sympathetic rings.

Alan:

> The question is: Does the ring get in the way of the music, or is it adding character to it?

Toms

The sound of the toms (originally and onomatopoeically called "tom-toms") can be the defining element of a record, and toms are arguably the parts of the kit that get the most attention for miking, tuning, and EQing. Some records will have them seemingly louder than anything, whereas the occasional producer will ask the drummer not to play them at all!

Simon Phillips:

> Even though a microphone may be only two inches from the head, if the source changes, then it's going to affect what it picks up. And the perspective thing—a lot of people don't understand how I can keep my toms totally open with no ring, and yet I can put a mic quite far away. But I can also still go close and it works. There's not a lot of excessive ring. And drummers ask me, "How do you do that?" I say, "Well, remember that drum is producing quite a lot of volume, so that mic gain is not having to be set so loud. If you put some tape on there, you're going to have to turn that mic gain up." Because, as well as changing the sound of the drum, you're taking the volume and the transients out of it. I learnt this by going to the studio, again, first session of the day, and I'd get the sound, the engineer would say, "The toms are bit ringy." OK, so I'd put a bit of tape here, and a bit of tape there, and a bit of tape there. And, great, it sounds great. So, I'd leave the drum kit, pack it up, go to the next studio, set up, and he goes, "The toms are a bit ringy." That's funny, that's what the other guy said. By the end of the day, I've got three strips of gaffer tape, and I'm going, "There's something wrong with this picture." So then, what I started doing was at the end of the session, I ripped it all off. Start at the new studio, same kit, set up, "The toms are a big ringy"—but I've never put more than one piece of tape.

Alan:

> The toms are really the engineer's chance to create some stereo. If it has been close-miked, each drum can be in its own stereo position. We don't necessarily have to follow the drummer's or the audience's perspective on this—it's just whatever panning gives the tom fills the best stereo effect. It's unusual to pan the kick or the snare anywhere but center.

Hi-Hats and Cymbals

A hi-hat is two small cymbals—one facing down and one facing up—that make contact with each other—either tightly or loosely and anywhere in between, according to the pressure on a pedal. The tone will be governed by size and shape.

Simon Phillips:

> You can't tune a cymbal. You're stuck with it, and if it doesn't sound any good, you throw it away and get another one. That's really what it's about. And that's an art in itself, and it takes years to really be able to choose cymbals properly. I'm still learning. Because sometimes what works well to the ear on its own, sounds very different in the context of the whole kit.

Miking

In the fifties and sixties, a drum kit was basically recorded as a single "combination" instrument. Beatles engineers Norman Smith and Geoff Emerick often used one kick drum mic and one overhead. The fashion of miking up each individual drum didn't start until much later.

In the late sixties, ways were found to make the kick drum sound more punchy and better articulated. Drummers started making more of a feature of it. Along came Free's "All Right Now," with its distinctive and prominent kick drum pattern, and the age of the truly discernible bass drum really "kicked in."

Simon Phillips:

> I think up to that point—and you'd know better than I—I know that a lot of studios, you had to use a certain microphone for certain instruments. You were not allowed to use this on that.

Alan:

> At Abbey Road it was viewed as a serious sin to use a ribbon mic or a condenser mic on a kick drum. There were "angry memos" hung up in the common room. "This mic will not be used for . . ." It made sense, though, really. Ribbons are inherently rather fragile, although condensers did get used despite the warnings.

Simon Phillips:

> The [Neumann] U 47 condenser became a very popular mic for bass drum, especially once the volume of the drum had been taken out, which does happen when you take the front head off and you fill it full of damping—you are also decreasing the volume. It's a more recordable sound. The hole's very important to the sound. The mic's already inside, so it doesn't reflect back onto the mic.

The classic kick drum mic solution these days is probably an AKG D112 or another dynamic mic right by the hole if there is one, or otherwise halfway into the drum at beater level. If you put your hand up against the hole, you're going to feel the movement of air. And in fact that's exactly what you are recording—the movement of air.

In recent times, it has become a popular practice to use a small loudspeaker, typically a Yamaha NS10, as a transducer to pick up extreme bass frequencies, and add that signal to the main kick mic. (Remember, a loudspeaker is just a microphone in reverse.) Yamaha made a ready-to-use system—they called it the

Subkick—but at the time we were going to press, it had been discontinued. Anyone with a few tools and a bit of determination should be able to rustle something similar up.

The snare drum is extremely important because it helps define the entire beat and feel of a track. Sometimes it can help define a genre, or even a complete era. In spite of the huge diversity in styles, types, and sizes of snare drum—all of which impact the final sound you'll produce—miking almost seems to have become standard nowadays: a dynamic mic like the classic Shure SM57 positioned at the side around two inches above the head. But that doesn't mean there aren't other choices and options.

Simon Phillips:

> There's this whole thing with using a standard 57 as opposed to a Beta 57. A Beta 57, from what I can tell, has more level and a little more top end. So, what sounds better: the Beta 57 with more top end, and then you put a little on, less EQ, or an older 57, which you have to doctor more? Which ends up being the better sound? I personally would go for the regular 57, because I think it sounds better once it's treated a little. If I don't think a 57 is going to work on the snare drum for a particular song, then I'll put a condenser on it; it's a really nice change. Also, when you're on a session and you've recorded four songs, you start getting tired of the same old sound and you need a change.

Alan:

> Rather than using a 57, I've had more luck with a condenser mic that's two or three inches away from the top of the snare. It's going to sound very thick. I think a lot of engineers would start with a condenser knowing that they are going to have to put quite a bit of top end on it—perhaps as much as +12 dB at 10 kHz.

Simon Phillips:

> Oh, definitely, yeah. And especially the way we're used to hearing recorded music and drums now, yes. I mean, I end up recording with some top end and bottom end on the snare drum, then when I mix I put on a whole load more, too. It's just, we like to have that nice, crisp-sounding snare drum most of the time.

Taylor Hawkins:

> It depends on what kind of record you're making. If you're making, like, a rock 'n' roll record that's just rock 'n' roll sounds, then I think it's cool to have a good drum sound all the way through that's consistent all the way through, so it sounds like a band.

Almost everyone will mic a snare from the TOP. But there are those who like to mic the top AND bottom—Taylor Hawkins, for one, and not only the snare . . .

Taylor Hawkins:

> Yeah, yeah. We record the top and bottom of the hi-hat sometimes!

Simon Phillips:

> I never use a bottom mic. I hate it, unless I'm engineering another drummer, and why I don't know. I kind of get into engineering mode then. It's because if I'm listening, I'm going, "You know what, that snare I think might need a little bit of help." I record it but I don't even monitor it. I just check it out—*OK, that's fine, put the fader down*. Because I just don't like the sound of it. So I'm not a big fan of the bottom mic, because I find a lot of people use it in the wrong way; they use too much of it, and it takes away the dynamics. It's kind of a soft sound, but underneath the drum, there's not much difference in volume when you hit the drum lightly and hit it loudly. Down there, it's pretty much the same sound. It doesn't really change that much. So, it takes away the dynamics of your playing.

The hi-hat is a hard instrument to record because it's a moving target.
Alan:

> As well as having its own mic, hi-hat will invariably be picked up by the snare mic as well, especially if the snare mic has a lot of top on it. I'll usually use a small diaphragm condenser deliberately pointing away from the snare, about four inches from the top half. I usually like to hear the hi-hat from the audience perspective to the right of the player. I'll pan the *mic* hard right, but only set the *level* of it so that it appears halfway between the snare [which contains a lot of it] and the far right of the stereo picture. If the hi-hat appears to be hard right, it is invariably too loud!

Overhead mics are used to capture the cymbals and the overall spread of the kit.
Alan:

> I have favored ribbons as overheads for many years. In particular, the Coles/STC 4038s. Another lesson learnt from Geoff Emerick. You invariably have to add quite a bit of top end—say, 8–10 dB at 10 kHz—but the result is a very smooth sound on cymbals that is

FIGURE 16.3. At left is a classic snare mic—a dynamic—the Shure SM57. On the right is a small capsule condenser mic—generally the preferred choice of Alan. Photos by Charlie Steves.

not in the least harsh. I'll place them about seven feet from the ground, each one directly over the center point of cymbals on each side, and pan them hard left and right. Sometimes I'll favor the ride cymbal on one side if it needs it. Because these ribbons have a figure eight polar pattern, they also naturally pick up a little reflection from above.

It has become a standard practice for most recordings of drums to incorporate at least a pair of "ambience" mics at the far ends of the room to give the feeling of space the room itself affords. The effect of ambient mics will be much more natural-sounding and quite different from adding artificial rooms or reverbs. Beware, however, that if there are other instruments going on in the room, they will get picked up by the ambience mics too—but that might be a good thing! Ambience mics can be mounted on tall boom stands so that they can be placed at the maximum height possible and as far apart as possible, which generally gives the best "ambient" effect.

Ambience mics are often set to an omni polar pattern, so that reflections are picked up from all directions and not just from the direction of the drums. Ambience mics can also work on other instruments, too, or even vocals when they are being overdubbed.

It is standard practice on classical recordings to use ambience mics to capture the sound of the studio or hall—in an effort to replicate, perhaps, what the audience might hear in the concert hall.

FIGURE 16.4. Ambience mics: capturing the sound in and of the room.

Phase, Gating, and Other Considerations

All consoles have phase buttons on each channel, and some engineers attach a lot of importance to the phase relationship between mics on drums.

Sylvia Massy:

> I'll carefully go through each mic, starting with the kick drum and muting all the other mics on the drum kit, and I'll listen to that kick drum along with one of the overheads put into center in mono. And I'll compare phase in and out, the phase button on the channel, just to see which way sounds better.
>
> It's like an optometrist, you know: "Is it clearer this way, or is it clearer this way?"
>
> And then I'll go and mute that, after I figure that channel out, and I'll listen to the next mic in relationship to the kick drum. And I'll do that all the way down the line, the same with the snare. It takes some extra time to sort it all out, but once you've got everything in alignment like that, it's fantastic. It just sounds really good.

With everything recorded onto its own track, it's tempting to feel that every drum has to be heard separately and independently, as opposed to being part of a whole. The "noise gate" has been a favored device that automatically shuts down an individual mic when the signal goes below a certain level (see Chapter 10). The idea is that when a drum isn't being played, you wouldn't be recording the spill from the other drums on that mic. But how important is such a squeaky-clean signal? Gating drums, of course, risks losing information that actually adds to the feel, simply because it fell below the threshold level. Players can be, and with some justification, very much against this type of technique. Would Simon Phillips ever use one?

Simon Phillips:

> Never. Only if I mix. And I'd rather use fader movement than noise gates. I'm not a big noise gate fan. Live is a different story, because I do tend to try to dissuade the engineer from using them, but I also understand why he uses them. The idea is that if I'm not playing, that all these channels will just close down and tighten up the rest of the stage sound—that's really what it should be. I should be able to even look at a drum and open that noise gate! Because I play very dynamically, and if I'm playing really soft, I don't want only half the notes to come out.

Headphones and Playing to Clicks

Being able to keep time is part of the drummer's arsenal, but metronomic accuracy seems to have become a theoretical requirement since the early days of disco, back in the 1970s. In today's DAW world, where everything can be cut and pasted and kept "on the grid," as they say, it's certainly a lot easier to move stuff about if you can rely on a consistent tempo throughout the track. (Assuming the track needs a consistent tempo, of course. There is *nothing whatsoever* wrong with a chorus that is "naturally" a BPM or two faster than the verse, etc., etc.)

The most common way to both help create and measure slavishly accurate timekeeping is to feed a machine or computer-generated "click" (normally playing four or eight beats to the bar or measure) into the players' headphones, so they can remain glued to the beat. Clicks don't literally have to be "clicks," of course. They can be drum or percussion loops . . . anything that helps keep the track "perfectly" in time.

Taylor Hawkins:

I just kind of go with what they have, usually. There's been some that are hard to play to, you know. The more space in between those clicks there is, the harder to play to, obviously, because there's more time to f*** up.

Simon Phillips:

It depends on the song. On a Toto album I engineered, we did most of it without click. Because what I wanted to do was capture the band the way it sounds live, and I don't think it's ever really been captured on record like that. I said, "Guys, we could play in time. We don't always need a click."

Playing to a click track is an art in itself.
Simon Phillips:

To play with a click well, you have to have very good internal time, that's really what it is. And one of the things I delve into a little bit doing drum clinics is that the sound of the click is very, very important. A lot of people, when they're putting up a track, they give you a click sound that's way too big. First of all, you're hearing it in the headphone. Every time you hit a bass drum, you've got that. Every time you hit a snare drum, you've got that. To me, it's wrong. Musically, it's wrong. I like to use a very small cowbell, a pretty horrible, measly little cowbell that I can have very quiet and doesn't really get in the way of what else is going on. It's not fighting you.

The other thing to do is turn the click down. If you're in time with the click, you shouldn't hear it. Sometimes I'm playing, and I'm going, "I really can't hear the click. Is it still going?" And what I do, I just kind of lean back a little bit, time-wise, and oh, there it is, and then just come forward again. But that takes a lot of years and a lot of confidence.

You're not going to sit there and listen to the click and the drum kit. That's not how you listen to music, because hopefully that click won't get mixed. But you can play with that click. You might play your verse kind of with the click. You might go to the B section and kind of push, go ahead of the click, and then you might get to the chorus and really sit back so the click is ahead of you. There's nothing wrong with that. You're playing music. Nobody is going to hear the click. The click isn't God, it's just a tool, and you can abuse it and use it any way you like. Music first.

That seems to be the general view from the drummer's perspective.
Taylor Hawkins:

Our last producer, Gil Norton, an English fellow, he actually had really great clicks. He said, "I don't want you to play to *dink, dink, dink, dink*, because then you're just paying attention to that too much." And then, he came up with these, like, salsa things, where it's, you know, things that you kind of play *with* instead of playing *to*. But I've noticed after being in the studio for a couple days, you're playing good to the click when you

> don't hear the click any more. That takes a little while to develop that, but I think if you're a drummer out there, start playing to clicks.

EQ and Levels

Any engineer will tell you that first of all a great drum sound comes from a drummer who can balance themselves.

Alan:

> I think if I recorded a kit flat, I would never be happy. I have standard practices for snare and kick that I would not feel were right unless I was hearing them that way right from the moment of starting a track. That usually means a lot of top on the snare, as I said before, and added low end to the kick. If I'm using a Subkick, the kick mic will usually be flat.

Simon tends to rely on his mic pres to create the tonality he's after, which then allows him to basically record flat, maybe adding a little top and bottom to the snare.

Simon Phillips:

> If I'm mixing, I ride all the tom fills, and so the fader is probably about 10 to 15 dB down. So you'd still get the sympathetic ring, but it's not overpowering, and the kick and the snare are cutting through nicely. And in every tom fill, I follow it, so I get the toms really in your face. I like to mix loud tom fills. I like to hear them.

Taylor Hawkins:

> I know when I like the sound of something, but that changes. I like a lot of different kind of drum sounds. In the studio, I try to pay attention, but I don't ever try to give engineers suggestions on miking or EQing my drums. I'll just say I don't like that. As far as really getting involved, I get involved in the mixing, "Can you make it louder?" Like every f***ing drummer. "It's not loud enough!"

Every drum track, every drum kit, and every drummer comes over differently. Sometimes you can set the levels, and the toms and cymbals will be well balanced without any "gain riding." Sometimes you'll be short of the ride cymbal and you'll have to favor the overheads when it's playing. Quality drums will produce a quality sound, but in the hands of a crappy drummer, they can sound like tin cans. It's a well-known fact that the whole basis of rock and pop stems from the drums, so their importance should never be underestimated.

17

KEYBOARDS

There's More to a Keyboard Than a Keyboard

Modern keyboards don't necessarily have any recognizable sound. A keyboard can sound like a piano, or an organ, or strings, or a sound effect—in fact, any sound can be triggered and played by an electronic keyboard.

It wasn't always like this. One upon a time, there were individual and easily recognizable keyboard instruments—a piano, a harpsichord, a church pipe organ, and so on. But from the turn of the twentieth century, electronic musical instruments have used the standard "ivory and ebony" style keyboard as the best way to deliver electronically generated or synthesized musical sounds. From the organ to the electric piano to the synthesizer to even the virtual synthesizer, these instruments have all hitched their wagons to the black and whites.

The piano and to some extent the organ are both "one-man orchestras" capable of producing the highest highs and the lowest lows in an essentially self-accompanying setting, where a single player can play melody, bass, and rhythm elements at the same time. Modern keyboards can reproduce sounds that aren't even distantly related to traditional keyboard instruments, and the concept of keyboards has come to mean literally anything you can hear on a record. So it's not surprising that modern keyboard players are often expected to perform the role of orchestrator and all-round sound wizard to find and deliver the almost limitless range of sounds available. However, this does represent a challenge.

For the keyboardist, it means he or she is no longer associated with particular sounds or roles within music—unlike, say, a drummer, bass player, or even a guitarist. For the engineers, be it in the context of recording or live sound, it means they have no idea what they are going to have to deal with from one moment to the next. A keyboard player might deliver you an airy, atmospheric pad sound one minute, and a rip-roaring bass the next.

So for all concerned, keyboards need to be handled with care and patience.

Keyboard Types

Several types of sound come under the general job description of keyboards, and the best known—the one to really stamp its mark on the world of musical instruments—is the piano. Developed in the early eighteenth century, the piano (originally the *pianoforte*, a name taken from the Italian words for "soft" and "loud") generates sound by keystrokes activating felt-covered hammers, which hit strings stretched across a wooden soundboard. The volume of each note can be varied infinitely, depending on the strength of the touch, There is a natural decay or a gradual reduction in volume as the note dies away. Decay is the length of time it takes a note to fade naturally or before a damping mechanism cuts it off when the note is let go. The "sustain" or "damper" pedal has the same effect as holding notes down even if the player lets go of the notes. The piano is fully "polyphonic." In other words, there is no limit to how many notes can be played simultaneously, provided there are enough hands and fingers on deck!

One of the very earliest forms of keyboard instrument was the pipe organ, essentially a mechanical wind instrument. Organs have no "touch sensitivity." In other words, it doesn't make any difference how hard the keys are hit; all the notes will have the same volume. Furthermore, notes will continue at the same volume or, as we say, "sustain" until they are let go. Note the difference: a piano "decays," and an organ "sustains."

Organs regulate volume mechanically or electronically. On a pipe organ, it's how much air hits the pipe. On an electric organ, the volume is dependent on the electrical sound output level. The most famous electric organ sound is the Hammond B3, first made in the 1930s and popularized during the 1950s. Although these (now vintage) instruments remain studio and live staples, they are no longer in production and only digital equivalents of them remain.

The synthesizer is a purely electronic instrument, initially named for its ability to "synthesize" or duplicate conventional sounds using different elements of sound-generating and processing circuitry. Since the mid-nineties, digital synthesizers or "synths," as they are more commonly known, have become predominantly "sample"-based and tend to produce more emulative than original textures. Sampling grew out of a digital technology first used in the early eighties on the Fairlight CMI ("computer musical instrument"). Samples are really just another word for "digital recordings." Instrument notes, effects, vocal parts, drum loops—anything that can be recorded—can be used as a sample. Samples are most commonly triggered by a MIDI "note on" command, courtesy of someone majestically pressing the appropriate key at the appropriate time. (See Chapter 7, "MIDI.")

Programmers and Players

With today's synthesized and increasingly virtual sounds, you have to wonder how much keyboard playing is still about playing and performing and how much of it is now about the technology and the programming. There are great keyboard players who cannot read music and who've never learned to play a scale and just follow their instincts and do what they feel is right. But there's also another breed of players who think everything is based around so-called "sound libraries," "virtual instruments," and sampled sounds.

Alan:

> I think you have "sounds" guys, and I think you have people who can play, sight-read any piece of music you put in front of them. Those are two different educations. If you have those two talents in one person, wow.

FIGURE 17.1. **Triggering a sample or loop might only take a single finger press, but what leads up to it might take hours of work.**

That said, even staunch, "purist" players still have the option of being able to manipulate their keyboard parts in post-production . . .

Michael McDonald:

> I might love a piano performance, but if I was sort of falling off the bench . . . well, you know, I like fixing.

Rami Jaffee:

> When I have the mouse in my hand, once I hear something, I'm tuned out, because I'm one-track-minded. If I'm trying to fix something while people are saying stuff like, "You like that bit at the end?" I'm like, "All I heard was the little pop sound in the first bar. That's all I could hear." I need to focus on one thing at a time. If I have to pee, I can't play a piano part.

Recording MIDI Versus Recording Audio

Related to the programming-versus-playing debate is the question of recording MIDI data versus recording a part as audio. Unless you're recording an acoustic piano or a vintage organ, most keyboards and all virtual instruments have the option of being recorded in MIDI. MIDI and audio can sit side by side. But is it really necessary?

With MIDI, you still need to choose a performance, as well as selecting from a range of sounds. You can save a lot of time by being decisive on the latter.

A lot of engineers and producers might, instead of calling in the impossible part to be played by an incredible virtuoso musician, figure out a way of programming it inside MIDI to make an impossible part manifest itself. You have to balance whether it might have been better with a real musician playing the real part or whether it's technically acceptable because it was played by a machine, which puts every microdot of the part into the right pocket. A lot of modern music decrees that things must be metronomic, absolutely in time, absolutely spot on. Whether this is good thing remains a matter of debate.

The other school says "ruff and ready": a few little indiscretions in musical parts are not so important. Just take it as is, flaws and all.

Alan:

> I think there's an awful lot of keyboard parts on records that are largely incompetent MIDI performances, corrected, retimed, rejigged, sounds added, layered. I know I'm a guilty party on such things!

Whether you decide to record MIDI or to go with just the instrument's own sound, it's a measure of how confident you are that what you're going to play or have played is going to form an integral part of your final record. If you're incapable of making decisions, then record the MIDI. A musician might often want to record in MIDI possibly just to repair a couple of timing errors or bad notes here or there.

Using either hardware or software instruments, both bases can be covered simply by connecting MIDI from the instrument to your computer or interface and, in addition to creating an audio track, enabling a MIDI track as well. The original MIDI drum loop that Alan created for "All Our Yesterdays," the track written and recorded during the making of the *Art & Science of Sound Recording* video series, was initially a MIDI loop created on a Yamaha Motif XS. This made it extremely easy to experiment with tempos, sounds, and even parts long before the track needed to be committed to the DAW. Although Alan only used this loop as a guide for the demo, it could have been used to further develop the idea if other live players were not to hand. Retaining the MIDI, we've got the ultimate control over manipulation of notes—volumes, velocities, shifting notes backwards and forwards in time, or up and down in level. And not only that, with MIDI we also still have infinite control over what sounds to use choose for the notes we choose to play. Decisions, decisions!

Producer Patrick Leonard looks back at the early benefits of MIDI:

> Years ago, when I'd go in to play a part, or especially something that I wanted to feel sequenced, or wanted to feel ultra tight like some sort of staccato synth sound, I'd be practicing at home for hours with a metronome to get it so it was exactly right. With MIDI, you just quantize it.

A musician might still want to record in MIDI just to repair a couple of timing errors, or bad notes here and there. You might not want to quantize anything, not make anything metronomic, but essentially just hold on the original performance to correct the little problems.

But the role of MIDI as Chief Fixit might be coming to an end.

Alan:

> I think I can honestly say that as recording has developed since the advent of MIDI, I'm seeing a little bit of a movement away from it. More people are concentrating on good performances and parts that work. So much of the corrective surgery that used to take place in MIDI can now be done on the screen as part of the editing of audio in the DAW.

Vintage Versus Virtual

The term "vintage" mostly implies and concerns some form of analog technology. OK, but what exactly is the real value of vintage?

Patrick Leonard:

> These guys would get in an ARP 2600 or a Minimoog and nobody had a clue what it was. So, I'd say, well, let me mess with it, and they'd give it to me and I'd take it home. I started learning what filters were, what envelopes were, how this stuff worked. I really learned that first, and then I had to sort of connect the dots to recording.

Rami Jaffee:

> With vintage Moogs and other old synths, I like how it just starts fresh. There is no program. There is no memory. You'll be lucky when you tune oscillators and it works in the track. But I'm a per-track player—you know, I want to hear it and just immediately go, "Oh, my gosh," turn on something and say, "This is perfect."

The point is that quirks in the sound can so often *define* a vintage instrument. That's why a real musician might get a different result playing the actual instrument as opposed to a programmer simply triggering a sample of it. But in a track, is it really possible to tell the difference between a sample and "the real thing"?

On the *Art & Science of Sound Recording* video series we experimented, playing the same piece of music on a real Fender Rhodes piano and what is generally acknowledged as one of the best samples of a Rhodes, on the Yamaha Motif. Although the Motif does sound really good and, at a first listen, very authentic, there is in fact a world of difference, largely due to the fact that any sampled instrument is going to make the same sound every time. Unless the voice programmers deliberately make it unstable or uneven, there is a uniformity and tidiness attached to the sound that any Fender Rhodes, Hohner Clavinet, or Hammond B3 could never produce. The irony is that keyboard players were granted perfection—exactly what they always dreamed of. Only now are people beginning to see the realization of those dreams comes with some baggage. As with timing and tuning, perfection in sonic properties is not always perfection in musical terms.

Dave Smith:

> There was a long period of time where pretty much everything was digital, and after a while it got kind of old to your ears. I think a lot of people forgot what they were missing. Because the only subtractive synthesizers around were digital emulations or software emulations, so when they heard the real thing, all of a sudden the lights come on, and they said, "Oh, OK, now I get it. Now I see what everybody is talking about."

The Recording Process

Electronic keyboard instruments normally offer mono and stereo line level audio outputs, and can be connected to an interface or DAW without additional amplification. If the instrument offers FireWire, USB, or Ethernet interfaces, these are likely to deliver an all-digital output signal.

The process of recording keyboards—both what is being recorded and how it is being recorded—has probably changed more than for any other instrument type in recent times. DAWs have been the catalyst for this. Firstly, keyboard players *at all levels* are able to deliver master-quality textures, effects, and tonalities from within their own rig, Equally, the modern recording process is now able to accommodate every imaginable punch-in, and merge and manage parts at all different levels and intensities with ease. Years ago, "keyboard" parts—given their enormously wide range of functions and textures—represented much more of a challenge to player and engineer alike. This has also had the effect of allowing a lot more keyboard parts to be recorded alongside the rhythm section, not as a guide, but as what we call "keepers."

The first synthesizers delivered sound that was dry as a bone. Sounds or instruments would be recorded one part at a time, one track at a time, with effects added on the console or using outboard gear. Reverbs, delays, and choruses started to appear on synths in the mid-1980s, and initially there was some resistance to such effects being recorded as part of the instrument's sound. But as the quality of instruments' digital signal processing improved, effects legitimately became part of the recorded sound.

In the modern era, a professional keyboard player is very likely to turn up to a session armed with just one or two keyboards, but positively groaning with firepower, thanks to sound libraries and processors within their Pro Tools rig or a virtual studio technology host like the Muse Research Receptor. Especially for textural, pad, and sound effects sounds, keyboard players will now premix and preprocess their "sound" and deliver a unified stereo output to the console (if you are fortunate enough to be in a studio), or simply to a pair of tracks on GarageBand!

Synths tend to have stereo outputs, but they often put out a mono sound with stereo effects such as reverbs and delays. If every keyboard is recorded in stereo, we might find we are losing the benefit in the mix of certain parts coming from extreme left and right. It's worth experimenting with placing synth parts on the extreme left and right, even if they are recorded in stereo and designed to be spread across the picture.

Conversely, a mono sound can be made to sound as if it is stereo by simply panning it to one side and adding a short delayed version of it and panning it to the other side.

Alan:

> So many records sound like they are mono, just because of the inability of artists, producers, and engineers to accept that panning to the extremes has value—it's fun to make stereo an extreme thing. I think creating interesting stereo is *the* most important part of recording. And in surround, the sky's the limit.

Some parts will probably always merit being recorded separately, though—a piano part, an organ part if it's not just playing sustained chords, or an "orchestrated" string part.

Nowadays, most keyboard parts are probably going to be recorded as overdubs—i.e., not as part of a tracking session. But it wasn't always like this. Take Michael McDonald's first studio experience:

> Rick Jarrard was the producer. Rick had produced [Jefferson Airplane's] *Surrealistic Pillow* album, [Harry] Nilsson's *Aerial Ballet*, and José Feliciano's records from "Light My Fire" on. So this was really the big time for me. It was really kind of an amazing trip to come

out from St. Louis to L.A. and live out there. I was eighteen at the time, and of course I would have signed anything just to get in the room and record—and I think I did. The experience was great, because it was Elvis' band as the rhythm section. It was Ron Tutt, James Burton, Jerry Scheff, and myself on keyboards. And I remember that they were very kind to me. Every once in a while, Ron Tutt would say, "You might just want to kind of pull it back a little bit. You're kind of getting ahead of us, you know." And I had no idea about tempo or anything. But I learned so much from those guys and so quickly—playing with, as you can imagine, a group of musicians like that, who were nice enough to not ask the producer to go get Larry Knechtel to come in and take over my part.

Some would say overplaying has always been a potential keyboard hazard. Now, with unlimited tracks and unlimited sounds, that trap is even easier to fall into.

Rami Jaffee:

Even on my own session, I'll go over and start playing, and just be like Dr. John over there, and I'm like, "Stop that." The guy over there just knows it's so polluting the song. So I have this, you know, kind of a band sense of playing keyboard, so it's more playful. The biggest thing I really miss is playing with everybody. And especially as a keyboard player, when you're tracking with a band, the mentality from a producer's standpoint—dialing the drummer in and a little bit of a bass and a little bit of guitar, and then keyboards are such a final icing, that by the time there's a take, I've got the coolest part under the sun, you know. That's the problem when I have to do it myself, that I'm not with everybody and hearing everything grow organically. I think that's a shame.

Being such a full-frequencied instrument, the piano in particular poses some special challenges. The biggest is not treading on someone else's toes. You can approach it from several directions. You can say to the keyboard player, "Your left hand is in exactly the same range as the bass, and you're not playing the same tune. So unless you decide you can play the same tune, then you should not play that part. Or you should take it up an octave." Another way would be to say, well, the piano is important, let's change whatever the bass end of the track coming from other instruments is playing. It's all about balance, it's all a little recipe between the instruments, that makes a balance sound like a balance. It's all just tweaking here and there, and suddenly when you hit it, you know—*That's where I want to be*.

Michael McDonald:

I don't like people around for when I'm doing a piano overdub. Because that's a real exercise in mindless experimentation, looking for the right voicing and stuff. The only thing a third-party observer could go away with is, "That man's insane," or you know, "He doesn't play very well." I mean, I feel a little self-conscious until I find a part.

Miking an Acoustic Piano

It's no accident that the piano is still the most popular keyboard instrument out there. Everybody wants to hear piano. It's an incredibly wide-ranging instrument, from the lowest of the lows to the highest of the highs. Even the most musically uninformed listener knows the sound of a piano. Piano parts can be great. It's almost remarkable what an essential a sound is produced by "the piano"—whether it's a concert grand, whether it's an upright, whether it's sampled piano on a synthesizer, people will say, "That sounds like a piano." There's something in its basic character of a piano recording; something in its attack and decay, harmonics and stuff. "That's a piano." Ask Elton John.

There are as many ways to mic and record an acoustic piano as there are pianos and mics. A very safe method is to use a pair of cardioid condenser mics placed in the treble and bass areas over the strings: Anywhere from about eight to twelve inches from the strings usually works well. For greater separation between the two areas of the keyboard, angle the mics away from each other. Sometimes you can get a good result from placing two or more mics right in the holes in the soundboard.

Alan:

> For the recording of "All Our Yesterdays," I set a pair of Neumann 87s a reasonable distance from the strings, giving a very natural sound. Thankfully, the piano was in an isolated space where other sounds were not allowed to penetrate. If the piano had been in the same room as the drums, it would have caused severe separation problems. The mics would have to have been much closer, and the lid would have to have been

FIGURE 17.2. Alan miking the piano for the recording of Soquel High School's choir (see Chapter 21).

> almost closed, with the gaps covered with blankets to prevent unwanted sound—in this case the drums—coming in.

PZM mics (see Chapter 3) can work well. It's a relatively muffled, but still pleasing tone. The best part is that they are inexpensive. PZMs also work well on the soundboard of upright pianos. Uprights can also be miked inside, near the strings, but it's more common to position conventional mics at the treble and bass ends halfway down at the back.

If you've got the three octaves above middle C and two octaves below middle C sounding good, chances are, the rest are probably going to sound fine too. It's such a classic sound. You don't have to play fifteen-note chords to make it sound like a piano. You can just play one note, two notes, a bass note, a simple rhythm. There will always be room for piano.

Because piano is both delicate and percussive, it's important to minimize any problems with latency on a DAW recording. This might be an issue if a piano is being overdubbed.

Alan:

> There was a favorite Steinway baby grand at Abbey Road, which used to get wheeled between the studios because it sounded really good. I think the piano on Paul McCartney's "Maybe I'm Amazed" was a great piano part. It has everything. It has that wonderful *du-du-du-du-du-du* in the bass end. And then in between the lines in the bridge section, there's this wonderful discord in the right hand with the thumping left hand. It's a classic discord. It's a wonderful piano part. I still enjoy hearing it to this day, and it's approaching forty years ago that we recorded it. The engineer was Phil McDonald. That was great night. The entire track, every note you hear of "Maybe I'm Amazed" was essentially recorded in one evening—very fast—and McCartney played everything. Linda did some backing vocals. But that was it. Just the two of them.

A piano will sound at its most natural when it is uncompressed and left to display its own natural dynamics. A little compression might help stave off peaks, but be careful about losing the naturalness. Having said that, if you want the "Lady Madonna" effect, then compress it beyond recognition.

A good piano should need little EQ. Studio pianos tend to be "doped," meaning the hammers have been artificially hardened to give a deliberately bright sound. An undoped piano might need some help—adding some top-end EQ. Classical engineers seem to be OK with a comparatively dull piano sound—as might be heard in a concert hall. "Great Gig in the Sky" was a full-size concert grand recorded in Abbey Road's classical studio, No. 1.

Organs: Recording a Hammond and Leslie

Organs provide sounds that can be infinitely sustained, and they can be used for anything from a "pad" to a screaming solo. Although there are plenty of synths and virtual instruments, if you want the real deal, you're talking about a Hammond, still as popular and powerful today as it ever was, despite weighing in at a cuddly three hundred pounds.

Rami Jaffee:

> The Hammond B3 is so diverse, and you can just make so many different sounds. It's not just an organ. You get in there and can create a lot of fun stuff. I call the drawbars my

> EQ. Got your lows, got your mids, got your highs. It doesn't really matter where I am on the keyboard—I can tweak the tone with drawbars to find a spot for myself.

The Hammond has always been associated with the Leslie, which contains speakers that rotate and produces a sound totally unlike any other. It was a remarkable invention in that it produces the Doppler effect, which is very difficult to create without movement between listener and source. That's one of the magic things about the Hammond. It produces this slight Doppler effect, which results in a subtle perceived pitch variation. A Leslie cabinet has two speaker arrangements: a rotating horn that handles the high frequencies and a fifteen-inch loudspeaker pointing downward toward a drum—a kind of rotating baffle—which puts out the low frequencies. Both actually receive their signals from a split mono source, but the result is unquestionably stereo. Both the horns and the drum spin at fast or slow speed, activated by a switch alongside the keyboard.

Rami Jaffee:

> Slow is great, and when there's a build-up into a chorus . . . you know, I use the fast speed for drama and then go back to slow to let the song stand out. I usually mike up my Leslie with two Royer ribbon mics on the top tweeter here . . .

A lot of engineers would mike the top and bottom. You can place a mic on the front of the horn, the back of the horn, side of the horn, the bottom of the rotor. You can go two mics, you can go six mics . . . there are all kinds of ways of dealing with it. You can use condensers or dynamics or Rami's choice, ribbons. The Hammond/Leslie sound is so distinctive that it's quite forgiving to record. It's really down to taste.

It's worth mentioning that if you get too close to the horn, you will get an artificially exaggerated "pulsing" effect as the horn rotates at its closest position to the mic. Be aware also of mechanical noises from the motors and other mechanical parts, which will be accentuated if the mics are too close.

Alan:

> One thing about the Leslie, which everybody kind of needs to know, is that the double-sided horn, which looks like it's producing sound from two angles, is actually only producing sound from one of those angles. The other one is just a dummy tube just to *mechanically* balance the rotating speaker. So if you think

FIGURE 17.3. **Miking a Leslie cabinet. Keeping it simple: one on the top, one on the bottom. Photo by Charlie Steves.**

> you're going to get sound out of both those orifices, you're mistaken. I have had the best luck with a bit of air around the organ—miking from, say, one or two feet away . . . one on the top one on the bottom, lovely stereo effect. That was usually good for me.

The Hammond is not the only organ in town, of course. There were the not so greatly revered fifties and sixties transistor organs like the Farfisa Compact and the Vox Continental, usually made of red and white plastic with lots of glittery paint. They had a particularly nasty tremolo effect built in. They just sounded so dreadful, it's hard to believe we called them organs, but they do have their time, place, and followers.

Alan:

> I love the sound of a big pipe organ. I went to the famous monastery at St. Florian in Austria once and heard the original Bruckner organ, which was just the most amazing sound. I actually went out and played a few notes myself. It was just life-changing. It has to be said you cannot go in with a preconceived plan to record a pipe organ. You have to walk about to see where the sound is coming from and where it sounds best. I recorded a great pipe organ with Ambrosia at the Royce Hall at UCLA back in the late seventies.

Thankfully, pipe organs have been extensively sampled, so a good pipe organ sound is much easier to achieve now than it used to be.

Sampling, Virtual Keyboards, and Sound Libraries

Most modern recordings use samples in some form or other. In one sense, "sampling" is simply recording or rerecording. A sample can be a sound, a snippet of a recorded song taken off a CD, or an instrumental or vocal passage. Samples can be recorded and played on DAWs or assigned to and triggered by notes on a keyboard or virtual keyboard.

Most engineers and producers now have access to a library of their own samples—either in hardware synths or virtual instruments. Also, by loading up the vast array of "sound libraries" now available, we have entered a new realm in sampling technology. Sound libraries from EastWest, Sonic Reality, and the Vienna Symphony series, for example, have become increasingly powerful and popular. Orchestral libraries have become so comprehensive that it is now sometimes hard to tell if a real orchestra is being heard or a sampled one. But here's the catch: If you play an orchestral sample like an organist, it's going to sound like a huge organ! So although the technology has improved dramatically, there is still very much a need for players and orchestrators who know how these sampled sounds should be voiced and articulated.

Sampling has become a serious business both as a technology and as a commercial enterprise.

Another form of "sampling" in recent years has been the practice of ripping an entirely unaltered slice of a commercially released track and using that either as the basis for, or a featured aspect of, an entirely new record—most commonly, in the hip-hop and R&B genres.

In 2008, Kanye West used a sample from the Alan Parsons Project track "Ammonia Avenue" for his song "Heartless." Such ripping/sampling/copying (whatever you choose to call it) is now an accepted practice, but much to the chagrin of many of the artists who indulge in the practice, it involves negotiated payment from the person doing the sampling to the copyright holders of the recording—i.e., the artist/record label and the writer/publisher of the composition. Sample away—but have your wallet handy!

Modern technology makes it possible to give, say, piano notes a sustain they would not normally have, and conversely, normally sustained instruments can be modified to cut themselves off virtually as soon as the note has been played, so that the sound only lasts for a few milliseconds. Also, a percussive instrument can be "softened" by reducing its attack or the transient at the front of its sound—almost fading it in sometimes. We refer to these characteristics as the *envelope* of a sound. It is defined by four parameters: attack, decay, sustain, and release—ADSR for short. You will see these parameters on virtually every synth out there.

The world of keyboards has become associated with a great deal of the sounds you hear on the average record, well beyond piano sounds, organ sounds, melodic synth sounds, pad sounds, etc. Every effect, every little thump, every percussion sound, every ethnic instrument you hear that melds into the overall effect of a record is quite possibly being played or triggered by a keyboard from a synthesizer or computer screen.

To some extent, keyboards are simply controllers, rather like knobs and switches, managing and orchestrating a world of sounds from a myriad of sources. Ivory and ebony keyboards were initially developed for organs and pianos, both of which are in themselves still very much one-person-orchestras. It's interesting how this underlying capability remains alive in the modern idiom.

18

BASS

The Importance of Bottom End

It's impossible to underestimate the role of bass in modern music recordings. From pop, to jazz, to rock, to hip-hop, people need to hear and feel those bass frequencies.

Alan:

> Even if it was a solo folksinger playing an acoustic guitar and vocal, the BBC would insist that that was not a full enough sounding frequency range, so they would bring on this upright bass player. No matter what the act was, there always had to be some bass in it. It's the completion of the spectral picture, the thing that gives the roundness at the bottom.

The bass can totally make or break the way a track sounds. We talked extensively to legendary session bass players Carol Kaye and Nathan East for this chapter.

Carol Kaye:

> We got on a date with Sonny and Cher, and Sonny had this one-chord tune called "The Beat Goes On." I thought, wow, you've really got to invent on this one, you know? So I came up with a line for the chorus and all of a sudden, it all came alive, and I thought, God, the bass line

can be a key thing to a tune, to a hit, you know. It wasn't, "Oh, Carol, you're so good"—I wasn't into that. It's just that it was a challenge to create lines to create hit records, and you could do that on the bass.

Nathan East:

The bass is one of those instruments I think you "feel" when you take it away. You realize how much you miss it. It's always been fun to have the responsibility of being that glue between the rhythmic and the harmonic elements.

Setting Up for Recording

Bass can be miked on a cabinet or recorded direct or direct inject—DI for short—right out of the instrument. It can also be taken directly from the amplifier's preamp stage.

Carol Kaye:

Most of the time, they miked me. In fact, all the time until about '68, they started to do a direct line, then half mic, half direct line. But the film studio always miked me. I used the Fender 410, and it was the Super Reverb with the open back. In about 1967, I changed to the closed amp, which is the Versatone amp, just a small studio amp, very quiet, and I had four of those then.

Alan:

I've been recording bass direct my entire career, and almost 99 percent of the bass I've recorded has been direct. I usually just don't even give any consideration to what's coming out of the amp. If you can get it sounding good on the direct, then that's what you go with. It's technically cleaner. The only time I've had occasion to use an amp is when a dirty, gritty sound is required—and in fact I did do that on a couple of tracks played by Nick Beggs for an album I worked on in 2012 by Steven Wilson of Porcupine Tree.

I've recorded Nathan a number of times right out of his DI box and never missed not having an amp.

Nathan East:

These days I always use the Radial Firefly direct box, made by my friends at Radial. It has become my standard DI.

The output of a DI box (see **figure 18.1**) can be fed straight into the mic input of a DAW interface or recording console. A direct box converts the low-level, unbalanced, high-impedance signal coming from the instrument into a low-impedance, balanced signal, using

FIGURE 18.1. **The Firefly DI box from Radial Engineering. Photo courtesy of Radial Engineering.**

a transformer. These are known as "passive" DIs—which have no power supply and do not amplify. "Active" DI boxes often contain their own preamp stage and so can be connected to an input on a DAW or console without further gain makeup or amplification. Active DIs can be battery-powered or phantom-powered (see Chapter 3) from a console. They can also incorporate a transformer, but there are also "transformerless" designs. High-quality transformers tend to produce a better sound, but will probably cost more. There will be a balanced output from the box, usually on a male XLR connector for recording, and an unbalanced output going to the amp so the instrument can be heard on the amp whether or not it has a mic on it. Nearly all DI boxes have a ground lift switch, which can help get rid of hums and buzzes caused by ground loops.

An alternate way to capture the sound is via an external preamp, as contained in Universal Audio's LA-610, which rather conveniently has a quarter-inch unbalanced input on the front panel to plug the bass into. This can be a great choice because it also has a limiter/compressor on board, which you will most likely want to apply to the signal anyhow.

Getting the Sound

There's no such thing as a great bass sound on its own. But there is "a great bass part" that works in conjunction with its sound to make what people think of as a great bass sound. You can't just get one bass player with what seems to be a great sound on one track and then expect it to work in the context with another record entirely or another style entirely. But there are certain people who never seem to miss—the great bass players we all know and love: McCartney, Sting, Carol Kaye . . . there's a certain degree of trust. "This is Nathan East. It must sound great!"

So the sound starts with the player, the instrument they're using, and how they're playing it.

Alan:

> I remember back in the U.K. listening to those classic Motown records, and all the engineers would gather round and listen to those records and say, "How do we get a bass sound like that?" In the end, it turned out it wasn't the sound. It was the part that made it great.

Carol Kaye:

> The engineers didn't do anything. I'm the one that got the right sound. [Oh really, Carol? —*Ed.*] Coming from jazz, you want a full sound for your bass. But sometimes, they wanted a clickier sound. Like for instance, when I did *Mission Impossible*, a lot of click, but I also palm mute it to do that. It's very rare that I'll palm mute, but I needed that extra snap for that, you know. So you hear the low end of the most clicky sound.
>
> Some of the bass, like the Electric Prunes and Nancy Sinatra, it was a lot of clicky sound that they wanted. That's not the sound I like, but you hear me doing that on some of those records.

FIGURE 18.2. **The palm mute technique in action; note the guitarist's palm resting on the strings below the pick.**

I noticed right away I had to mute [damp] the bass, because if you don't mute the bass, you've got a lot of extra overtones and undertones that kill your sound. I use a doubled-up piece of felt, because I played with a pick, taped with masking tape where the strings exit the bridge. So the strings still ring, but when you're playing, you don't have all kinds of other sounds happening. I used the felt on all the records.

You know, if you're playing with a pick, you've got to use a hard pick, because it gets a nice sound. You want a pick close to the end of the neck here, not back here near the bridge, where it's really thin.

Flatwound strings were the strings of choice that everyone used back then, in the sixties, too, because it got that impact sound real fast, and you didn't have to work real hard to get a sound out of it.

Nathan East:

One of my big things when I was starting was, I used to just pull pickups out of my Fender bass that I had purchased at Manny's Music in New York. And I was always looking for a sound . . . I said, "I wonder if I'll ever find what I'm looking for?" Then, I moved to L.A. and I heard Abraham Laboriel playing a session at A&M Studios, and I said, *What bass was that he was playing?* It sounded amazing. It was a Yamaha bass. And he introduced me to the Yamaha people, and that was in the early eighties. They put a bass in my hands and it changed my life. It was just the right sound for what I had to do.

I had sort of a combination of Motown James Jamerson meets the Beatles with that McCartney real percussive sort of hollow sound, but still you could hear every note, you know. And then, you mix in a little Earth, Wind & Fire—Verdine White with that very sort of tribal approach—and then groups like Tower of Power, where it was just, you know, funky. I was looking for that thing where it was really warm and fat, but percussive and would cut through.

Although EQ and dynamic control will generally be handled by the engineer, some bass players also like to add their own special touches at source.

Nathan East:

I use the NE1 EQ box, made by Yamaha—my top-secret equalizer. It adds a lovely fatness and warmth to the bass. It's sort of hard to find, but I love it. Never record without it. It has an EQ setting for my bass that I've used on everything. And I use that in conjunction with my own direct box. I've always felt that if I could have control of the front end, it will at least give the engineer something good to work with.

You'd think that for a bass, you'd only need to EQ at bass frequencies, but that's not the case. There are a lot of mid frequencies in a bass sound, even high frequencies. You'd think that 4 kHz or so would be too high, but no, it's not—you can definitely hear a difference. 4 kHz is way above what you'd expect a bass to respond to. It would normally affect the clickiness, rather than the actual resonance of the notes themselves; it'd be the attack you'd be EQing at 3 or 4 kHz. But there are no rules. You can turn a sound completely inside out with EQ if you choose.

Alan:

> I'm usually a bit of a decision maker on bass sounds right at the beginning. I prefer to know what EQ, limiting, compression, or processing of any kind that I'm going to put on it, and I'll apply it right then and there and commit to it. It would be unusual that I would apply further limiting or compression after it's recorded.

Limiting will catch any unexpected peaks, and if used properly will even out the overall sound so that all the notes will be heard. It will often increase sustain, as well . . . Bass responds well to limiting or compression, but if you print or commit to your processing, you need to be cautious, as you can't "uncompress" after the event.

Alan:

> It would be on very rare occasions when I did not apply compression of some sort to a bass guitar. I'd be less likely to put echo FX, phasing, flanging, delays, and so on unless I knew it was going to form part of the arrangement of the record. We're a bit spoilt in the digital world in that we don't have to commit to anything. We can apply any kind of processing to the recorded track after it's been recorded and then go back to the original raw sound. That was more difficult in the old days, when tracks were not as plentiful and you had to make more decisions early on.

Carol Kaye:

> I had a Gibson box, the octave divider, which I used on films like *Airport* and *True Grit* and so on. It had a real good fuzz tone, and we did one of the dates of "Good Vibrations" with the fuzz tone, too.
>
> On a Phil Spector record, he had a lot of echo in the phones, and then the bass player and the drummer weren't jiving, so I just kind of like knuckled down to try to make it congeal, you know. And so, Phil heard that and he put a slap back on it, and it came out great. It's subtle, but it's there, and so it helped the bass player and the drummer kind of connect.

Parts and Arrangement

The rhythm section should be a cohesive unit. The rhythm section can be thought of as being bass, drums, guitar, and keyboards, but it can also just consist of the bass and drums. You want to make sure that the patterns being played by the drums (specifically the kick drum) and bass are compatible with each other and are playing as a unit.

It has almost become a requirement when recording drums and bass that bass must not overpower the kick drum and the kick drum must not overpower the bass. We need to look for sounds that work with each other. Obviously, they fall into in the same frequency range, so EQ adjustments will be crucial. Also, you don't want a drum fill to conflict with a bass fill. That's all down to the chemistry between the bass player and the drummer.

On a session there's always a degree of experimentation that happens if you just have a chord chart. You can't expect, say, six musicians, no matter how well they know each other, to instantly just come up with something that's actually going to work with just a chord chart and a tempo. They have to interact and hear what the others are playing. A good rhythm section is also good at not getting in each other's way.

Alan:

> Of course I'd love to have been a fly on the wall at some of the classic sixties Motown [sessions] to see whether Carol Kaye or whoever was playing did literally originate every bass line that you hear, or whether the arranger or writer had some kind of idea what needed to be played.

Carol Kaye:

> When I got on a date with Joe Cocker, for "Feelin' Alright," I hadn't heard that tune before. It's Paul Humphrey on drums, Artie Butler on keyboard, and a fellow by the name of Laudir De Oliveira on congas, a wonderful guy. We kind of fell into the groove, with Joe in the studio singing it.
>
> When Paul was playing upbeats, I was playing downbeats, downbeat fills, you know, so you do the opposite of what the drummer does, and so that's how I composed the line. It's just automatic. You do it that way, with statement and answer and like that kind of thing. It was a big hit twice, you know—must have done something right.

Nathan East:

> When I'm in the studio, I sort of pretend I'm playing live, and that kind of keeps your studio performance fresh. So sometimes I literally visualize an arena full of people and just try to give it something special, so you don't just come up with a part.
>
> And not only is it the notes, but many times it's that space between the notes too that you create, that give the notes more meaning. I think with bass you're always in a sort of in a balancing act, covering the bottom, but stepping out there from time to time.
>
> You need to get to that point where you learned the song but you're not confident enough just to be playing a part that's etched in stone. You're still fishing for parts but listening to what's going on around you. And that's where you get the magic, because people are still, like, looking.
>
> When I hear a demo, while I'm listening, I try to just imagine in my mind what lines would be memorable, how can I inject a little magic and just put some love into the part without it calling too much attention to itself—however, doing a little more than just playing whole notes, you know. And that's a very challenging thing, you know. That's more challenging than if you had a part that had, like, a bunch of notes already preconceived.
>
> I'm still lucky that I'm playing on a lot of projects that are band-oriented: B. B. King, Eric Clapton, Fourplay, where all the guys are in the room. And, that's a good thing; because nowadays lots of people send me files and say, "Add bass to that." I mean, that's fun, but there's nothing better than playing with the other guys at the same time.

Bass in the Mix

One issue that concerns people when they're not recording in a pro studio with large monitors, is how to judge the bass sound on midsize or *near-field* speakers that can't reproduce a full bass spectrum.

That can be down to just knowing the system, knowing the player, and knowing what to expect of an instrument being played in a certain way in a certain style. Even if monitoring is compromised in some way, you should be able to apply the rules that you've applied in the past and say, "Well, I can't really hear what this bass is sounding like, but my experience tells me this will sound all right when I get out of here."

Alan:

> I'd be hard-pressed to trust a bass sound listening on speakers on a laptop, but on full-size headphones you can get a pretty good idea of what the overall spectrum is sounding like. Not everybody has big speakers. Even if you have the greatest speakers in the world in your recording studio, that doesn't necessarily translate into the real world. You've got to make compromises and appeal to the masses. It's one of the aspects of the job. You can't expect everybody to have THE most brilliant sound system. You've got to take a view, and say this will work for most systems—and that's what you go with.

If you're working with some mega-monitoring system that goes down to 10 Hz—you're going to know everything about that bass sound. Whether it's rattling the room, or whether it's going to break windows or whatever. But there's a downside to that as well. You could say to yourself, "This bass sound is sounding absolutely huge on these speakers, but it may not necessarily sound huge when I get it out of here." You've got to apply your own rules and work from experience.

A little bit of tweaking of bottom-end EQ might happen on the mix just to make sure that it's filling out the track adequately. That's one of the skills of engineering and production that you set a good-sounding track right at the beginning and then you don't have to worry about it. A good sound should carry through right to the mix, so the mix becomes more of a formality.

Alan:

> Are you getting "Value for Money"—are you getting enough loudness for the level that is showing on the meter. In other words, if you have a crappy sound, it'll have to be too loud to be heard. If you want to feature a sound that is bad value for money, then it has the potential to send your mix into the red, which means the overall level of the mix will have to be decreased [not a good thing]. The expression is particularly applicable to bass because it consumes meter level, as opposed to "what you hear" level.

Final Thoughts

Alan:

> I've had the tremendous advantage of working with some great players in the past . . . McCartney, for example, would occasionally just go for the simplest thing to play with the band—no room for mistakes. Other times he would come back and spend all night overdubbing until he got a really great, interesting part that people would prick up

their ears and say, wow, what a great a bass part. And that was never more evident to my ears than on *Sgt. Pepper*, where there were just absolutely magic, carefully worked out bass lines.

Without bass providing the foundation, a lot of music would feel thin and spineless. Singers and guitar players might hog the limelight, but bass players—even if they don't always get the credit they deserve—are often the real heroes of the game.

19

GUITAR

Most people accept that it all started centuries ago in Spain. The Spanish or classical guitar remains very much in evidence and its distinctive sound much revered. But as far as acoustic guitars are concerned, we are more likely today to encounter acoustic guitars with steel strings, which have been popular since the 1900s. The steel string was an important milestone because it meant guitars could then be electrified.

Hello, rock 'n' roll!

Electric guitars rely on the same electromagnetic principle as dynamic microphones, except that the vibration causing the current is coming from a metal string, rather than a diaphragm.

Electric guitar is the heart of nearly all rock, pop, and country music, and there are as many sounds an electric guitar can make as there are, as they say, guitar pickers in Nashville. And that's a lot.

Alan:

> I remember when I was a boy, before I got into this whole recording thing, I saw a photograph of a microphone in front of a guitar cabinet. I said, how can that be right? Surely, an electric guitar is an electric instrument that should be picked up through electronic means. I thought, "How crude is it to put a mic on an amplifier or a cabinet?" There's the reason why I didn't become a recording engineer until I'd learned why this was. Interestingly, my concept worked well for bass guitar, but almost never for any other guitar type.

And "type" is very much the operative word here. Guitars and guitarists come in all shapes, sizes, and temperaments in both senses of the word.

Alan:

> I've recorded countless celebrated band guitarists and the top session players in the U.K. and the USA, and never got the same sound twice!

For the *Art & Science of Sound Recording* video series, the team spent time with one of Los Angeles' premier session guitarists, Tim Pierce, who has recorded with everyone who is anyone in L.A. since the eighties. Tim's meticulous approach to recording guitar substantially forms the backdrop to this chapter.

FIGURE 19.1. Ace session guitarist Tim Pierce.

Guitar Types and Sounds

Tim Pierce:

> If you had a good Les Paul and a good Stratocaster, you could do 90 percent of what you need to do.

While this is undoubtedly true, there's still a vast range of sounds that can be produced by different types of guitar and a myriad manufacturers. To have any meaningful dialogue about guitar sounds, all the parties concerned need a language through which they can communicate. A "Strat" sound. A "Les Paul" sound . . . even different types of pickup—standard *single coil* (see **figure 19.2**) or *humbucking* (see **figure 19.3**). Each has its own characteristics.

FIGURE 19.2. A guitar with three single coil pickups.

FIGURE 19.3. A guitar with two humbucking pickups.

Tim Pierce:

> I use humbuckers all the time, and they're great, but really, non-humbucking pickups have a lot more expression and a lot more nuance, and a lot more crazy stuff will hap-

> pen. Like with a fuzz pedal, if you use a single coil pickup, it just has so much more teeth and bottom end. It's really more open-sounding in a sense. A humbucking pickup does have a lot less high and a lot less low than a non-humbucking pickup. The P90 pickups are single coil, and they're noisy. They kind of behave like little microphones, and there is so much more top and bottom. Stratocasters are that way, too—they're really much more expressive, because the pickups are single coil.

It goes without saying that guitarists should know their instrument and be able to select which instrument (and also which amplifier or processor, of course) will get the result they're looking for. But at least a good working knowledge of the subject is going to help the engineer and producer, as well. For engineers, knowing what to expect from a particular guitar setup can only help the recording process, while a producer who can identify and reference a tone he or she thinks would be appropriate probably stands a better chance of getting it than the person who just says, "OK, try another one." Valid points of reference can also be players, bands, or even particular records.

Tim Pierce:

> If I plugged into this old Marshall Plexi, this would sound much more rich and full in the bottom. If you brought this forward to modern day, it's kind of . . . Hendrix becomes Chili Peppers.

We also discussed guitar sounds with producer John Fields, who's been extremely successful with powerful, guitar-based pop productions—in particular, a Rooney track called "I Should've Been After You."

John Fields:

> Strangely, it sounds like the Brian May kind of guitar sound, but for me it was like a Genesis thing, actually, like *Abacab* zone, maybe—I'm a super Genesis freak. And these guys are a lot younger. They're like in their early twenties, but they're the only guys I've met at this age who love Jeff Lynne and Queen and the Beatles. These guys understand where it came from.

This raises the question: How important are classic, "vintage" sounds? You are not going to get the same sound as a vintage Strat on an old beige Fender combo with a cheap Squier or Strat copy and a $50 amplifier. If you are looking for a vintage sound, you need vintage gear. And possibly a vintage player, as well.

John Fields:

> Yes. Of course I'm going to use those sounds or I'm going to spank them up to a certain kind of competitive level. But I mean, it's more about the musicianship than the sound.

Amps and Speakers

A good guitar sound is affected by the amplifier just as much as the instrument. In other words, we could describe a sound as a classic Les Paul using a humbucker through a Marshall 4x12, if we wanted to be more specific (see **figure 19.4**). And through a Marshall 4x12 using a particular amplifier head, if we wanted to get even further into the DNA of a guitar sound.

Many great guitar sounds have relied upon the coloration and distortion produced by amplifiers. It's virtually universally accepted that guitars sound better through tube (or "valve," as they say in the U.K.) electronics.

Tim Pierce uses a wide variety of tube or valve amplifiers, all of which, interestingly, can get fed into a Marshall 4x12 cabinet that he has imprisoned in a sort of soundproofed nuclear fallout shelter in his garage.

FIGURE 19.4. A Marshall 4x12 cabinet.

Tim Pierce:

> I have an amp switcher that allows me just to choose. It runs everything . . . It's basically a patch bay on a rotary switch.
> The whole definition of what we do as electric guitar players is just about the tube. That's the distortion, it's everything. It's amazing that something this old and antiquated is basically at the heart of what we do as electric guitar players.

Tim has a wonderful lexicon of descriptive terms. Here he is describing some of his favorite amps, the first from Naylor:

> This is good for really smooth distortion. You can really hear the articulation of the strings, and it's really spongy. I call it a friendly distorted amp.
> This is my Divided by 13 head, and it's great for really classic kind of slightly broken-up sounds. It's really useful. Really natural sounding.
> I have Vox amps, but I also have a Matchless amp that sounds like a better Vox at times, so I can get a Vox sound out of that Matchless, and sometimes I prefer to use that.
> This Diamond head is a super heavy metal head. Even though I don't look like I would play heavy metal [Agreed. —*Ed.*], it's something I get called upon to do a lot. And, it's just super overdrive-saturated. It's marvelous. It's also good for solos, too, because it's so distorted. It's nice when you're soloing to have a really, really distorted signal.

Not every player can afford a showroom's worth of hardware, but the moral of this particular piece of the jigsaw is to really know what you do have. Experiment. Find out the strengths and weaknesses. For students of engineering and production, it may be helpful to keep a diary of guitars, amps, and settings and build up your

knowledge—and your own preferences—over time.
Alan:

> I have always favored Marshall heads and 4x12 cabs. But I've also done well with Fender combos. The guitar amp used on *Dark Side of the Moon*? It was a Hiwatt head and cab, but David Gilmour had a lot of processing between the guitar and the amp, like the EMS Synthi Hi-Fli and a Binson Echorec [see **figure 19.5**], as well as early MXR stomp boxes.

FIGURE 19.5. **A Binson Echorec. Photo courtesy of Phil Taylor of Effectrode.**

Microphones

The recording chain doesn't stop at the amplifier and speaker cabinet. A cabinet will need to be miked to get the signal into your recording medium, of course.
Tim Pierce:

> One of the most frustrating things about miking an electric guitar is that when you hear an electric guitar and you're standing in front of the amp, there's a tremendous amount of air being moved, and you feel it in your chest and your stomach. You take that same sound, that glorious sound, and you hear it through the microphone and the recording chain, and it sounds way smaller, because it's going through something that is smaller. And so, you have to make slightly different choices with sound and tone to bring it back to size.

Why is LOUD necessary in guitar recording?
Tim Pierce:

> You can with a small amp that's quiet, simulate the sound of a large amp that's turned up very loud, pretty closely. There are just certain aspects of it that don't sound the same. There's a bottom end, like a fist, a bottom end fist, that comes from having an amp turned up all the way on a large amp that you can't quite reproduce coming from a small amp. It's softer around the edges. And that can be great for recording, but you really get a punch from having the real deal, the thing turned up all the way, the loud amp turned up all the way.

In Tim Pierce's soundproofed bunker in his garage he has two mic setups—a Shure SM57 going through an API mic pre and a second SM57 going into a Chandler mic pre.

Tim Pierce:

> The Chandler sounds very much like a Neve, gives you a little more mid-range attack and bite.

John Shanks is another *guitar-orientated* producer we met up with.
John Shanks:

> I switch amps much more than I think I switch microphones. I mean, basically, in my room, I love old Sennheiser MD421s for guitars. And I've done where you put 421s in the back of a Vox and then a 57 in front. I like blending amps at times—you know, Voxes and Fenders, and you just kind of find that spot where the part is speaking or you get what you're looking for.

Alan:

> I've always had more luck with condenser mics on guitar cabinets, because they just tend to have a smoother response. Dynamics tend to have a mid-range nastiness that a condenser mics don't have, and guitars are famous for mid-range honk. If you can minimize that by using a full-range mic, you'll be better off. You can make a guitar sound really nasty by putting the mic in the wrong place, too close to the center of the speaker cone. If you go right to the midpoint of the speaker cone [see **figure 19.6**], you're likely to get a shreddy tearing sound, whereas if you mic it a little further back and perhaps favor the outside edge of the cone [see **figure 19.7**], it's definitely going to be smoother.

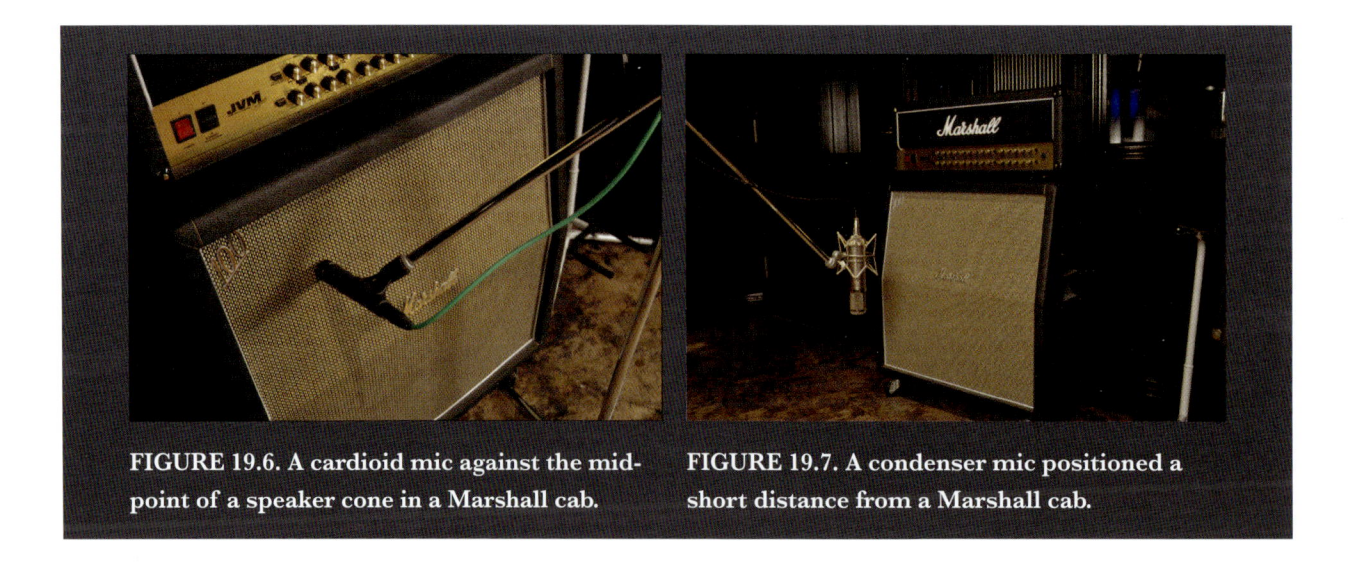

FIGURE 19.6. A cardioid mic against the midpoint of a speaker cone in a Marshall cab.

FIGURE 19.7. A condenser mic positioned a short distance from a Marshall cab.

Of course, you don't have to use just one mic. You can use several mics, at different distances. If you have a cabinet with several speakers, you can put a mic on each speaker, you can mic one at the bottom and one at the top, take a mic six feet away from cabinet, put a mic at the other end the room, and so on. It's just down to taste. If you want to capture the sound of the guitar in the room, you're going to need a room mic. It's always surprising how live sound engineers almost invariably have a 57 or a 58 right up touching the cloth of the cabinet. Alan has always avoided that. He always feels that electric guitar mics should be several inches away from their amp source.

Tim Pierce:

> You get a fist from the 57. It's mid-range. And I think a lot of what we've heard over the years on records has been that mid-range fist. So it's kind of in our DNA at this point as listeners, that we hear an electric guitar through a 57. But what has happened in recent years is a craving for more air around it—so if you put a Royer or maybe an old C37 Sony or any other bigger-sounding microphone, you get the fist from the 57 and then you get all this pillowy bottom end and all this depth from the Royer. When it's close-miked. I like to get right where the paper meets the cone, that way you get plenty of top end, but it's not harsh top end. If you get right in the center of the cone, you have harsh top end. How far away? Maybe just a couple of inches. But I like trying different mics, and I like blending microphones.

Pedal Power

Tim Pierce:

> A nice thing to do is just use an overdrive pedal to hit the front end of the amp kind of hard. Here's this pedal called the Z.Vex Super Hard-On that just explodes the front end of the amp a little bit. So you take the amp sound, you turn on the pedal, it kind of adds a really nice push to the front end of the amp.

Guitar tone has a love/hate relationship with volume—that's love from the player's perspective and if not hate, then "somewhat less love" for the person trying to record it. One of the byproducts of volume is the level of buzzes, hums, and assorted noise a fully cranked guitar and amp will spit out. While you want to capture the tone, you probably don't want to capture the accompanying noise that's present when the instrument is not being played. One solution is to apply a noise gate.

Amp Modeling: Hardware and Plug-ins

An alternative to the analog method of using microphones, amp, and speakers for recording guitar, is to use a processor that digitally re-creates or "models" it. This can be through a hardware unit like the SansAmp, or plug-in software you can call up on your DAW.

One of the pioneers of amp modeling is Andrew Barta, from Tech 21/SansAmp ("without amp" in French, of course!).

Andrew Barta:

> I felt that it was very inconvenient to have to haul around huge amps and speakers. Many times you wanted to have different sounds that meant not only one big amplifier but several sets of them. Moving projects from studio to studio can be very burden-

> some. I thought, let's make this choice more compact and go direct. Every time you mike up an amplifier and move it like a quarter of an inch, it's a totally different sound. Add to that equation another couple of microphones, or changes in the room—there are infinite variables. My idea was, by going direct you can get a consistent sound.

There's no denying the instant effect of devices like the SansAmp or the Pod by Line 6, but some people are concerned that if you use too many artificially re-created sounds at one time, there can be a cumulative negative effect.

Tim Pierce:

> Modeling devices are amazing in their way, but the people I work with require something different. I mean, we can all tell the difference. It's really great for me, at least, that they can't get guitar sounds out of a computer that sound like amplifiers quite yet. It gets a little closer all the time, but the dynamics and the harmonics and the distortion are just too complex.
>
> If you throw down one part with a modeling device, it can sound pretty good. The minute you throw down the second part, you hear a buildup of certain harsh frequencies and a sort of blanket over the sound. Once you've overdubbed three or four parts, it's really apparent that you're not using the real thing.

John Shanks:

> If your budget is limited and your environment is limited, yes, modeling is amazing. I can hear the difference, but there's certain records that I've heard, where I found out after the fact that they were done with guitar plug-ins, and I'm a big fan of those records. I think there was a Cardigans record with all guitar plug-ins, and I thought the guitar sounds were amazing. For me, I love the process of mixing tubes in with other devices, because nothing to me speaks better than that. I like the sound of air moving. You can feel it with the speakers moving. I think sometimes you miss that with plug-ins.

Amp modelers and plug-ins in the wrong hands can sound truly awful. But a knowledgeable and talented player will get a good result no matter what he plays through. There is never a substitute for talent.

Pedals and Stomp Boxes

As soon as technology had developed sufficiently for an electric guitar to produce a pure, clean-as-a-whistle tone, someone came along and invented a device that made it sound utterly distorted, shredded into oblivion, and then a lot more besides.

A stomp box, as its name implies, is something you can stomp your foot on. It's a pedal, which will give us the effects so many guitarists know and love, like distortion, wah-wah, overdrive, delay, fuzz, phasing, tremolo. The list goes on . . .

Tim Pierce:

> I have so many pedals that if I had them all on at the same time, it would totally degrade the sound of the guitar. So what I have is a homemade pile of pedals—in other words, a loop switcher. Each one of these loops goes out to a matrix of different pedals.
>
> The loop box allows me to bypass everything in the chain, so I'm basically sounding the same as if I plugged directly into the amp. I leave the tuner and the volume pedal on most of the time, because that's what I need. I need the volume pedal for swells and also to hide noise, and I need the tuner to keep tuning all the time, because I'm constantly tuning.
>
> So I have these on. If I bypass them, there's no change in the tone whatsoever. That way, I know nothing is degrading the tone.

Alan:

> On some pedals, "bypass" is not a true bypass, and there may be some coloration occurring within the box despite it being in bypass mode. A real bypass behaves like a piece of wire—it sends out *exactly what comes in* . . .

Tim Pierce:

> The older vintage pedals, many of them are not truly bypassable, and the Boss pedals, I think, a lot of them are not. So, you just deal with it. And it's good to have loop switchers to bring things in and out, meaning they are not in the circuit at all.

In the U.K., the name Pete Cornish is synonymous with the best of the best in terms of pedal *boards*—literally platforms on which a range of carefully selected and exquisitely wired pedals live permanently in one ergonomically pleasing environment.

John Shanks:

> When Pete Cornish was making these elaborate pedal boards for Jimmy Page and [David] Gilmour, he always included a line driver at the end—a boost, which kept the signal level up, so you didn't really lose fidelity.

John Shanks:

> Using a lot of pedals and chaining them up, even though they're theoretically bypassed, you still are going to get signal loss, you're still going to lose some of the sparkle. And so, Pete said to me, "Let me come up with stuff that's good for you, because I know how your mind works and you're always trying stuff." So he made me this box, where it splits the signal in stereo. It's stereo in, because I come out of a Line 6 delay into a four-channel box—four outs, so I can basically plug in four combos and they're in stereo. There's another one now that gives me more flexibility, as far as switching on different amps and turning them off. Now, there are other companies that do it, but Pete's stuff is handmade and it's worth the wait.

> It compensates for the cable lengths. It keeps the highs. And also, what's great is, he includes phase switches. So, if I am daisy-chaining or combining amps, I can just quickly change the phase if necessary.

See www.petecornish.co.uk.

Building Up Overdubs

We've been looking at the tools of the trade, but of course the most important factor to consider when recording guitar is the guitarist.

Tim Pierce:

> As you overdub, it's good to create different colors on a track, like a palette of paints. Sometimes it happens on tracking sessions that guitar is kind of a low priority. But that's part of the magic of it—knowing that there's nothing on the line, that it's not a "keeper" part. You can kind of "go for it" in a way that you wouldn't otherwise.

Alan:

> I've always liked the guitar overdub process, especially when you've got a guy who really knows how to lay down a part. Tim Pierce was an absolute joy to work with on the track I wrote for the *Art & Science of Sound Recording* video series, "All Our Yesterdays." His technique is so good, his sounds are so great, and he's very open to ideas. In the space of two hours, we transformed the song from a simple backing track to something that sounded like a record.

The following is a transcript of some of that guitar overdubbing session. We print it here because it demonstrates the process more effectively than describing the process ever could.

Alan:

> There's a lovely picky pattern from the tracking session that I think we could do with on all the verses.

Tim Pierce:

> Yes, I actually thought the same thing. I got a sound up for it. I put a little delay on it . . . kind of Gilmour . . . Pink Floyd may be the first time I ever heard a delay effect like this. I don't know if it was ever used before. It became, like, the sound of U2 after that.

Alan:

> There was a track called "One of These Days." Roger had to set it up with a Binson every night onstage. Rick would have to go over and start tweaking the delay. This is onstage, with the audience waiting for the encore!

Alan:

> I wonder if we need it on the intro as well?

Five minutes later . . .
Tim Pierce:

> So here I would do ambient stuff. I thought maybe kind of mirroring the basic track we did, but just fuller.

Alan:

> But the vocal will come in at that point.

Tim Pierce:

> I understand what you're saying, though. It might be more hypnotic to have it from the top. Then you wouldn't notice it entering.

Alan:

> You could bring some other little motifs in there, as well. Good word—"motif." Maybe a little more of the delay effect. We're printing, right?

Tim Pierce:

> Yes.

Alan:

> Probably be nice to have a stereo delay. Are you set up to do any stereo?

Tim Pierce:

> I had the same thought, and I'm set up to do a double of it.

Alan:

> Same thought process! How did you set up the delay? Take the tempo and enter it? What are you actually using for that?

Tim Pierce:

> It's this Eventide Eclipse. And it's great because you just choose the tempo and it automatically calculates the delay.

Alan:

And it's a dotted eighth?

Tim Pierce:

Dotted eighth, yes. What you do is . . . you play the note . . . without the delay it's just eighth notes. The dotted eighth gives you this percolating . . . this other syncopated rhythm.

Alan:

It would be much less interesting if it were just a shorter delay.

Tim Pierce:

So here's an eighth note. It's just going to shadow.

So how important is the touch of the player as against the instrument and the amp?
Tim Pierce:

One of the hardest things I had to learn about recording the guitar was, when I started out, I hit the guitar very hard. And the irony of recording guitar is that the best tones come from hitting the guitar as lightly as possible—having the monitor level of your guitar up in the mix as much as possible and hitting the thing as lightly as possible. It blossoms. It gets bigger. The softer you play, the bigger it gets. It's a total paradox.

The problem with having it that loud and playing that soft is, every little nuance, every mistake just comes up. Every little thing that you do explodes. It took me a lot of years to be able to play very soft and under control. For recording, the best guitar tones come from a feather-like touch, and it took me years to get, you know, sort of good at it.

Double-tracking guitars can make a huge difference to the perceived size of the sound. Sometimes tripling or going even beyond that can really help. Sometimes on solos, provided a solo can be duplicated, double-tracking can add an effect like no other.

When double-tracking, the great thing about electric guitar in particular, and acoustic also, is that when you do try and get it exactly the same, there are still a lot of differences, and those differences are usually absolutely magical. There's a fine line. You can step over the line, and you realize you have to make it closer.

The sound of the room the guitar is recorded in can be important, although in Tim's case, he only has the dry sound inside his "amp room." There are a lot of very good and versatile studio effects boxes and plug-ins to simulate room sounds without going to the trouble of using distant mics on a cabinet in the studio. Live echo chambers work well if you have access to them. On *Sgt. Pepper's* for "A Day in the Life," the Beatles used the entire Number One classical studio at Abbey Road as an echo chamber! There is also the story of Simon & Garfunkel using the building's elevator shaft as a chamber on *The Boxer*—Li Li Li—BOSH!

Tim Pierce:

> A great room sound is great once in a while, but generally, these days, guitars are just bone dry.

John Shanks:

> I was in London and working at SARM West, and it was the room where Zeppelin had recorded in and some Queen records, and in that room I really tried to take advantage of the room. So, less guitar overdubs, not as dense, where it's really the one guitar with a lot of room. And then when the chorus comes in, it's a twelve-string that comes in and just enhances that part, where it's a more Zeppelin-y kind of recording, more minimal overdubs, where you're taking advantage of the room.
> When you listen to modern rock bands, more dense, layered, or power pop, or some of these kind of artists, where you're creating dynamics and layering sonically with amps—Diezels [German amp. —*Ed.*] or big Marshalls coming in the choruses, and fuzzboxes, etc.—to create dynamics.

John Fields:

> Part of my style is to change it up, to change the guitar part's subtlety from chorus to chorus, or whatever.

Another often used effect, particularly on guitar solos, is reverb. But fashion plays a big part in this.
Tim Pierce:

> There's rarely a reverb you can use these days. Just because tracks are dense, there's no room for a reverb. I mean, if you listen to Van Halen's first record, a three-piece band, you've got his guitar on the right, and then a huge room sound on the left. That's awesome, but there are no records made that way right now. I mean, records are dense. So, guitar parts are generally bone-dry. You rarely hear reverb.

Solos

The guitar solo was a staple item in pop records right up to the seventies. It was generally played over a verse chord sequence as light relief from the lead vocal. In blues, or blues-based rock, guitar solos had long enjoyed a more prominent status, of course. But by the 1980s, guitar solos started to get phased out of pop and, with some very notable exceptions like Dire Straits' "Sultans of Swing" or Eddie Van Halen's solo on Michael Jackson's "Beat It," the guitar solo has continued to slide out of fashion. But perhaps they are coming back?
Alan:

> I like 'em. And on the track recorded for the *Art & Science of Sound Recording* video series, it never entered my head not to have a guitar solo!

Tim Pierce:

> When Kurt Cobain showed up in probably 1991, the door was shut on guitar solos. It has just opened, and people say it's because of the games, *Guitar Hero* and so on. And it's amazing to have spent seventeen years being denied the opportunity to play a guitar solo. But now I'm kind of glad they're back.

Recording a guitar solo is an extremely subjective and personal thing.
Alan:

> George Harrison did spend a lot of time—he would just essentially plod his way through a solo in the early stages. He would just keep playing it and playing it until he didn't make a mistake. It sounds cruel to describe it like that, but that was his methodology. Keep playing it, keep developing the tune, keep the good bits and take the bad bits out. He would just keep playing it until it was a good take. He'd spend long hours on a song. Because he could. The Beatles had a recording budget from heaven. No one would ever say they'd have to cut down on their studio time.

There are different ways of working. You can record several complete versions; you can build it up, punching in phrases one at a time. You get a great solo, but it's great except for the last bar, so you might punch in just for that.
Alan:

> It used to be pretty seat-of-the-pants in analog days—when you punched in, you'd lose what you were punching in on. Of course on a DAW it's all nondestructive. The process of building up a guitar track is much less likely to give you a coronary. It was pretty nerve-racking in analog days to actually punch in—and out—on a guitar solo. You had the opportunity to destroy a piece of magic just by mistiming your punch. And the worst thing—tape ops were paid a pittance for their huge degree of responsibility!

Here's John Shanks talking about an experience with Lindsey Buckingham:

> We were doing a guitar solo, and it was interesting. He goes, "Well, I'm not sure what to do." Sometimes people are so isolated in their own world that they don't realize how much I've analyzed their sound or their playing, sonically. And as a fan, I think, "No, this is what works, this is what moved me, and maybe we should explore some of that." And so, with Lindsey, I picked up the guitar and I said, "You know, kind of your double stops and the high E ringing," and he went, "Oh, yeah, yeah—that's cool." And I go, "Well, that's me doing you." And he said, "Oh, I get it now." And so, I'm running out and tuning up his amps and getting the delay sounds right and moving mics around until we find it.

There are no rules on solos. Sometimes the producer has a line in his head that he hums to the player. Sometimes it's just echoing the vocal lines. Or maybe you are just looking for the craziest, manic headbanging (or hairbanging?) outburst ever recorded. Did Van Halen really calculate every note he was going to play on the "Jump" solo?

Tuning

The tuning of any acoustic instrument—including the piano—is both, to coin a phrase, art and science. Getting your guitar to the point where it'll play several different chords "in tune" is a constant battle, as everyone who's ever picked up a guitar knows!

Tim Pierce:

> Guitar has never been totally in tune, it never is. There's a lot of trickery involved in recording and making guitars sound in tune. And one of the things about modern recording that's very frustrating, is that the emphasis is greater than ever on having things be perfectly in tune, and it's so hard with some guitars. For instance, the Les Paul guitar was designed in an era when the strings were really thick and nobody was bending strings and guys were playing jazz on them. The thing that makes it hard to tune is that the strings turn at certain points. Fenders are much easier to keep in tune because there's a straight string pull to the headstock and machine heads. You really have to struggle as a guitar player to record in tune. And there are times, even at this point in my life, when I have to punch one chord at a time.

John Shanks:

> Sometimes what feels good is not exactly perfectly in tune. It's the micro tones. I always related it to guitar players or violinists. I mean, part of Jeff Beck's thing is playing in between. It's not major; it's micro tones. That's what creates the tension. And, you know, with Clapton's playing with Cream, or Jeff Beck's playing or Jimmy Page's, it's the bending, it's the subtleties, it's the vibrato.

Left-hand guitar technique also has an effect on tuning, because of the way the guitarist is stopping a fret, or what pressure he's applying to the fretboard in what direction. If a guitar player is producing consistently in-tune results, it often means he has great technique. A guitar is not just in tune or out of tune. You can actually PLAY a guitar in tune and out of tune as well. Strings can also can effect intonation—especially old, rusty ones.

Tim Pierce:

> It depends on the part. If I'm going to do a solo, I'll try and pick up a guitar that has 9s or 10s on it. But if I'm playing rhythm, I'll use a guitar that has 11s on it. So it just depends on the part for me.

Tuning is particularly bothersome on chords with distorted sounds or what we call *power chords*.
Tim Pierce:

> On power chords, everything is so much more complex, and the harmonics get just so out of control that they rub against each other in such an irritating way. I mean, the way you solve it is by building the chords on different tracks. You do the root and fifth on one track, and then maybe you'll do the thirds on another track. It will sound like one guitar, but it's a really good way to create the full chord, you know, with multiple guitar parts.

A recent technology, the all-mechanical EverTune bridge, is set to revolutionize guitar tuning. Gerry Dale and Robin Millar's extraordinary and brilliant Snap Dragon Tripper guitar is a folding instrument that unfolds perfectly in tune. It's quite uncanny. There are various videos online—well worth checking out.

Acoustic Guitars

This chapter has focused unashamedly on electric guitar, but of course the acoustic guitar is hugely important as an instrument, and its sound is very distinctive. (See also Chapter 20, "Recording Acoustic Guitar with Vocals.")
Tim Pierce:

> Playing the acoustic guitar, there's a certain amount of pain in extracting the sound from it. It takes a lot more "oomph" to get a tone out of the acoustic guitar. When you hear it, it can sound effortless and amazing, but when you're actually playing it, it really takes muscle, and it's painful sometimes.

Wrap

Tim Pierce:

> To get a good guitar sound, maybe you need to do five or six or seven things right, and not do a thousand things wrong. If you have a good set of pickups into a good guitar going straight into a good amp into the right speaker into the right microphone into the right mic pre, you're done.

Of course the one item Tim left out of that menu is the most important, and that's the player!
Tim Pierce:

> Then, there's a touch involved, a touch and a tone. Unfortunately, guitar players get caught up in, "Ooh, I just bough this amazing amp. It was only $2,000." Well, it was the wrong amp. I'm sorry. Or, "I just got this amazing guitar. It has these really high-tech

pickups and they're battery-powered." Well, no, that's not the right pickups. You know, you really have to give up your prejudices and kind of get the right gear, and the right gear, historically, doesn't change, with regards to guitar.

With all the changing technology, especially with synthesizers and virtual instruments and special effects becoming more dominant in modern recording, there's STILL no doubt—the guitar ain't gonna go away.

20

RECORDING ACOUSTIC GUITAR WITH VOCALS

Something countless musicians need to do at some stage is to record themselves playing acoustic guitar and singing at the same time.

What you want is a reasonable degree of separation, so that you can add a touch of reverb to the vocal without the guitar going swimmy, or brighten up the guitar without the voice going sibilant. So, how best to achieve this?

During the making of the *ASSR* video series, we discovered singer-songwriter Matt Lucca in Santa Cruz, where the filming took place, and he became our guinea pig for solving this age-old problem.

Microphone Choice

The first things to consider are what microphones to use and which polar patterns.

On the guitar, it's ideal to use a mic with a cardioid or hypercardioid polar pattern, which will be very focused on the source you want to capture but hopefully won't pick up much if any signal from anywhere else.

The same applies to the vocal, although we are more likely to choose the vocal mic for its intrinsic quality characteristics rather than its ability to reject unwanted sources—in this case, the acoustic guitar.

Alan:

> I've had some success with two mics on acoustic instruments—notably Jake Shimabukuro's ukulele—but in this situation, we are more concerned with the vocal sound and how it works with the acoustic instrument. It's perfectly natural for both to be in mono—a little stereo reverb will make it become stereophonic.
>
> There's a vintage LP by blues veteran Leadbelly which the label felt would sell more if the mono recording was converted to stereo. Vocal and guitar—hmm . . . how to make it stereo? Well, what they did was hilarious. Whenever the guitar was on its own, it was panned left, and whenever Leadbelly sang, both went in to the center. Totally laughable!

> In the studio, I would always favor condenser mics both on the guitar and the vocal. On the live stage, where things are not so easily controlled or where there are budget constraints, dynamics might be a better choice. Proximity effect on the both the mics may be an issue, which might be easier to deal with on dynamics.

Mic Placement

It's best to position the mics in such a way that maximizes the natural characteristics offered by the cardioid polar pattern—in other words, to capture the maximum amount of source that you do want while minimizing the one that you don't on each mic.

In general, it's best for the performer to stand rather than sit, as this adds another few vital inches to the physical separation between the vocal mic and guitar mic. Angle the vocal mic upward, away from the guitar, and at the same time, angle the guitar mic down, so as to minimize the vocal going into the guitar mic (see **figure 20.1**).

One problem we might encounter when trying to get the vocal mic as close as possible to the singer is "popping." We experimented with some different proximities with Matt's vocal mic, both with and without a pop shield. A sponge pop shield may help, but a screen "popper stopper," as in **figure 20.2**, will mean there will have to be a little more distance between the singer and the mic, thus worsening the separation. Screen popper stoppers don't work live, of course.

Finger squeak may be an issue when the acoustic guitar is very exposed, but really the only way round it is a change in the playing technique—making an effort to take the left hand off the strings when changing position.

As far as effects are concerned, we may have to be careful that any effect we apply to one mic has a pleasing or complementary feel on the other. We wouldn't want the guitar to sound like it's in Carnegie Hall and the vocal in the pub down the road!

The whole point of this exercise is to create a recording environment where the performer can forget about technology and just perform. So once we are set up, we should try to avoid too many last-minute changes. It's best to just go with what you have.

FIGURE 20.1. **A guitar mic pointed downward, away from the vocal, to maximize the instrument's input. Photo by Charlie Steves.**

FIGURE 20.2. **A singer using a screen "popper stopper" pop shield in front of the mic.**

RECORDING ACOUSTIC GUITAR WITH VOCALS | 205

21

RECORDING A CHOIR

When we record people en masse, such as a choir or an orchestra or a band playing live, logistics change. Inherent uncertainties come into play as we deal with a large group of people all performing at the same time.

Often, such recordings will happen in a remote environment outside a conventional recording studio. Some of the best orchestral and choral recordings have taken place in ballrooms and town halls, for example. When we're away from our home base, in addition to carting the recording hardware for the session, we'll need several mics, mic stands, and cables long enough to stretch from the performing area to our recording setup in a makeshift control room.

Ideally, we want to create as much separation as we can between the live sound in the room and the location where we are monitoring the recording. If your recording rig is in the same room as the performance, it's going to be difficult to assess exactly what is being recorded. We may also have to deal with unfamiliar and problematic room acoustics and extraneous noise.

Most schools, colleges, and churches tend to have a few microphones and some sort of recording device or software tucked away somewhere—so recording your local choir is not something that should require a huge investment, just some planning and a little bit of know-how.

During the making of the *Art & Science of Sound Recording* video series in Santa Cruz, California, an opportunity arose to record the choir of a local school, Soquel High. We captured some extraordinary performances, creating a piece of musical magic from what we discovered was an amazing group of young singers.

This chapter examines all the processes of recording a choir in the context of that recording session. No matter who you are or what your budget, you will almost undoubtedly confront the same challenges and questions we faced.

Approaches and Preparation

Preparation and planning are a good thing for any session, but for a remote location ensemble recording, planning is absolutely key.

First, we need to decide exactly what we want to achieve. Are we trying to make a master recording for potential release? Are we simply recording for the amusement of the current group? Or maybe it's just an experiment. Even if your goals are modest, it's best not to cut corners and to make the best recording you can.

There are countless ways to record a choir. A simple pair of mics out in the audience area would certainly capture the sound in the room. The audience area can be either "real," as in the case of a theater or arena, or "virtual," as in simply at the back of a large studio or hall. At the other end of the spectrum, we may be tempted to give each singer his or her own mic. While this may seem like the ultimate means of control, in reality it is more likely a recipe for chaos. A choir, as any choir director knows, is a single body and is most often more than the sum of its parts. The same goes for the *recording* of a choir. The choir should sound like a cohesive unit and not just a collection of individual voices.

Close-miking a *section* of the choir as opposed to each individual member is a popular method and could involve, say, four mics, one each for the sopranos, altos, tenors, and basses. However, when you, "the listener," hear a choir, it's not likely to be "close" unless you are the conductor. The audience typically hears a choir from at the very least thirty or forty feet away. Distance tends to reduce individual detail, helping fuse and blend voices into the single unit we want.

So does that mean it's best to mike a choir from thirty to forty feet? Not necessarily. Exactly where to place your mics and how many you should use depend on a number of factors, including basic equipment, such as the number of mics you have at your disposal, and the number of channels available on your recording rig. The recording may also be governed by the natural acoustics of the room . . . If the room is an old church with beautiful natural reverb, you may want its characteristics to be featured in the final recording. If the location is a "dead" room or a room with some harsh reflections or problematic areas, you may prefer to create an artificial "space" with digital reverb or an echo chamber and focus on close-miking.

For the video, we spent several days planning, and so should you. These were our thought processes:

Planning

1. *Our goal* was to capture the spirit and energy of a school choir in a simple school hall environment, as opposed to recording in a dedicated recording facility with a full-blown control room and isolated studio. We were not trying to produce a "pristine" recording, since the Soquel High School multipurpose room, where the recording would take place, is adjacent to the school kitchens!

2. *Our approach* was to use a combination of close-miking and "room miking" techniques, plus to experiment with an interesting recording technique called Mid-Side—usually referred to as MS (see sidebar on p. 212). We had sufficient mics and channels to try three different approaches and then choose which combination worked best when we mixed. (See "Creating the Mix" later in this chapter.)

3. *Our recording rig* was Cubase on a laptop with an eight-channel MR816 interface and a couple of pairs of decent (closed) headphones.

4. *Our choice of mics* was based on availability from Alan's and Keyfax's collection, and also polar pattern—the Mid-Side technique requires one mic to be configured in a figure eight pattern.

5. *Reconnaissance* is a good idea, and we made a brief advance visit to the location to measure the distance between the performance area and the room where we would be setting up the recording rig—and also to check that there would be no major surprises.

6. *Setup time*. Based on the above, we concluded that we would need two hours' setup time before the performers arrived. Here, timing was crucial. Twenty or thirty people milling about, wondering what's going on, makes a terrible start to the day. Some hanging about time is unavoidable, but it is important to minimize it.

The Equipment

The MR816 has the capability to handle eight mic inputs and has phantom power, which was needed for the condenser mics we had chosen. We went straight from the interface to a laptop and recorded the Cubase audio to our trusty portable LaCie USB hard drive at 96 kHz 24-bit.

We decided to use condenser mics exclusively, which would be typical for a session such as this. On a very tight budget, dynamic mics (and maybe a low-cost ribbon mic for the figure eight to use the Mid-Side

FIGURE 21.1. **A Mid-Side microphone setup, with a figure eight mic at a right angle above the cardioid mic.**

technique) would still do the job, but would be at the expense of compromised signal-to-noise and fullness of frequency response.

Alan's much-favored Neumann KM 84 cardioid mics were chosen for the basic left, center, and right areas of the choir. The directional characteristics of a cardioid polar pattern (see **figure 3.16 [left], p. 20**) focus each mic on its own area of the choir, so that when they are panned left, center, and right, we get a decent stereo spread.

For the Mid-Side or MS signal, we chose the Audio-Technica AT4050 switched to figure eight, pointing with its active pickup areas at right angles to the forward plane. For MS to work, it's a requirement to use one cardioid and one figure eight set perpendicular to the center cardioid mic (see **figure 21.1**).

The piano was miked with a pair of SE Electronics SE1s. Cardioids give us the best separation between the bass and treble strings of the piano, especially if they are angled slightly away from each other.

Finally, the ambience of the room was captured with pair of AT4050s set to "omni" mode. It's common practice to use omnidirectional mics to record room ambience, so that not only the sound of the room will be captured from the direction of the source, but so that the mics will also pick up reflections from above, below, and behind.

So-named "room mics" are normally placed high so that you'll capture as much general ambience as possible. In a performance venue, you'd want to capture the room as a whole, rather than pick up focused coughing and shuffling from the audience. A normal mic stand, fully extended with a boom, may only reach six to eight feet, so it's best to use larger stands that can reach up to ten to twelve feet. If the building's construction and your cable lengths permit, you could also suspend the room mics from the ceiling.

Inevitably, some little detail gets forgotten, and we discovered that we didn't have enough of the right size microphone clips and suitable stands and attachments for the mics we'd chosen. So long as you don't forget the duct or gaffer tape, you can probably improvise your way around most physical problems like this.

Mic Placement

Mic placement is always crucial, but in this situation it was complicated by the fact that we were familiar with neither the choir nor the room. We also weren't able to hear the results in a control room monitoring environment. All we had was a pair of headphones at the recording station.

You have to rely on your experience, plus a degree of trial and error, to get the result you're after. A bit of luck also helps—no engineer in the world always gets perfect results.

If you only mike a choir from relatively close range—say around eight feet, as we did with the left, center, and right positioned mics on our session—the result won't represent the sound the imaginary live audience hears—i.e., what the choir actually sounds like in the room. This is where the "room" or ambience mics come in. Exactly where the room mics should be placed will depend on the size and shape of the room. For our session, we placed two mics approximately twenty-five feet from the choir, as high up as our mic stands would allow. In general, ambience mics are best placed at the extremes of the space, but be aware that long distances from the source will result in a time delay. You can't change the laws of physics, but modern technology allows us to adjust time delays after the event. A variety of placements like this gives us options when it comes to mixing the final recording. Options are good.

Setting Levels

Even so-called "close" mics are probably not going to be that close on a choir, so the signal coming through might appear low on the DAW. In our session, the signal from each mic was generally peaking at around −10 dB. If there aren't going to be any huge peaks in the performance, there shouldn't be any need to apply any limiting. For a choir, manual gain riding is probably more appropriate if necessary.

The Actual Recording

It is important that the producer of the session regularly goes out into the performance space, so that he or she knows what is actually happening in the room and to hear the "real sound" of the choir. On our *ASSR* recording, one such visit educated Alan to the fact that we had inadvertently got the main choir left and right microphones the wrong way round on the cabling into our control area. It was only when we actually did some playbacks that he noticed that the voices on the right were coming from the left and vice versa. This was easily corrected, repanned, and relabeled on the Cubase session.

In a perfect world, take one would be "the one," but rarely is that the case. It is perfectly acceptable to do multiple takes and maybe to edit between two or more for the final version. Be aware that the choir director may conduct at slightly different tempos between takes, which will make editing more difficult. It might be appropriate for him or her to use a click track or a visual metronome. On overdub sessions there is always a reference to work to. Often we will have to make edits to deal with extraneous noise as well as performance-related issues.

In our current "non-studio" environment, we had to expect and live with the odd creaky floorboard, rustle, or squeak. Digital recording will almost certainly allow us to edit out or minimize unwanted noises, but if a plane buzzes the building or one of the choir has a coughing fit . . . it's best to stop and do another take.

One hilarious incident happened on our recording: at the end of the first piece, Alan raised his finger to his mouth to gesture *Shhh* . . . as the last chord faded away. Our stills photographer thought it was a great shot and pressed the shutter button on her camera at the precise moment to ruin the take! She was very red-faced, but we forgave her and got a perfect take of the ending a few minutes later.

S*** happens on live recordings. Don't be too hard on yourself, or others.

Creating the Mix

If we have used a combination of close mics and room mics, there will be a dramatic difference between the heavily focused and perhaps too "close" sound of just the front mics and the softer, more diffuse and distant sound captured by the room mics.

In our DVD session we had effectively three sets of mics to choose and create our blend from:

1. The three Neumann 84s to capture the immediate, close-up sound of the choir, left, center, and right
2. The center cardioid 84 with the figure eight Audio-Technica AT4050 in a Mid-Side or MS configuration
3. The pair of ambience or room mics, which could be added in both the above cases

For this session, we eventually chose a blend of the MS configuration and the room mics. In this combination, we created a quite dramatic stereo effect, complete with precision and articulation you'd expect from close miking, coupled with the softer, more distant, but more cohesive sound of a choir heard from the audience's perspective.

The Mid-Side Technique

This is a recording technique that creates a dramatic stereo picture using just a pair of centrally located mics, one directly above the other (see **figure 21.1**).

The concept—originally devised by EMI engineer Alan Blumlein back in the 1930s—requires that one of the mics (normally cardioid) faces the source (in the middle, hence "Mid") while the other, set to a figure eight polar pattern, is positioned with its active pickup areas at right angles to the forward plane (capturing sound at either side, hence "Side").

On playback, the recorded signal from the cardioid is combined with the figure eight as a "sum," which is panned left. Reversing the phase of the figure eight track means we "subtract" the figure eight signal from the center cardioid and that signal is panned right. Combining the two—the so-named *sum and difference* technique—rather uncannily creates a wonderful stereo image.

Despite having been invented more than seventy-five years ago, MS recording is ironically more easily dealt with on a DAW than it is on analog gear. All we have to do is take the cardioid signal, pan it center, and take the figure eight signal and pan it left. We then duplicate the figure eight signal onto a new track and reverse its phase on the DAW—easily done. The new reverse-phase figure eight signal is panned right.

22

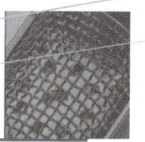

APPROACHES TO LIVE RECORDING

Mixing live shows for the audience in a venue involves all the same principles you apply to studio recording—especially the need for separation. The main difference is that on a live show, everything happens at once and you only get one chance to get it right. But on a live recording you get to reassess things at a later stage, do a whole bunch of repairs, and fool the public into thinking what amazing, flawless performances everybody gave on the night.

FIGURE 22.1. The Alan Parsons Live Project in a live concert performance in 2010. Photo by Annie Colbeck.

Alan:

> You could say for a live recording, you can replace everything except the audience! But be careful not to destroy the atmosphere, the heat of the moment, or the vibe generated by the occasion.

Capturing a live show is still a recording, with all of the issues and physical properties of each instrument that we have to deal with in any environment. But there will be special cases, such as cymbals, which are going to carry acoustically and ambiently. Because of their frequency, they're going to cut through and you're going to get a lot more of that in the house.

The magic of digital means you could record several shows and mix one band member's performance into an entirely different show—provided "sync" and "wardrobe" (if you're also shooting video) allow. But if you value your sanity, the best route is still to record everything you want to capture as cleanly—and as independently—as you can from the get-go. And this first involves getting the best quality signals from the instruments and mics that you possibly can.

For the making of the *ASSR* video series, we worked with Alan Parsons' own live sound engineer, Kevin Kennedy.

Kevin Kennedy:

> As far as backline is concerned, it's all pretty standard. You've got keyboards, we have microphones, we have computers for playback tracks, guitars, we've got amps . . . from a backline point of view it's just like what you'd start with in a studio.

And as with studio recording, a click track coming from a laptop or keyboard workstation can provide synchronization security if you want to make repairs after the event. Often, just the drummer gets a click on headphones or in-ear monitors. Clicks on loudspeaker monitor wedges onstage obviously don't work. An advantage of playing to a click is that prerecorded sequences or parts can be added into the mix—*shhh!* Don't tell anyone.

Kevin Kennedy:

> For the keyboards, we're taking stereo line outputs to the DIs. DIs have a transformer with ground-lift capability. And that will take each line signal and convert it into a balanced feed so you don't get noise and buzz.

Microphones

You'll see different mics onstage from what you'll find in a recording studio for a number of reasons. Roadworthiness and cost are the two biggest differentiators, but there are also technical and specification considerations, such as sensitivity and polar patterns.

Dynamic mics are generally considered the best to use in live performance (eight squillion people who use Shure SM58s can't have got it that wrong), but if you are *recording* a live performance, then it's worth pausing and considering your options.

Traditionally and generally, condenser mics were thought to be a little too fragile to withstand the rigors of the road. But this is changing, and there are now several brands and models of condenser mics that can be used quite safely on a live stage—especially on something like a guitar cabinet, which shouldn't see too much "action," unlike a mic for vocals or drums. A Shure SM57 draped over a Marshall 4x12 cabinet might be the classic miking "image" for electric guitar, but again, if you are recording your live performance, consider a condenser—something that may help you capture a little more fidelity along with bark and bite. Moreover, it is almost certainly worth also taking a direct out from the guitar amp so you have another source to play with when it comes to assembling your live recording.

For acoustic guitars, it's best to use instruments with a built-in pickup going into a DI box. It will be a lot safer (feedback-wise) than any form of external miking. Miking an acoustic guitar on a rock show is asking for trouble.

For drums it's common to close-mike individual drums, including toms and hi-hats. Cymbals can be captured using overheads, much as you would on a studio recording.

Stage Volume and Separation

Separation is very important if you want to have the option of making repairs later, and that means not having too much signal from one instrument spilling into the microphone for another. So the volume of each instrument is crucial.

It's a very different job mixing for the audience at a live show and mixing the monitors for the musicians. A monitor engineer has the unenviable task of getting each musician's ideal balance into his monitor wedge or in-ear monitors. Not usually a part of a recording, but worth a mention because they're in charge of what the musicians hear. And what they hear will have great influence on what they play.

Kevin Kennedy:

> We have what's called a splitter system, and all of the inputs that come from the stage go into a rackmount unit. And that splits every input into three, sometimes four, depending on need. We want to split one of those feeds to go to the monitors, and then one comes out to front of house. If there's going to be a recording, like a multitrack recording to a truck, you'll need a third splitter or sometimes a fourth splitter, and that would go to another source for an independent mix. The neat thing about splitters is that everyone can do their own thing.

Alan:

> A major act might choose to hire a sophisticated mobile recording unit, but if you can't afford a recording truck, you can still take a separate split feed from the stage mic and line sources into your recording system, which will give you a completely fresh set of outputs to record from.

You will need as many mic pres as you have microphones or a separate console that can feed out to as many track outputs as you need. A cost-effective alternative is to take a feed of each channel from the front-of-house console using the mic pres of that console. This is usually called the direct out. You'll usually want to record from a point in the console chain that will not be affected by the fader movements at the show and will be independent of any EQ and other processing.

You can achieve excellent results recording direct to a laptop, but remember, you'll need multitrack software and a channel of A-to-D conversion for every microphone or instrument you want to have separate control over in postproduction. One very interesting solution comes from American company PreSonus, whose StudioLive 24.4.2 desk comes with the company's own Capture software, specifically tailored to multitrack live recording.

The simplest recording of all is to capture the actual stereo "mix" of the show as heard by the audience. But the danger is that whatever "happens" on the night will also be recorded and, in the case of any performance cock-ups, or misuse of compression and gates, for example, you won't be able to do anything about it after the event.

A point to bear in mind, no matter what hardware and software you're using, is that if your recording system is set up at the front-of-house console in the venue, chances are that the monitoring facilities for your recording are going to be compromised. So make sure at the very least you have the ability check that each recorded track is clean, hum- and buzz-free, and contains the information it should contain—e.g., the hi-hat track doesn't have a vocal on it.

Kevin Kennedy:

> For a live recording, a lot of people will use ambient mics in the house to pick up the sound in the house as it happens through the speakers, and to pick up audience applause and noise. And they'll then mix that into the final recording. A lot of times if you take a direct split into a live recording, you'll end up with a pretty dry-sounding mix. It'll be live, but you won't hear the audience or the room as it happens.

Provided you have everything that happened recorded, you should be able to re-create it or even improve on it.

A live concert recording needs to capture the excitement of being at the show without revealing the warts and possible train wrecks that may have occurred during the concert itself. It's a delicate mix of compromise and deception.

23
MIXING

Back in the day when we were recording to wax cylinders, the only way to get a well-balanced recording was to move musicians around in front of the single large horn microphone or to get them to play more loudly or quietly.

With electrical recording came greater control over the balance, as a result of being able to combine the outputs of multiple microphones pointed at individual performers or sections. Once a "live" sound balance between the various mics had been created, the result was recorded to tape and became the master. Easy!

But ever since we've been able to record instruments or groups of instruments on multiple tracks and add new material (overdubs) onto existing recordings, we've had to go through a process of rebalancing the recorded tracks for the final piece of music that people hear in the real world. This really is a delicate balancing act, a continual adjustment of levels, tones, textures, and placements until the final "recipe" is to our liking. The final mix is the point where we let go and commit our work for the ears of the masses.

Mixing can be the make-or-break point of a hit; and the mix, depending on its complexity, can take many hours or even days to complete. The mix is extremely subjective and is often the source of conflicts between musicians, producers, engineers, and record company A&R departments. Often a label will take on fresh ears for a mix and employ the star "Mix Engineer of the Week" to hopefully create a dazzling finished product.

Alan:

> Some engineers, myself included, get really uncomfortable when their work is passed on to someone else. My work is very personal to me.

Others feel it's all part of the game.
John Shanks:

> I just went through a recording where it was appropriate for a mixer out of Nashville to mix it. It was better for that format. And maybe if we do a pop version of the record, you know, we'll mix a pop version of it. But it was the right thing to do—you have to be a team player. You have to know what's best for the project.

FIGURE 23.1. Mixing Through the Ages: (1) Real time. (2) Reel-to-reel time. (3) Real time. (4) Non-real-time.

Mixing Methods—"In the Box" or in the Studio?

Depending on how you work, mixing can be something of a formality, because all the balance subtleties might have already been automated in the DAW during recording. But if you do want to reassess your recording and create a new mix for your final product, there's no fresher or better way to do it than to look at the raw, unprocessed sounds, on their own tracks. This could simply involve a fresh look at the material wholly as digital data on a DAW. Or it could involve going into a professional recording studio, routing all the individual tracks through a large-format console, and making use of thousands of dollars worth of outboard processing equipment and monitoring systems that cost as much as a house.

Up to the end of the seventies, the mix had to be "performed," almost like a performing band, often by several people at a time. A common scene was to see several pairs of hands on a desk, muting and unmuting tracks, furiously panning, moving faders up and down . . . It wasn't until the late 1970s that any real degree of automation started to creep into the process.

There are those who wonder if there is or was a real benefit to what can be termed "performance mixing." Some feel that it adds excitement to the record. The other side of the coin, now that we are fully immersed in digital and virtual technologies, is that we can now achieve perfection (whatever that may mean, of course), and so if every fader movement, pan, and on-the-fly EQ adjustment can be recorded and replayed . . . why on earth would you not want to do it?

An extension of the latter approach is to effectively mix as one goes along and bypass the entire process of "mixing" as a subsequent event altogether.

No matter how it's done, we will at some point need to combine our series of individually recorded tracks into files representing a stereo or 5.1 surround mix that can be replayed on a consumer playback system. The approaches you can take loosely fall into the following categories:

1. A hands-on performance mix in the analog domain using an analog console. *(Very human, captures a moment in time, requires potentially expensive hardware.)*

2. An automated mix in the analog domain using analog console. *(Precise, possibly time-consuming/expensive, requires expensive equipment.)*

3. An in-the-box mix where tracks remain in the digital domain and adjustments are made simply by using a mouse. *(The least expensive, unless you quantify your time, which can be almost limitless.)*

4. An in-the-box mix where tracks remain in the digital domain, but with hands-on adjustments made using a "controller." *(You push real faders up and down instead of a mouse and get a better picture of what's going on.)* It's worth noting that professional controllers are sometimes as big as the room they are housed in, but even a large-format controller is in essence just a very large mouse!

Jack Joseph Puig:

> Mixing in the box has its beauties. There's a certain sound to it. It's fantastic, actually. But I think given the choice, anyone in the world most likely would pick mixing through an analog console if they could.

Your situation, budget, style of engineering, and production will dictate what works best for you. And realistically, there is no "right" way. In the *ASSR* video series, we try to give you a flavor of all these different approaches. No matter whether you are flanked by five assistants at a large-format console or making adjustments parameter by parameter at the kitchen table on GarageBand, you'll face many of the same challenges and decisions. For the remainder of this chapter, we look at those processes and choices.

Mixing for the *ASSR* Video Series

FIGURE 23.2. **The control room at Record One.**

Figure 23.2 is the main room at Record One where we undertook the mix of a track we recorded for the video series.

Alan:

> Record One has one of the largest consoles I have ever sat at. It's got ninety-six channels. The main reason for this to exist is for the film work at the facility, which often requires an enormous number of channels. The building itself at Record One is best known for a gentleman by the name of Michael Jackson, who did a lot of work there with my heroes Bruce Swedien and Quincy Jones. So the building is kind of the American equivalent of Abbey Road, in a way.

For our mix of "All Our Yesterdays," we came out of the DAW and back into the analog domain, bringing up the individual tracks from Pro Tools on the studio's SSL 9000J console.

We did this mix in the analog domain, bringing each track from the DAW up on its own fader. The studio can handle up to sixty-four D-to-A outputs, which was plenty for our purposes. At the end of the session, the analog stereo mix from the console was converted back into the digital domain and recorded onto two tracks of our DAW.

Preparing the Ingredients

Back in the days when we recorded onto tape, it was almost impossible for parts or takes to get out of sync, because everything was recorded in a linear fashion, sequentially on the tape.

On a DAW, each recorded part exists as a separate WAV file, which can be used in a "nonlinear" fashion. Nonlinear means any part can occur at any time and be repeated any number of times—or even be played backwards! So it's vital, unless we are deliberately doing crazy stuff, that all our various tracks remain in sync with each other.

It's very easy for files to get detached from their originally intended place if your project goes cross-platform between applications, or gets handed over to the Hot Shot Mixer of the Week—i.e., not the person who originally made the recording.

We don't want every punched-in vocal phrase, for example, to appear in the list of available files. We want all the individual takes of each part or performance to be combined, or "comped," into a single entity. Any unwanted material should just not show up.

"Consolidation" is the way to ensure that everything we recorded starts and stops as originally intended. We might have dozens of files that need to be accessed on a single track during the song. This will appear on the screen as a series of waveforms with gaps in between them. Consolidation creates one file for each track that accesses all the needed source files at the correct start time (normally the very beginning of the song) and runs continuously as long as they're needed.

The important thing is to make consolidation part of your normal working practice, which will ensure you don't incur the wrath of any puzzled engineer—or frankly even yourself—looking at your work later down the line.

Jimmy Douglass:

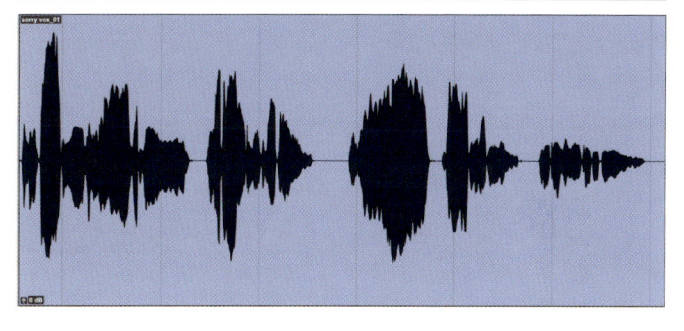

FIGURE 23.3. (*Top*) **A non-consolidated track, where each individual recorded part is marooned in its own time capsule;** (*bottom*) **a consolidated track joins everything together from beginning to end.**

> A record is no longer made one place, one idea added onto another—"You make a part and then this other guy makes a part. Then another guy makes a part . . . Oh, you're a great guy. You mix. Here, do it." And, that's kind of what I'm getting a lot of, and that makes it totally not fun, and it takes up a lot of time just trying to figure out where all the bones are buried.

Elliot Scheiner:

> Sometimes you get a drive with no written notes, so you're dependent on going into the drive and seeing what the information is, whether it's good or not, whether it's to

be used and so on. Often, they don't eliminate files they're not using. Worse than that is that even when you call and say, "Please, consolidate the files before you send them to me," they don't, or it's something they don't think about. And so, you get a drive and you open up one of the songs and there's three hundred files in there. And every time that happens, I just go ballistic.

Alan:

Even on analog multitracks, a little time spent cleaning up unwanted or extraneous material will prove to be a benefit. Personal experience with a certain Beatle who was not very careful about erasing unwanted material meant that we spent endless amounts of [non-automated] mixing time trying to remember to cut tracks that burst forth with "Hold it" or "Let's try that one more time" or chattering over the intro before vocals came in. It was a different mind-set in those days—if you erased something, it was gone forever.

Computer Power: Recall and Automation

Of course, a mix goes beyond just getting a good balance or blend of ingredients. We may decide not to use a particular track or tracks in particular places in the song. Or we might need to switch tracks to get the best performance of a particular section. So, some of our mixing time will be spent selecting or deselecting a track so that it only plays exactly when we need it.

Also we might want to change EQ or other processing during the course of a track. Level changes are almost inevitable to emphasize important passages or boost weak notes or phrases.

As veteran record producer Jim Dickinson once observed about what it takes to create a hit, "It's simple: You just turn the good parts up and the bad parts down."

Alan:

That sounds like a philosophy to base an entire career on. And I think I have!

Chuck Ainlay:

I like coming out multichannel into the desk and mixing things as an individual item and using analog EQ and compressors on the console or plugging in some vintage bit of gear that I think is going to give me a good sound—although there are certain plug-ins that I rely on heavily.

Working purely in the box is, by definition, an "automatable" environment (at least we've never heard of a DAW that doesn't offer it). Sound and level change commands are written into the song so that each move or adjustment only has to be performed once. The computer will now automatically reperform these moves every time the moment passes.

Consoles such as the SSL at Record One have full "recall" facilities, including fader movements. With motorized faders, all such movements can be recorded and replayed. In the past, people used that recording device called the human brain and those motorized objects called fingers.

Jack Joseph Puig:

> Automation has become very important because at this point in time, recall is something that everybody in the world wants to do and does. It's funny, I think I would give a Grammy to SSL! [SSL produced the first Total Recall console in 1977. —*Ed.*] It gives us the ability to go in, listen to, fiddle with, and change things if we like. Every button, every switch, every knob, every send, and so on is recallable.

Bringing Up the Tracks

Mixing is about making decisions. Now is the time when different takes, blends of different mics, even maybe entire parts themselves vie for selection in the final product. Whether we're working in the box or bringing up tracks on a large-format console—which we did during the mixing section of the *ASSR* video series, the process begins with listening, track by track, to the material we recorded and seeing what we've got and what needs to be done with it.

If you are fortunate enough to be working on a console with lots of faders, the time-honored system of using a marker pen on masking tape to name your tracks is simple, direct, and very helpful. So too is bringing up all your tracks in some sort of logical order: bass, then all the drums, percussion, guitars, keys, vocals, etc., etc.

Alan:

> I have tried to stick to the same tracks and channel numbers for the rhythm section of everything I've done for years—so I don't need to mark the console for anything basic. So I know the bass is on track 1, the kick is on track 2, the overheads are on channels 3 and 4, and so on.

In rock and pop genres, as well as in metal, hip-hop, R&B, electronic, dance, and almost all forms of "popular" music—drums are the engine room of the recording. Unless we just have a stereo loop from a drum machine or a sample generating the drums, drummer-played drums will generally have been recorded on several tracks. So, for reasons both artistic and practical, it's common practice to look at the drum tracks first, make some basic choices, and get the drums as a whole to sit well together.

On "All Our Yesterdays," there were actually twenty-six tracks of Simon Phillips' drums! Viewers of the video series may recall that the song was recorded at Simon's studio. That's drummers for you!

We had some interesting material. The kick drum was represented by three different sources: Simon's left kick drum, his right kick drum, and a speaker contraption along the lines of Yamaha's Subkick that gave it some really nice bottom end. The overheads were panned left and right; the snare drum, on its own track, was kept in the center. The hi-hat also on its own track, we panned hard right, but at a level that makes it appear half-right (more about hi-hat panning later). The toms were panned out in a stereo spread. Note that this is seen from the audience perspective, not the drummer's.

Sometimes EQ and intrinsically important effects will already be printed or committed to on tape or disk, but the balance between the component parts needs to be reassessed, starting from scratch.

Then we listen: Is the kick drum punchy enough? Is the snare laying down a strong enough offbeat? Are the tom fills and cymbal crashes coming through clearly?

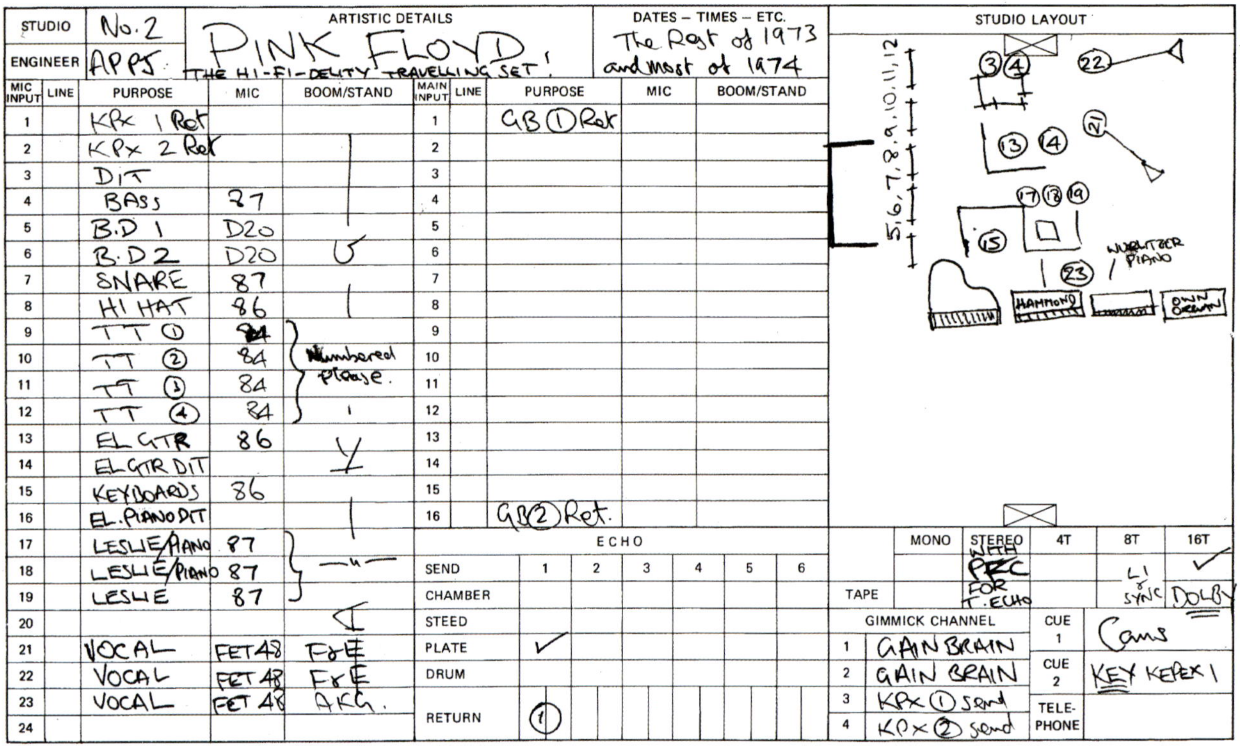

FIGURE 23.4. Alan's recreation of a mid-1970s Pink Floyd track sheet.

Alan:

> When I solo the snare, it's going to have a completely different sound from how it sounds when it's mixed into the whole kit, so it's always worth bearing that in mind. It's important to realize that the snare mic is probably never going to sound very good on its own, but in context it'll hopefully sound pretty good.

Elliot Scheiner:

> I spend a good deal of time working in drums until I get it to the point where I think that everything that goes in after that is going to work well. And then I add instruments and make a mix of an individual instrument to the drums, and then that becomes the foundation.
>
> So, the next thing that goes in for me is bass. I'm always listening for the relationship between the bass drum and the bass. And after that, it will go to percussion, and then I'll bring in instrument by instrument, but it's always with relationship to the drums.

A popular technique is to add each instrument one at a time to the drum mix at a level that feels right, gradually building up the mix until all the ingredients are in the "mixing bowl" in the right proportions. But there are no hard-and-fast rules, as Alan explains:

> In fact, what I generally do at mixing stage is put everything in *excluding* bass and drums, so that I can tell we're hearing everything else that's going on. Bass and drums

are so dominant in rock 'n' roll, but you really need to address the melodic parts as a separate process. When I have a good basic balance of the rhythm section—i.e., bass and drums—contrary to what most engineers would do at this point, which would be to start adding other things, I like to take the bass and drums out and then start listening to other things on their own.

I prefer to start with the other instruments in the rhythm section, like rhythm guitars and keyboards—a technique I learned from Beatles engineer Geoff Emerick. If all the basic instruments, apart from bass and drums, are in the correct proportion, not only level-wise but also their position in the stereo picture, I should be able to feel a good balance in the rhythm section . . . the guitars, keyboards, percussion, and so on. I'll even think about adding in backing vocals and orchestration before finally bringing in the bass and drums and adding in the lead vocal and any solo instruments.

The mix is when any shortcomings in the track will be revealed and need to be addressed. For instance, on our mix for "All Our Yesterdays," we felt that the keyboard pad part played by Rami Jaffee sounded a bit "too mono" (even though it was recorded in stereo). A trick you can use to create more of a stereo feel is to put a small delay (around 30–80 milliseconds) on one side, with both the original tracks on the other side.

The Stereo Picture

Consumers often find it hard to grasp the really quite simple concept that stereo is made up of a "panorama" of sounds spread between the left and right speakers.

On a console—physical or virtual—"panpots" allow us to move each source anywhere from extreme left to extreme right. We're not changing the volume of the sound, just its position in the stereo image. Different stereo pan positions are based upon how much of a sound is being fed to each speaker. With the panpot set to extreme left, the right speaker has no information at all. Moving the panpot to the center, the sound is heard as a "phantom center" image between the speakers—not just "in both speakers," as the uninitiated would say. Continuing to move the panpot to extreme right position means the right channel will get gradually louder and the left channel correspondingly quieter, until at extreme right no sound is present in the left speaker.

Each recorded sound has to be placed somewhere in the space between left and right, although some sounds will have their own inherent stereo spread on two tracks and will generally be simply panned hard left and right. But we might decide that a stereo source sounds better on one side or in the center. Filling the stereo space and holding the balance and interest between left and right is an important skill in the mixing process. Bad mixes will favor one side too heavily or have too much information in the center and sound effectively mono.

Alan:

> Creating interesting and engaging stereo is something you will be given credit for—trust me.

Backing vocals or clusters of instruments recorded on several tracks spread across the panorama can help create stunning stereo spreads. Stereo reverbs and delays can also enhance the feeling of space.

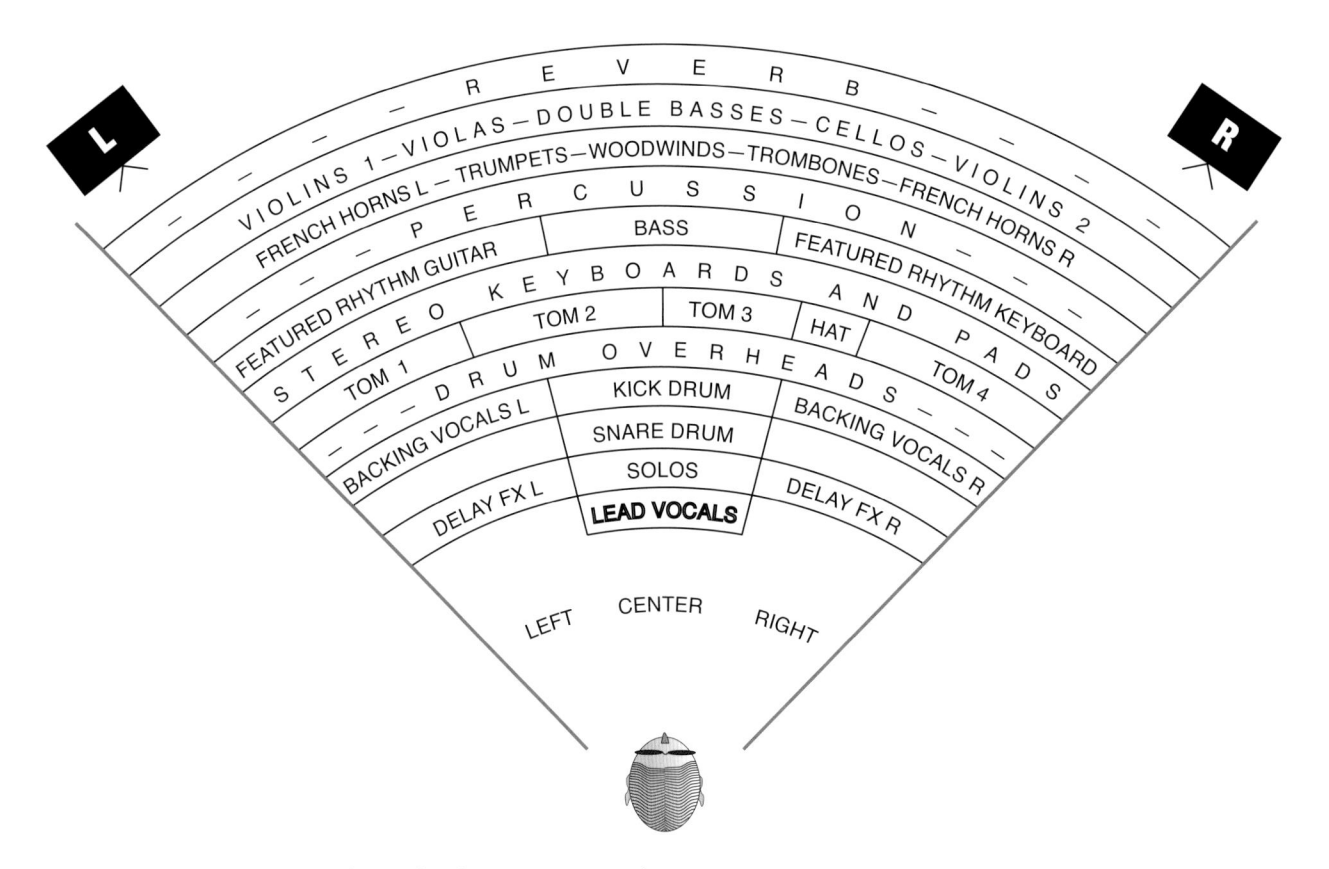

FIGURE 23.5. **A good starting point for your stereo picture.**

Drum Panning

On a set of drums there are left, right, and center sound sources that you can both see and hear. It's a good starting point to pan the individual drum tracks, so as to re-create a drum kit's natural stereo image. It's a question of taste whether you like to create the stereo picture as from the drummer's or the audience's perspective.

Alan:

> I like to bring each drum/track up on its own and set the pan position for each drum/track accordingly. I often re-pan the toms from their natural position to give tom fills a more dramatic stereo effect.

"Center" drums would commonly be kick and snare drum. Toms can be panned as required, and overheads would be generally hard left and right.

Alan:

> A lot of people ask me about hi-hat panning. Here's a little trade secret: I usually pan the hi-hat hard right, but mix it at a level which makes it appear slightly to right of center. This is because the snare mic inevitably has a lot of hi-hat on it and so will appear to be center along with the snare. So gradually increasing the hi-hat level [panned right] to place it a little bit to the right of center gives it the necessary definition and place in the stereo. But if the hi-hat track is actually heard hard right, it's always too loud. It sounds natural a little to the right because that's where it is on the kit.

With any ambient mic tracks, as well as overheads, you'll create the most "space" by panning those hard left and right.

Processing

An important aspect of mixing is the choice and application of EQ, reverbs, delays, and other audio goodies. The choice of reverb, especially on the vocal, will set the scene and give the listener an impression of the size and type of space the music is being played in.

Jack Joseph Puig:

> Different types of equipment all have different types of feelings and perspectives and sounds, and I like making a collage of what I think is the best of the different pieces of equipment. Not only that, each piece of equipment has a sound and an attitude and perspective that another piece of equipment doesn't have. So I like the idea of having a box of sixty-four Crayolas, as opposed to eight.

Mixing is a process of continual assessment and reassessment. Initially, we might be looking at individual tracks to make sure they are all generally in the right place and space. But eventually we might start to notice shortcomings in a sound that can be addressed by EQ or some kind of effect to enhance it . . .

For example, if the drums are a little lacking in overall brightness, we might try EQing the overheads to give the cymbals a bit more splashiness. After adding EQ, it's a good idea to check the sound with the EQ in—and then out—to assess what the change is achieving in the mix.

Elliot Scheiner:

> Usually, once everything gets in, I'm either changing a little bit of the EQ on the bass or a little bit of the EQ on the kick. I generally use the Steinberg EQ, because I really like the way it sounds and what it does and how gentle it can be.

Alan:

> I'll usually establish a reverb "type" for the vocal first, then think about what instruments need similar treatment. Sometimes I'll bring up a different style of reverb so that certain instruments can appear to be in a different space, if it works for the song.

Elliot Scheiner:

> A lot of the times when I get music to mix, I try and think about this being recorded in one room at the same time. That's the way I grew up, that's the way I think music works best. When you see musicians working off one another, you know, the bass player played something, and the guitar was motivated by that lick to do something else. A lot of times, you don't get that benefit, but you try to create that idea in the studio.

Alan:

> I would normally spend time looking at the lead vocal and solos on their own first without, then with their effects and processing before adding them to the mix, in the same way you would check the quality of the main ingredient before adding it to the mixing bowl.

If the reverb you already have on the drums and percussion and guitars is sounding pretty nice, it's worth trying the same reverb on the voice. See how it sounds. Are there any problem moments or words?

Reverbs and delays are often governed by the style of the music, which will most likely have been established during the recording. A mix session is a good time to experiment if you haven't found the perfect vocal sound by now. But if the effect you've been listening to during the recording still works well, don't tempt disaster by tweaking minute details. It's a mistake to feel you need to change things *just because you're mixing*. The "if it ain't broke" rule can apply to the mix as a whole. You might want to think about saving key parts as dry unprocessed stems in case you want to come back and redo any processing, or if you think there's a question mark on the effects you've applied.

It's very easy to spend too long in a mixing session and get nowhere, as Tony Brown explains:

> A lot of times, I tell you, man, the tracking rough has been the final mix of the track. Because they've just been impulsive and just throwing things up and flying by the seat of their pants, and it's so amazing, when I like that, they get upset. They go, "Man, that was a rough mix." And, I go, "But it was your rough mix, and I love it." You should be flattered and say, God, thanks man, as opposed to getting upset with me for taking a rough mix.

Groups and Stems

Once you've achieved what you feel is a good drum balance, it's useful to group the drum tracks so that a single fader will adjust all the drums at a set balance. On a large analog console this may be possible using VCA groups. There's plenty of explanation about VCA grouping online. Digital consoles take all this in their stride, and you can even group the groups.

David Thoener:

> If I have maybe twenty backing vocals—instead of bringing up all the backing vocals on the console, I'll bring them up in Pro Tools. I'll EQ them, compress them, process them in Pro Tools, and bring them up on the console in stereo. It makes my console mix a lot easier to deal with. Sometimes, I'll have the entire drum kit come up in stereo. So, I'll have stereo groups come up and then use the console for my summing, which is why people ask me to use a console in the first place.

Similar to groups, in that they're combinations of tracks sub-mixed to a pair of tracks, are *stems*, which are often created within the mix so that key elements of the track can be rebalanced later on. Stems can be groups of like-minded instruments or sounds—in other words, all the keyboards, all the guitars, backing vocals, drums, strings, and so on, complete with their reverbs and effects. It's sensible to leave the bass as a separate stem. When all the stems are added together at the same level, you should theoretically end up with the same balance as on your composite mix.

Labels will often hire a remix engineer to work from stems, as opposed to working from the original multitrack—often a frustration to the guy who created them!

Jimmy Douglass:

> Yes, my work gets farmed out to other mixers, and usually it gets farmed out after I've already mixed it, and I've given them stems of my mix, and all they have to do is basically just kind of open it up and just fix all the little things, and then they'll call it their mix. That's kind of the new world, and, you know, I'm not bitter over it, because it is what it is.

Alan:

> It's always a good idea to have a song recorded in such a way that when all the tracks are open at roughly the same level, we hear a reasonably good balance. You will get credit for good technique if the faders on the DAW are in a reasonably straight line and not showing every track at totally different levels. As well as being convenient for the next time I work on the track, it's also a kind of courtesy to another engineer working on the track for the first time.

Sylvia Massy:

> There's another advantage to having everything sound good when you push up those faders. Because, if your project leaves your hands and goes to another mixer or another engineer, there's very little that they can screw up at that point; it's more they have to work to screw it up, because you've done the work for them. And also, if you've summed all the drums to a stereo pair, everything will be placed the way that you intended on it being placed when you recorded it.
>
> Actually, my strategy for recording these days is to record everything in a way where if you just push up these faders, monitoring back what you've recorded, and you have panning in left and right pairs, that everything just is premixed. Not that it would have a bunch of effects like delay or anything on it, but that the sounds are recorded in such a way that there is very little work to do to get the basics sounding good.

A *straight line mix* is a kind of holy grail.

The Vocal Level

The relationship of the lead vocal to everything else is a crucial part of mixing, and the most likely subject of criticism. If it's too loud, it will weaken the perceived power of the backing instruments. If it's too quiet, it will sound insignificant or lacking in importance. It can be a fashion thing, a genre thing, or just a case of whether the words can be heard. It's always a good idea to do a mix without vocals, so that the vocal levels can be reassessed later without having to call up the whole mix again. The same applies to solo instruments, which generally need to be at the same apparent level as the vocal, or they will sound strange. Some producers will print mixes with the vocal deliberately louder or quieter, so that they can accommodate their own changes of heart or the criticism of others constructively

Checking the Mix

Having achieved a satisfactory mix, you'll probably want to compare it on a number of different systems, and since this is the iPod generation, you'll want to see if it works on headphones or even on the worst invention of the century—earbuds. You might also want to check how much deterioration is going to be caused by MP3 encoding. There's no substitute for knowing your own studio sound system, but there's also no harm in checking your mix on a small pair of speakers or in other listening environments. You may even want to copy your mix to a USB stick or CD and check the mix in the car.

Alan:

> One of the things I've always done is to step outside the room, and just listen to the mix from the passageway outside. That way you just get an overall impression of the mix as a record—I'll just listen almost as if I'm a consumer hearing it coming from a radio or TV in another room, I'll make sure that everything is there and that the vocal is at the right balance, and so on.

Jack Douglas:

> What I like the most is a Bose wave radio. If I do my final mix on there, my mix will be competitive, and if you listen to it on your iPhone or headphones, or if you listen to it on your computer, it's going to sound right.

On the other hand, some engineers will argue that every last detail has to be heard—on the best system with the best response and lowest distortion characteristics. But not everyone agrees.

Jack Douglas:

> I love it, too. I'm as crazy about masturbation as anybody, but really, no one is listening like that anymore. You know, I like to create pieces of music that you can appreciate at that level, so I try to make that kind of depth and fidelity work in that little wave monitor. And when I do, it's rockin' everywhere.

Levels

It's important that the mix we deliver is at a level comfortably below the distortion or "clipping" threshold. If we don't allow enough headroom, even if the meters tell us that we're at a comfortable level, we might still actually be dangerously close to distortion on transient or percussive sounds. If you're using VU meters as your level reference, zero VU should be somewhere between 12 and 18 dB below digital zero. We recommend −14. You can calibrate your system to the required level by using a professional test disk like Sound Check (see **figure 4.4, p. 40**). (Shameless self-promotion. —*Ed.*)

Alan:

> Although a good balance is a good balance, there are other parameters that need to be taken into consideration. One of these is what I call "spectral" response—in other words, is the sound of our mix going to stand up against other commercial recordings? This tends to be a fashion thing; at one moment in time mixes may tend to be very bright, or at another be completely dominated by a thumping kick drum. This is where we have to decide whether the entire mix needs EQ, compression, and of course the big debate in the industry: how "loud" should it be? This hot topic has become known in the industry as the "Loudness Wars."

We talk about compressing mixes in Chapter 9, but it's worth mentioning here that countless engineers base their entire approach to mixing on the application of mix compression.

Elliot Scheiner:

> At some point in my career, maybe ten to twelve years ago, I was using bus compression and bus EQ compression or EQ across the whole mix on the stereo mixes. And I guess four or five years ago, I eliminated the bus EQ. I felt it was way too much, way over the top. I do keep the bus compression, though.
>
> I've got to say, as far as the bus compression goes, it's not to compress the mix; it's more for the sound of the device. It will just catch occasional peaks, but it's barely hitting the overall mix. I use a Neve 33609, and I really like the way that particular box sounds, and so I use that across all my mixes. I have it in my home studio—I go D-to-A, A-to-D, you know, just because I like what that box does.

Alan:

> Call me old school if you like, but you won't find a compressor on my mix bus. I prefer to hold onto dynamics as long as humanly possible. I think decisions like this are best left until the mastering stage. Mastering engineers are well equipped to make judgments about these elements, particularly in the context of current trends. Different processes might be needed for online delivery, CD, TV, radio, and other media.

Sylvia Massy:

> One trick I learned from Rick Rubin for mixing with automation is something he calls "slippery fader." That's where you take . . . when your mix is nearly finished, if you want

> to give the choruses an extra punch, you just take your master fader, your stereo bus fader, and you just give it a little boost right on the choruses or in a bridge, or wherever you want it, just give it a little more excitement. And it's so subtle that you can't really hear it, but you feel it. I thought that was always a really great way to use automation.

In the days of mixing to tape, we had to keep a very close eye on our meters. If we had even a momentary peak, it would cause a problem—particularly on mastering to disc for vinyl. For those who are rediscovering vinyl, you'll need to take heed of this issue, as well as other problems like phase and excessive bass when mastering.

Destination Media

The nice thing about mixing on a big console is that you have each individual sound on a fader—faders you can actually touch and feel. You really do get a different perspective on how sounds have been combined, and get a good visual indication of everything that's going on right in front of you.

Of course, as well as mixing our tracks down to stereo and putting the mix back onto the hard disk, we might choose to also record it to quarter-inch tape. Many producers still swear that the analog-ness of tape can be recaptured at the mixing stage.

Jack Joseph Puig:

> I'm still mixing to tape, only because it's the only time that we will have used tape at this point. And sometimes, it can be great. I think to speak in absolutes is idiotic. Digital has everything that's wonderful about it, and so does analog. Neither one is better than the other one. So, like the blonde and the brunette, sometimes you like both, and sometimes you have your eye on the redhead, and that's equally as great. My style has always been pinching from the different decades and pinching from the different styles.

Housekeeping

Elliot Scheiner:

> The idea of taking notes has been completely forgotten about. I know some of the schools still teach it. I don't know if these kids come out and they just ignore it, or it's once they get into the studio, nobody is telling them, please keep a track sheet or keep notes, or something. You never get any of the benefit of that.
>
> I don't think that's a problem anymore, except with consolidation. I guess if you keep notes in the files that you're using on another proprietary system, you don't get the benefit of that on another system. I've seen occasions, like in Pro Tools, where under the track, they'll write a little note here and there, you know, "Use this in second chorus only," or something. But, generally, I haven't seen anything that transfers over like that. So that could be a cross-platform issue, which reinforces more the need for somebody to take physical notes.

Jimmy Douglass:

> My example would be like if I got a tape to mix something from you [*smiles knowingly at Alan*], I can tell you what I'm going to expect to see. If it was a multitrack, I'm going to expect to see *X* amount of tracks, they're going to be laid out, their effects with them, and so forth. And, pretty much I can put it down, open it up on the board, and then right off the bat, I've got a basic record I can now play, and now I can do what I need to do. As opposed to what I will expect today—I will get a file from here, a file from there, a file from here, a file from there, and a file from here, and I've got to put them all together. There's duplicates; they're not really duplicate, because they punched in one line on one of those ones. Well, which one is it? Well, I don't know, you have to listen to it and find out. So now, I'm sitting here listening and comparing for half of my time—most of my time just listening and comparing. I'll do a mix, and they'll go, "Did you listen to the rough?" "Actually, I didn't want to listen to the rough. I wanted to give you what I *thought it should be*." "Oh, we love the rough. We love the rough." Don't you understand? So now I'm sitting and comparing everything in the rough to all the stuff, and now, you know what, I'm not giving you anything that I wanted to give you, because I'm tired.

Alan:

> For the record, that's my favorite quote in the whole book.

The moral of this story—take notes until you're blue in the face, preferably on paper or in readme text files that explain anything and everything. Make sure every track is identified, when it is to be used if there is doubt, and once again CONSOLIDATE—if you don't, it will end in tears.

The mix is the final statement. The culmination of all the work you've put into your track. Is your mix just a formality representing what you've been building up with tracking, overdubs, and refinements, or is it a complete reassessment of what you've recorded? Or a revamp of work created by someone else? Whatever happens, it's important to make sure the mix contains your stamp and your personality. You should fight for that at all costs.

24

DEALING WITH DISASTERS

A studio disaster comes in many forms. You can spend time and money on a session that simply doesn't produce anything worthwhile. You can produce something worthwhile, but at the end everyone hates each other. Or you can produce something worthwhile, everyone loves everyone, and then you lose it all because you didn't make a backup.

In this closing chapter we're going to look share some studio horror stories and look at various ways to make sure all your studio experiences have happy endings.

In the days of analog tape, there was the master tape and that was your record, period. It could get lost, erased by magnetic fields on a subway train, or get mangled up by a tape machine, almost all of which could get laid at the door of human error.

Chuck Ainlay:

> One of the early recordings I did on a 3M digital machine out at the Castle when I was working with Deborah Allen. One of the songs was a first take. Although we had done subsequent takes, it was the first take that we decided to use. Back then there wasn't another machine to make a safety to. That was it. And the machine was fragile. So, it was Fourth of July, and at the Castle we had a big window on the side of the control room. I remember there were fireworks going off and everything outside there, and I walked by the tape machine, and it had these little wires that hung out of it where you could bounce one track to another. There was just some dangling other wires and my leg brushed against the multi-pair, and it threw one of those wires into the open card cage and all of the sudden the machine went into fast-forward and rewind at the same time and snapped the tape. I mean it stretched about this much tape [a lot!], so there was no way to cut it and put it back together.
>
> I called her, and she came out and I had the broken bit of tape in the wastebasket. She walked in and saw the tape, and she just clutched it in her hands and went crying out of the studio, knowing

> that was it, you know . . . But I figured out a way to use one of the other takes and repair that section. I had to do it because there wasn't a machine to make a safety to it. It all had to be done through the 4-track digital machine, back to a slave machine, and rebuilt. But I was able to put together something, and in the end it was actually a cooler little piece that got put back in there.

There's usually a way to fashion a happy ending to most disasters.
Jack Douglas:

> On John Lennon's *Imagine* album, I worked with Phil Spector. I kept a book when I was a kid working on these projects of what works and what doesn't. And Phil, well, he pretty much filled my book of what doesn't work. Including pulling guns in studios.

While Spector is currently making license plates, Jack runs a course on studio "etiquette" at Expression College in California. And truly, etiquette is more important than you might think.

Some Studio Rules

- Artists are allowed to arrive late. As an engineer, you're not. And as a producer, you should not.
- For engineers, if the producer or artist asks, "What do you think?" that's the only time you should offer any creative input. And any comments should always be positive. "This track sucks" is not going to win you any gigs.
- Phone calls and texting are fine on a break, but don't do it while the singer is pouring his or her heart out in the vocal booth. Multitasking is a myth—sorry, folks.
- Finally, just be pleasant, no matter how unpleasant your coworkers are. There's nothing like a glum expression to get everyone's juices flowing back into wherever they came from.

The biggest disaster any session can encounter is where the personalities are in conflict or the mood isn't right. Equally damaging to the vibe of a session is when equipment breaks down and things grind to a halt.
Jack Douglas:

> One of my early gigs was cutting a Patti LaBelle track. She was really wonderful and very patient. I was cutting the track on this wonderful old custom-made board, just full of . . . you could fry eggs on it, if you know what I mean. One of those tube consoles full of transformers. And, I thought the tracks were good R&B tracks that were really hot and popping, and I thought, oh, this is great.
>
> Patti came in for a playback, and I was so happy that it sounded so great. The bass player came around behind me and put his beer between me and the remote, and when I reached for the remote to hit playback I spilt the beer, which went directly into the transformers. The whole board went up in flames. Most of it melted, and the rest was destroyed by the fire extinguisher.

Notwithstanding an extreme experience like Jack's, one of the skills an engineer should develop is dealing with technical problems without disrupting the session.

Chuck Ainlay:

> The first thing you try and do is find a workaround without anybody knowing about it. Particularly during tracks, the last thing you want to do is stop the flow. So you try and find a way to just get by, because it's really more about the music than the technical aspect. A little bit of distortion you can cover up in a mix or something. So, not that you're trying to mislead anybody, but it's really more about capturing the music and keeping the vibe intact than making the perfect recording. Who gives a shit, you know? But if it's something severe enough, then you bring it up. Everybody's been in those situations—the producers, the artists. And so, maybe it's lunchtime; they can take an early lunch break or something while you deal with it.

The best engineers and producers just know what to do when things aren't going to plan, whatever the reason.

Niko Bolas:

> The best producers I know are the guys who show up a little bit early and they always give 100 percent. They also know that the only difference between getting a take and not getting a take is being able to admit that we didn't get it. But the effort is always the same. You're always trying to get it. It's just that the really good producers don't push it. Music happens when it happens. You don't get a take just because you want it—you know: "I really want to get a master today, so we're gonna just beat this into the ground." No, the really smart guys are the ones who say, "Let's go to dinner. It ain't happening."

Equipment: Preparation and Troubleshooting

First, know how—and that—your equipment works before the session starts. A session is not the place to learn a new piece of kit, and the words "Oh, wow, this monitor/compressor/mic/you-name-it . . . doesn't seem to be working" uttered at nine-fifteen in the morning are going to be about as welcome as hearing something similar from your pilot just as you clear the control tower. Don't risk sending your session into a tailspin either.

Carry spares, especially cables and connectors. It's a good idea to keep your software updated and your hardware (and underwear) maintained. (Personal hygiene is definitely a deal-breaker!)

It's best to make sure you always have plenty of space on your hard drives. If things do go wrong—and they will—a technical problem can ruin the atmosphere on an otherwise happy session faster than an A&R man saying, "It didn't bother me, but let's try another mix." Technical problems can and always will appear from time to time. The only difference between a pro and an amateur is how you deal with it.

Here are some approaches:

Without letting on that there is a problem, quickly switch channels, switch the mic, change the cable, whatever you need to do to keep the session alive.

Experience will dictate how quickly or efficiently you can troubleshoot problems, but as a general rule it's best to work backwards along the recording chain. In other words, if you hear a crackling out of the speakers, for example, try to determine if it's just that—is it just coming from the speakers or the monitoring section?—and not affecting anything you might be recording at that moment. Then try to assess whether it's on all channels or just one channel by soloing the outputs one at a time. If the crackle has reverb on it, you know you can narrow it down to the sources where you have applied reverb. Or is it the reverb unit or plug-in that's causing the problem? Once you've found the problem at a particular output, patch that output to a different channel and see if the problem goes away. If not, continue going back along the chain. Logic prevails. So once you've found the crackly channel . . . does it still happen when the source is brought in to a different console or DAW channel? Still there? Try another A-to-D converter, then eliminate the equalizer or any other patched in processing like a compressor or limiter. Bypass them and see if it cures the problem. If it's a mic source, change the mic pre and finally the mic itself. It's sometimes best just to change everything in the chain, get on with the session, and figure out the problem later. Sometimes the nature of the problem will dictate the course of action.

Chuck Ainlay:

> I wouldn't say I'm technical, but I'm technical to the point to where, you know, if it's a crackling, I probably know that it's an analog thing. Or, if it's a sort of spiky little thing, that's a digital thing.

Causes, Effects, and Cures

In the days of analog tape, the most common "disaster" was accidentally erasing something. Younger readers may be shocked to learn that "undo" is a very, very recent concept. If there was a possibility of wiping something, you always tried to find an option where it was less likely to happen. You could make a backup or "safety copy," as we called them, but usually if something got wiped, barring miracle cures, the only way to get it back was to record it again.

Alan:

> I remember early in my tape-opping days that I was asked to play an earlier take of a completed "live in the studio" pop orchestra session conducted by Brian Fahey, recorded on 4-track. The producer said, no, that's no good, we'll use the later take. I got distracted while the orchestra was preparing to record the next tune and on the cue to "roll tape," I did so. A few seconds later, I noticed that the tape counter was showing numbers that it shouldn't—I had forgotten to fast-forward past the "good" take. After a brief period with head in hands while the band was still playing, I walked up to the engineer, Peter Bown, apparently white-faced by all accounts, sheepishly saying, "I have bad news." He immediately said, "Have you wiped something?" I said, "Yes, we are a minute in to the good take of the last title—I can stop tape now if you like." The decision was made to break the news to the producer after this take. I was amazed to be greeted by the producer, Norman Newell, with "Oh, bad luck, Alan—thanks for owning up," rather than "You stupid dimwit." As luck would have it, there was plenty of spare time on the three-hour union session to rerecord the ill-fated tune entirely, and in fact all concerned said they thought it was much better than the take that got erased. I hadn't lost my job and everyone seemed happy! I got drunk that night.

Today's nightmares are about data loss—either a complete one, as in "My hard drive's crashed," or temporary ones, as in "Where IS that USB stick—maybe it's down the back of the sofa?" Or "Where's that file on my computer and what did I call it?"

There are all kinds of stories about the wrong take or mix being sent to the factory, and in extreme cases the consumer even hearing the wrong version. One case in point was a Rolf Harris release in mono that only contained one side of the original stereo mix. Entire vocal and instrumental performances were missing. Another was a bagpipe recording that got to the factory with the master tape having been played backwards at mastering.

Well, would you know?

Now more than ever, it's best to avoid the words "final" or "master" in a filename. Just date it. Abbey Road's policy was to mark a take BEST rather than MASTER and only mark it MASTER when there was absolutely no doubt that it was the definitive version. It's worth the time spent to go back to any previous unwanted versions and either erase them or put them in an "OLD VERSIONS" folder so that there is no room for error. It's also a good idea to mark the drives themselves, but avoid meaningless labels such as this classic that Alan's father once found on a can in a film archive: EDITS FOR TOMORROW.

Backups are absolutely key, as we've said over and over in this series, and you might want to devise your own personal backup schedule. Storing physical backup drives in a different location is always a good idea, in case of fire or acts of God. Allegedly, a number of classic Bob Marley tapes were lost in a fire in Ghana. Storing the data online on a server or FTP site is also an increasingly viable option. During the mix of "All Our Yesterdays," recorded for this series, we inadvertently lost some material—but because we had data stored online, we were able to save the day on that occasion.

A word or two about "power conditioners" with battery backup, and other general protective devices and systems that protect you against power surges and interruptions. Good idea!

We look at basic housekeeping in Chapter 23 on mixing, and certainly the more organized you are, the better your chances are of averting disaster in the first place and dealing with it should one occur.

Disasters can also be caused by "misunderstandings."

Alan:

> I have a vivid memory of recording an overdub of a brass section. We recorded a good take, and then the producer started talking about different voicings and inversions of the instruments and the brass section rehearsed the new arrangement without the track. Then the producer said, let's record it. I erased the original track to make way for the new version. Then the producer says, "I'm only hearing the new part. Where's the first part?" "STOP!" I yelled at the tape op, who of course was completely without any blame for this. Well—to cut a long story short, the section had to rerecord the first part again before we finally added the second part on a separate track. A very red-faced me that day.

Although this scenario would have been totally curable on a DAW, the moral of the story is, always be clear about what's happening on a session and make sure there aren't any misunderstandings.

Although we now live in the high-tech age of nondestructive recording on computers, and backups are possible, we still have to deal with an occasional computer crash. Several supposedly magic moments have been lost to the whims of microprocessors. The best attitude to take is that the next crash is just around the corner. Backup, backup again, and backup the backup is always a good policy.

Just one final word about computer crashes: If you're working on an important file that hasn't been bocked ip, gdfget hdgry jkshfdk ckl s dlllfjjds kajdhgfu.

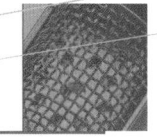

GLOSSARY

A440 Hz: A tuning standard for the frequency representing the musical pitch of the "A" note above middle C. Some countries use 442 Hz as the standard, which is slightly sharper and can cause tuning problems. Electronic tuners or mechanical standard tuning forks allow instruments to be tuned to the correct pitch.

ADAT: Alesis Digital Audio Tape—initially described a popular digital recording hardware unit made by the Alesis company in the 1990s. Currently, ADAT is the name commonly used for the ADAT Lightpipe protocol, which can communicate eight tracks of digital audio along a single fiber-optic cable. ADAT is used by A-D converters and digital input devices.

A-D/D-A: Conversion of an audio signal from analog to digital, or from digital to analog. This can be carried out at different resolutions, with accordingly different quality levels.

additive synthesis: A type of synthesis that creates sound by combining ("adding") harmonics at varying pitches and levels. A Hammond organ employs, in effect, an additive synthesis system with its drawbars.

ADSR: Attack, Decay, Sustain, and Release. These are the four most commonly used segments of stages of a synthesizer's envelope generator. Attack controls the time it takes an applied parameter to reach its initial level; Decay, the time it takes for that parameter to transition to a "sustain" level; Sustain governs the time an applied parameter will remain at the level to which is has settled; and Release, the duration of an applied parameter to fade out once a "note off" is generated. While envelope generators are most commonly found as sections or panels on a synthesizer, MIDI does provide for general control over these parameters.

AES/EBU: A professional format for exchanging digital audio signals. AES/EBU can communicate two channels of digital audio using a variety of transmission cables. Stands for "Audio Engineering Society/European Broadcast Union."

after touch: A MIDI parameter that measures the level of intensity applied to a note after it has been played and continues to be depressed. After touch can be polyphonic (different notes will respond individually in a cluster of held notes) or monophonic (one value will apply to all notes held down). Typically, after touch is useful for adding vibrato or pitch bend effects.

AIFF: Proprietary file format for storing and transferring audio data on the Mac platform.

All Notes Off: A MIDI channel message that tells a MIDI sound-generating device to shut off all currently active notes. This is a life-saving panic button to cure "hanging" MIDI notes.

ambience: Ambience mics capture the atmospheric or ambient sound in a room as opposed to a direct recording focused on and close to the sound source.

amp simulation: Electronic circuits that mimic the sound of a guitar amplifier.

analog: Used to describe devices/outputs/processes that deal with sound on the basis of variable frequency and amplitude—i.e., in a non-digital, non-computer-based way. In the case of synthesizers, a word that describes old-style, voltage-controlled synthesis systems.

arpeggiator: An automatic playing feature on a synthesizer that generates sequences of notes when a note or chord is held down.

ASIO: Audio Stream Input/Output is a driver protocol developed by German music software ("und hardware") giant Steinberg. ASIO is a popular choice, enabling low-latency and high-fidelity communication between software applications and computer hardware.

attack: See "ADSR."

attenuate: To reduce the level of a signal. An attenuation might also be referred to as a "pad."

automation/automated mix: The process of specifying and recording data to control real-time changes in a mix to sounds, signals, processes, levels, and more. Such maneuvers recorded within a DAW's timeline can then run and operate "automatically," without the need for constant hands-on human control.

Aux: Short for auxiliary. Most commonly, Aux is seen in conjunction with "Send" and "Return" to describe a channel or bus of communication along which a signal can be routed.

balanced cable: A professional cable that uses three wires—two to deliver the electrical signal and the third, a wrapped conductor, to act as a shield to help reduce interference along long lengths. The "balance" refers to equal impedance at both source and load. XLR and TRS are common connectors used for balanced cables.

band-pass filter: A type of filter that eliminates both higher and lower frequencies around a specified "band" of frequencies. More inclined toward special effects than "natural" tonalities.

bank: A collective storage location that houses multiple sounds, samples, patterns, etc. In MIDI, an individual bank can hold up to 127 items. MIDI also allows for many different banks to be selected using "Bank Select" commands.

binary: A system of numbering using only the digits 0 and 1. This is the foundation of computer language. MIDI is a binary system.

bit/byte: An abbreviation for "binary digit," a *bit* is the most basic unit of information used in any digital system. There are normally 8 bits to a *byte*, but in MIDI there are two additional bits: one to signify "start"; the second, "stop."

bit depth: Bit depth is the number of bits (1s or 0s in a binary number) used to describe digital data at a given point in time. One such point in time is a *sample*. Each added bit doubles the number of possible ways to describe each individual sample. A 16-bit sample can be described with any one of 65,536 values, whereas a 24-bit sample has 16,777,216 possible values.

buffer: An area of RAM used to temporarily store data.

bus/buss: A signal route within a device or section of a device such as a mixer (software or hardware).

CD (compact disc): A five-inch optical disc developed by Philips and Sony in the 1980s offering good-quality digital sound reproduction. CD uses a 44.1 kHz sampling rate and, upon its introduction, offered near-indestructibility compared with its predecessors the vinyl "record" and stereo cassette tape. CD remains a media storage option, albeit one with a low capacity.

channel: A discrete path of signal flow. On a console, a "channel" strip comprises all the controls and processors that can be applied to an individual signal. See also "MIDI channel."

chorus: An audio effect that superimposes two or more versions of a sound upon itself at different or varying pitches, so producing a thicker, sometimes "swirling" effect. Chorus thickens a sound.

controller: A hardware device providing immediate, hands-on control over a software program. Controllers often resemble recording consoles, with their faders, knobs, and buttons, but controllers do not actually pass audio.

CPU (central processing unit): The brain of a computer; the silicon chip that performs the major calculations.

crossfade: A smooth and gradual transition from one sound or signal into another.

cutoff: A parameter found on filters. A filter, as its name suggests, removes various frequencies in a sound and so changes its tone. A filter is basically a tone control. The cutoff parameter selects the frequency at which filtering takes place.

DAT: Digital Audio Tape. Slow-moving but high-quality digital tape on a small cassette that enjoyed a brief period of success in the 1990s, when it became an industry standard for master recording. Typically, DAT stores two tracks of audio, plus subcode and track info. In an attempt to fight off "master quality" bootlegging, the SCMS protection code was built into most DAT players, which prevented copying from a copy.

DAW: Digital Audio Workstation. The name given to computer-based recording tools.

dB: An abbreviation of "decibel." A decibel is a measurement of sound pressure level—i.e., loudness. This can be both a fixed measurement, as in jet aircraft noise producing 150 dB (enough to rupture your eardrums), and also a logarithmic, *ratio-based* measurement, when applied to reducing or increasing the level of an audio signal by a certain number of dB. Increasing the level of a signal by 3 dB (only a slight perceived increase) entails doubling the power requirement to produce it. Thus, a 100-watt amplifier only produces 3 dB more level than a 50-watt amplifier.

delay: See Chapter 12.

digital audio: The representation of sound as numeric data. In order for (analog/real live) sound to be digitized, it needs to be converted via an A-D (analog-to-digital) converter. To hear digital audio, the data then needs to be converted back into analog via a D-A (digital-to-analog) converter. The quality of digital audio is dependent upon many things, from the quality of the A-D and D-A conversion to the resolution and bit depth of the digital audio data itself.

digital zero: 0 dB FS (full scale). The maximum level possible of a digital audio signal. This means that all bits are 1s rather than 0s.

dither: The process of adding a small amount of noise to a digital audio signal to compensate for artifacts that inherently cause distortion.

dongle: A small piece of electronic hardware plugged into a computer, most commonly into a USB port, that acts as a physical protection device against piracy. Without the dongle plugged in, you may not be able to run a particular piece of software, regardless of how the software was obtained. Dongles are only used by certain manufacturers.

driver: Software that facilitates communication between computers and connected hardware or software programs. Drivers are frequently updated, so it is best to make sure you are using the latest one.

drum machine: An electronic unit dedicated to drum sounds and the generation of drum patterns. Drum machines originated from organ accompaniment systems developed in the 1960s and came of age just prior to MIDI, with the first *digital* drum machine from Roger Linn. The hugely popular Akai MPC series drum machines, initiated by Linn designs, fueled the beats that would go on to define hip-hop—though, ironically, the sounds themselves harked back to the days of synthesized drum sounds made popular via such drum machines as Roland's TR-808.

DSP: Digital signal processing.

dynamic range: The ratio between the softest and loudest signal that can be detected. It is measured in dB.

dynamics: Fluctuations in volume—i.e., the difference between the loud and the quiet. Dynamics can be essential to create music that sounds "real" and not overly electronic. Conversely, dynamics might also need reining in to produce music that sounds consistently loud.

echo: A delay long enough for two or more sounds to be discerned as separate events. Generally, the delay needs to be at least 50 milliseconds to produce an echo effect. What is technically "reverb" is often referred to as echo—a case in point is the echo chamber, which is in essence a reverberant room.

envelope: A term used to describe the overall shape of a sound's tone, pitch, or volume. ADSR (see entry) are the most commonly used parameters in a synthesizer's envelope generator.

EQ: Equalization. An audio process used to cut and boost individual frequencies present in a sound to change its tone. The name originated from its initial purpose: to make a sound more natural, balanced, or equal.

Ethernet: A widely used computer networking interface.

fader: A slider found on consoles and controllers to smoothly adjust the volume of a source.

feedback/acoustic feedback: A phenomenon that occurs when the output of an audio device, typically a loudspeaker, is "fed back" into itself via input from a microphone or pickup. Feedback normally generates a whistling, squealing sound that can be painful to experience. In the hands of a guitarist, feedback can be deliberately created and controlled (to some degree) for artistic expression (with a bit of luck).

filter: In audio terms, a filter rejects certain frequencies in a signal or waveform to alter its tonal characteristics. Low-pass, high-pass, and band-pass filters let certain frequencies "pass" through, filtering out the others.

FireWire: A serial interface standard developed by Apple, also known as the IEEE 1394 interface. It can be found on digital instruments, audio devices, hard disk drives, and computers and is an alternative to the (still more common) USB interface. Special cables and connectors are required to connect between devices. It appears to be a dying format. At the time of going to press, Apple uses the Thunderbolt interface on its new products.

flanging: An audio effect created by combining two identical sounds with a short but variable delay or pre-delay time. Flanging was initially devised by an engineer physically pressing down on the "flange" of one of two synchronized tape machines, thereby minutely changing the playback speed of that source and, as a result, the relative delay time between the two signals. The effect creates a chorus-like thickening of the resultant sound, but rather more dramatic due to its comb filter effect, which produces ever-changing harmonics and overtones. The effect is similar but not identical to to phasing.

frequency response: A measurement of the consistency across the audio spectrum that audio devices are capable of handling and/or reproducing. It is expressed as a range from a low frequency to a high frequency (e.g., 20 Hz to 18 kHz) usually followed by a tolerance of level variation over the frequency range (e.g., +/− 2 dB). A frequency response specification is meaningless without the level variation tolerance—but that doesn't stop countless manufacturers from failing to state it.

General MIDI (GM): A standard developed in the early 1990s, based around sound types, that enables sequences (stored in .MID format) to sound at least OK when played back on any "GM" sound sources. The establishment of a unified system of "Program Change" numbers allows piano parts to call up piano patches, acoustic guitar parts acoustic guitar patches, and so on.

As with most things MIDI, 128 basic sounds are specified, with provision for additional sound *subsets* that can be offered on more sophisticated devices.

Championed initially by Roland, whose Sound Canvas modules quickly became the de facto GM sound set, GM was for a long time the savior of both the game audio and cell phone industries, where standardization was key. Though not as vital as it was in the 1990s, GM is still a useful tool for transferring song files, and the GM drum map (specifying which keys trigger which drum sounds) continues to be the norm on all but the most sophisticated synthesizer drum voices.

graphic equalizer: An EQ device that provides control over a fixed set of frequencies, each frequency offering linear cut/boost control. The controls are usually a set of faders each marked with a frequency.

headroom: A buffer zone of safety in audio signals (both analog and digital) between the loudest transient signal and the maximum level the system can attain before clipping—i.e., going into distortion.

hertz: Abbreviated "Hz," this is a unit of frequency measuring how many times a sound wave occurs per second. The abbreviation kHz stands for "kilohertz" or 1,000 Hz.

impedance: A measurement of resistance for alternating current signals, of which audio is one. It is important for the specification of inputs and outputs of electronic equipment—particularly loudspeakers. It is measured in ohms, represented by the omega symbol—e.g., 15Ω.

in the box: A term that refers to the practice of processing audio recordings entirely within computer programs and applications and not incorporating "outside" equipment such as analog mixers and outboard processors. Using a digital controller on a mix is still keeping it in the box, as the controller is in essence a giant mouse.

latency: An interval of time between an action and the response to that action. Such "delays" can typically be found in the course of digital processing and signals traveling over large geographical distances. Latency is almost never a good thing, but a challenge to be overcome or compensated for.

level: The strength or volume of an audio signal.

line input/line level: A high-level input sourced from keyboards, DAWs, or tape machine track outputs, CD players, etc., unlike microphones and guitar pickups, which are low-level sources that need amplification to bring them up to line level.

Local On/Off: A MIDI channel message that sets whether your keyboard is going to trigger its internal sounds (Local On) or not (Local Off). This is a vital parameter to have control over to avoid loops and double-triggers when your keyboard is part of a larger, computer-based rig of equipment. A stand-alone keyboard with Local set to off will produce no sound—a common irritation.

loop: Like it sounds, a segment of music or data that repeats endlessly. Loops have their origins in "tape loops," where an audio tape recording was spliced top to tail in a loop, to achieve a continuous pattern. Loops are easily obtained within DAWs with a couple of mouse clicks. MIDI loops are an undesirable phenomenon that occurs when MIDI data is inadvertently fed back on itself, causing system crashes.

low-frequency oscillator (LFO): The use of ultra-low frequencies (beyond audio range) to modulate another parameter, such as volume, pitch, or tone.

MADI: Multichannel Audio Digital Interface—one of the professional standards (with its accompanying coaxial or fiber-optical connections) used to implement the communication and delivery of multichannel digital audio. Alternatives include AES/EBU, ADAT, and S/PDIF, but these formats only carry stereo on two channels down a single cable.

mastering: The process of making final adjustments—to overall tone, volume, and possibly effects—before a recording is ready for publication or duplication. Mastering for vinyl includes a disc cutting process.

metronome: Originally a physical, mechanical device featuring a "clicking" and speed-alterable pendulum, used to help musicians set—and keep—strict time when they play. Modern electronic alternatives exist in DAW software and on miniature hardware boxes.

mic pre: Short for "microphone preamplifier."

MIDI: Musical Instrument Digital Interface. A serial interface and control language developed by Dave Smith in the early 1980s initially to allow synthesizers made by different manufacturers to connect and communicate. MIDI went on to enable and drive the revolution in sound recording, fueling "sequencers" that would go on to become Digital Audio Workstations, or DAWs.

MIDI cable: Standard cable used to connect MIDI devices featuring five-pin DIN connectors on both ends. MIDI can also be transmitted by other means: USB, FireWire, and even wirelessly.

MIDI channel: MIDI data is communicated using a system of 16 discrete "channels," each of which can be used to send and receive specific commands between connected devices. When making connections between instruments/computers/devices, you normally will choose a MIDI channel (between 1 and 16) on which you want to communicate. On DAWs, you will frequently want to use several MIDI channels—one for each track of a song. You may also need to use several MIDI ports, each of which can communicate using its own 16-channel system.

MIDI clock: Real-time system message that drives and synchronizes performance data among MIDI devices. A more common means of synchronization is MIDI time code or SMPTE time code.

MIDI controller: Any electronic device that can generate and send MIDI data. Most commonly seen are MIDI keyboards, but there are many others, from MIDI guitars to MIDI drum pads, MIDI human breath controllers, boxes of knobs, gloves, and more.

MIDI file: "Standard MIDI File" (SMF): sequencer files that adhere to certain protocols. Most DAW/sequencer applications can save and load sequences in this easy-to-transfer format, in addition to generating their own proprietary file formats.

MIDI In, Out, Thru: Names and functions of the MIDI ports found on most MIDI devices. MIDI In will accept incoming data only. MIDI Out will transmit data. MIDI Thru passes on data being received at the In port to another device.

MIDI merge: The function of a device that accepts MIDI data from various sources and merges it into a single (output) source.

MIDI message: Packets of data that form a MIDI transmission.

MIDI port(s): The point or points on a MIDI device where you connect to other MIDI devices. Initially, five-pin DIN connectors were used exclusively. A MIDI port could also be a USB/FireWire/Ethernet port nowadays.

MIDI time code (MTC): System comprising the information contained in a SMPTE signal in "MIDI" form that can be recognized by certain MIDI devices.

mod wheel: Wheel controller found on synthesizers that players can use to progressively introduce modulation depth to a sound. The mod wheel itself can normally be assigned to many different parameters, selected by the user, though it is most commonly applied to modulate pitch to produce vibrato.

monitor: As a verb, to listen to a sound. As a noun, a speaker. In live sound circles, it represents an onstage speaker for musicians to hear each other.

mono: In audio terms, mono describes a sound or signal that is recorded or replayed using a single channel. Your mouth is mono. But your ears are stereo—two channels. Although we live in a multichannel world for entertainment (stereo iPods and 5.1 surround movies and home theater systems), it's important for mixes to work "in mono" because music is still heard in mono on many public sound systems where music needs to be delivered "complete" to consumers on the move. Mono is short for "monophonic." It is often used as a short form of "monaural," but the dictionary definition of monaural implies sound received by one ear!

MP3: In the opinion of the authors, the curse of modern music. Short for MPEG-1/2 Audio Layer III, MP3 is an encoding format for digital audio that uses variable data compression to reduce file size. Based on a "lossy" compression algorithm, MP3's undoubted value in enabling the easy transfer of music files on portable music players, computers, and over the Internet must be set against the fact that the music itself is severely compromised in audio *quality*.

multitrack: The capacity of being able to house (and so record, and play back) multiple "tracks" in a recording device such as a tape machine sequencer or DAW.

near-field: A term used to describe a size of monitor loudspeaker designed to be listened to in the "near" field—i.e., relatively closely, typically four or five feet from the listener.

notation program: Programs that focus on presenting music data on a stave, in conventional notation form. Almost exclusively, input to such a program (or indeed a notation feature within a DAW) is via MIDI.

Note On/Off command: A MIDI channel voice message indicating when a note is to begin sounding and when the "fingers are taken off the keys." Depending upon the envelope of the voice being triggered, a Note Off message may not necessarily result in the sound actually stopping, of course.

It's important to keep track of your Note Off commands (not normally displayed as a default on most DAW platforms), because it can be easy to edit a note before its Note Off message, which can lead to hanging notes and messy sounding loops, or, on certain platforms, irregular bar lengths being displayed. Motto: Keep an eye on your Note Offs when cutting and pasting.

octave: The interval spanning eight notes in a Western scale at which point the frequency of a note is either halved or doubled. In simple terms, the octave above middle C, for example, is the next C note up the scale.

oscillator: The circuitry that generates the sound wave that forms the root basis of a synthesizer sound. There are various wave types—e.g., sine, square, and sawtooth, which describe the graphical pattern or shape of each cycle of the wave. Consoles and DAWs usually offer a simple sine wave oscillator for equipment lineup and calibration.

overdub: To add a new part on top of existing parts, or a backing that has been previously recorded. Overdubs are recorded separately on their own tracks so that they can be individually controlled. Headphones allow the performer(s) overdubbing to hear the existing material.

pan: A term derived from "panorama," referring to a parameter that specifies the location of a sound within the stereo field, i.e., between left and right. Normally, if a sound that is originally stereo is assigned to two mono channels, the pan controls of the two channels are set to far left and far right, so that the sound can be monitored in its original spatial state.

parametric equalizer: A multiband equalizer that offers precise control of the three main EQ parameters: amplitude, center frequency and bandwidth (Q). The amplitude control determines the amount of boost or cut at the chosen frequency. The desired center frequency can be found by sweeping one of the frequency knobs in the desired range while boosting or cutting. The Q control adjusts the sharpness or bluntness (in graphic terms), or in other words, the amount of focus on the frequencies surrounding the center frequency.

patch: A throwback to the days of modular synthesizers when different modules and parameters within them could be connected using physical patch cords. The final sound, which resulted from multiple patching, eventually came to be known as a "patch." Fast-forward to modern synthesizers and the word is now used to describe any single and identifiable "sound," as in a brass "patch," a piano "patch," etc.

phantom power: A means by which DC power can be transmitted down mic cables to power microphones and other equipment requiring a power source. Phantom power is found on consoles, manifested as a switch that can be turned on or off, either globally, or per channel. Without phantom power, a microphone that has active electronics will need to use a battery. N.B. Some older equipment can be damaged by the application of phantom power.

phase: If two similar waves are very slightly delayed with respect to each other, they can form a mirror image and cancel each other out. This effect is called "out of phase." If loudspeakers are out of phase, it means that as one cone is moving out, the other is moving in. This results in a very eerie effect on the ear, as if the sound were coming from outside the speakers. Inadvertent phase reversal can happen in a miswired balanced cable or connector. Most consoles have a phase reverse button, which can be useful to change the phase of microphones with respect to each other. "Phasing" is a popular recording trick achieved by gradually varying a short delay, which causes a shift in phase, producing a "swishing" effect.

pink noise: A test signal that theoretically contains all frequencies in the audio spectrum at equal intensity.

pitch: Used to describe the frequency of a note; in very broad terms, high (pitched) or low (pitched). Pitch is also used to describe a sound (be it a vocal or instrumental) in relation to its accuracy to a note or notes in a scale—i.e., off pitch, on pitch, relative pitch, perfect pitch. "Pitchy" is a term that entered the global vocabulary on the TV show *American Idol*, when it was used (seemingly endlessly) to describe a singer who was having difficulty singing in tune. Related terms are "in pitch" and "off pitch," meaning, respectively, in and out of tune. "Perfect pitch" is a person's rare ability to tell that a sounded note is, say, a B-flat or a D and whether or not it is in tune.

pitch bend: A MIDI channel voice message, generally initiated by a pitch wheel (though any other controller set to manipulate pitch will do), that smoothly raises and/or lowers the pitch of a note or chord. This can be achieved in real time during a performance or can be recorded into a sequence.

pitch wheel: A control wheel, normally found to the left of a synthesizer keyboard, used to manipulate the pitch of a played note or notes. The range of the pitch change caused by full rotation of the wheel to an end stop in either direction can be adjusted.

plate reverb: A type of reverb in which large metal plate inside a box enclosure is made to vibrate to the signal applied to it. For years it was the only professional alternative to a real live echo chamber. Plates are still much revered, and there are many software emulations available.

plug-in: Software designed specifically to work inside (or alongside) a host application. Plug-ins are designed to provide additional content or functionality for the host program. The most common uses in audio for plug-ins are EQ, reverb, delays, compression, etc.

polyphonic: Describes an instrument that is capable of playing more than one note at a time. A flute offers one note of polyphony, whereas an acoustic piano offers full polyphony—i.e., every note can be played simultaneously and will sound. A synthesizer may commonly offer 8, 16, or even up to 128 notes of polyphony.

Pro Tools: A DAW platform created in the 1980s. Pro Tools is generally credited with establishing the viability and popularity of multichannel digital audio recording using personal computers.

Program Change: A MIDI channel message (from 0 to 127) that tells a device to switch to a particular patch/voice/preset, etc.

It is essential that Program Change messages are placed at the beginning of GM sequences (MIDI Files) so that piano parts will be played back on piano sounds, guitar parts on guitar sounds, etc.

punch-in/punch-out: The process of quickly going in and out of Record on a track, often done when a passage needs to be rerecorded within a longer part that is otherwise OK (i.e., a repair), or when a part comes in midsong. Punches can be preprogrammed at specific points or performed by the operator "on the fly"—i.e., while the music is playing. An equivalent British expression is "drop-in" and "drop-out."

Q: See "parametric equalizer."

quantization: Within a MIDI sequence, the automatic adjustment of timing values to some formula or pattern other than the one originally recorded. At its most basic level, to *quantize* a passage to 1/16 notes will drag all notes to their nearest sixteenth note, so making the passage sound very in-time, but also potentially very stiff and mechanical. There are many more subtle settings and styles that can both "correct" timings, in a more natural manner, and even create human-feel "groove quantizing."

In digital audio, the term indicates the process of converting audio samples into numeric values.

RAM: Random Access Memory. Temporary storage medium that operates only in the present—i.e., it gets cleared when the computer or instrument is switched off. If data currently stored in RAM needs to be saved permanently, it needs to be saved to a hard drive or other external storage device such as a USB stick.

release: Normally the final parameter in an envelope generator. This governs how quickly a sound will fade away once you have taken your fingers off the keys.

reverb: An effect that re-creates the sound reflections found in various rooms or contained physical spaces. Adding such reflections thus creates the impression that a sound is taking place in a large concert hall, a small room, in the Grand Canyon, etc., etc.

ROM: Read-Only Memory. Permanent storage in a computer or electronic musical instrument that cannot be overwritten. Synth presets, and waveforms used to create sounds, are stored in ROM.

sample: A sound bite stored as a digitized waveform in a computer, or sampling-enabled synthesizer. A sample can also refer to single slice of a digital audio wave.

sample accurate: Where two digital devices are synchronized to the precision level of an individual sample. Such "tightness" represents a tiny increment of time, but can be important to keep sounds in phase, as well as in sync with each other.

sampler: Computer application or hardware device that can record, manipulate, and play back digital audio.

sampling: To musicians, sampling involves the digital recording of sounds (into a sampler program, app, or equivalent) in order for those sounds to be replayed or retriggered in a different context. Applications range from sampling single notes played on a flute, for example, so that a keyboard player can then "play" the flute, to sampling entire sections of other people's songs and lacing them into a new "composition." Unauthorized sampling of copyright material helps get lawyers very busy!

sampling rate: The resolution at which a sample recording is taking place. Sample rates indicate of the number of times per second the audio is being converted into digital data. Logically, higher numbers offer higher resolution, and so higher-quality results. The higher the sample rate, the higher the memory requirement, so there often needs to be a trade-off. CDs are recorded at 44.1 kHz, which translates to 44,100 samples per second. It is never a good idea to use different sampling rates within one project. The process of "sample rate conversion" allows all elements to be at the same resolution—but it may be at the expense of a loss of quality.

SCSI (Small Computer System Interface): A specification (with attendant connecting devices) used to transfer data between a computer and an external storage device. This type of connectivity has now largely been replaced by USB and FireWire.

separation: Where a sound can be captured (recorded) without a signal leaking or spilling in from another source being played at the same time—i.e., every sound is captured "separately." Separation is often regarded as desirable because it gives you maximum control over the recorded sound without affecting other sounds.

sequencer: A musical word processor: a software application, or feature found on a hardware keyboard workstation, that can record, process, and play back events in a defined sequence to form a newly compiled piece of music. Though sequencing began life as a MIDI-only entity, sequencers eventually embraced audio recording as well. Modern software devices that can record, process, and play back both MIDI and audio are now generally referred to as Digital Audio Workstations or DAWs (sometimes referred to as "dahs" or "doors," according to where in the world you hail from).

serial interface: A form of communication that transmits information sequentially—i.e., one piece of information (bit) after another. MIDI is a serial interface. The alternative is a parallel system, which transmits bits simultaneously.

sibilance: The name given to the phenomenon where an "s" sound on a vocal is prominent to the level of harshness. Sibilance can be a natural feature of a person's voice. Plus, it can be created or exacerbated when using a particular microphone compression or EQ setting. Sibilance is generally reined in using some form of dynamic or frequency-based compression. Individual "s" sounds are referred to as "sibilants." "Sh" and "ch" sounds can also be troublesome.

SMPTE time code: Standard adopted by the Society of Motion Picture and Television Engineers for synchronization between audio, film, and video devices. SMPTE data uses a 24-hour clock for its code and identifies every "frame." There are different types of SMPTE for a number of different international video and TV frame rates. The code can be recorded as audio or embedded within a DAW file. Some MIDI devices can use SMPTE.

solo: The action of listening to the sound of only one channel or track (most commonly, using a channel's Solo button).

S/PDIF: Stands for Sony/Philips Digital Interface Format. The specification is formally called IEC958, but is more generally known as S/PDIF, and is a consumer format for transferring digital audio signals. S/PDIF simultaneously transmits or receives two channels of audio, usually stereo.

SPL: Sound pressure level, a measurement used to assess and perceive loudness. Sound travels to our ears through sound "waves." Larger waves create more "pressure" on our eardrums, which living creatures perceive as volume.

Standard MIDI File: A standardized format enabling MIDI sequences to be exchanged among different manufacturers, products, and platforms. Though frequently related to a General MIDI sound set, SMFs do not have to include any program information, and indeed are commonly used simply as a base-level (notes and parts) method to transfer sequence data for the purpose of ongoing music production.

sustain: Where a note or signal reaches a point where it continues at a constant level for a determinate period of time before it decays or releases.

System Exclusive message (Sys Ex): A way for individual manufacturers to add or create proprietary data within a MIDI stream. MIDI manufacturers each have an ID code that heralds a command unique to that manufacturer's products. A typical use of "Sys Ex" is to transfer voice or program information back and forth among devices and/or computers.

TDIF: Tascam Digital Interconnect Format. A bidirectional format for the communication of up to eight channels of digital audio.

tempo: The speed at which a piece of music plays or is played. In human terms, tempo is more of a guide to the pace of music; but in computer-driven recordings, tempo has become more of an absolute, measured and set in BPM or beats per minute. In film circles, tempo is more often measured in frames per beat (FPB).

Thru: The MIDI Thru port passes "through" to the MIDI Out port data that is being received at the MIDI In port.

Thru-box: For units that don't have a Thru, port you can purchase one of these physical boxes. Generally they will provide a MIDI In socket and several Thru output ports.

Thunderbolt: An interface between devices—notably those by Apple and Intel—offered as an alternative to USB and FireWire.

tick: The smallest increment of a beat; based upon the resolution of the device or application being used.

timbre: Tone characteristics or color.

time code: See "SMPTE time code."

time signature: Numerator/denominator. A bar or measure of music is divided up into smaller increments—beats—that allow people to read, or simply to understand, what a composer or producer has in mind when instructing you what to play. The time signature is a guide to how beats fit into a bar of music. Time signatures are presented as two numbers, one on top of the other. The top number indicates the number of beats in any given bar and the bottom figure indicates the note value that represents one beat. For example, a time signature of $\frac{3}{4}$ means there are three "quarter notes," or "crotchets," in a bar.

touch sensitivity: The ability of a keyboard's sounds to respond to how hard you hit the keys. You can adjust the response of the keyboard to suit your own particular playing style. See also "after touch" and "velocity."

transpose: To change the key of a musical performance by raising or lowering its pitch by a predetermined musical interval.

tremolo: Steady, rapid up-and-down fluctuation in volume; used as an effect.

unity gain: The result of passing of a signal through a device without any increase or decrease in level.

USB: Universal Serial Bus. An industry-standard protocol (using several types of physical connector) for communication between computers and electronic devices including peripherals, instruments, mixers, microphones, and more. USB also delivers a small amount of power (5V), but at a current level insufficient for many devices to operate properly. Such devices may need their own individual power supply.

USB MIDI: Where MIDI is being delivered via a USB interface.

velocity: Measurement of the speed—and so in practice the intensity and resultant *volume*—at which notes are being played. More velocity equals more volume. MIDI provides for velocity levels from 0 to 127. See "touch sensitivity."

VST plug-in: "Virtual Studio Technology," a format initially offered by Steinberg (but now widely adopted as standard) for the creation of instruments and effects used within a DAW environment. Although the results of these plug-ins are audio-based, they are MIDI-driven and operated.

WAV: A file format for uncompressed digital audio initially devised by Microsoft/IBM. AIFF is the Mac equivalent. Nowadays, either format can be used on either platform.

word clock: A synchronization signal used to ensure that audio data is received at the same rate it is being transmitted. When multiple devices are digitally connected, all need to use the same word clock to avoid problems of audio transfer and, most likely, unwanted noise in the signal. It is vital that there is only one "master" word clock that is distributed to all the connected digital devices.

XLR connector: A professional three-pin connector in widespread use for analog audio connections. It has a locking mechanism that prevents the cable from being pulled out accidentally.

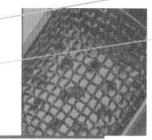

INDEX

2-track, 2
4-track, 5, 27, 236, 238
8-track, 2, 27, 62
16-track, 2, 27
24-track, 2, 3, 27
24-bit, 43, 49, 209

A&R department, 98, 217, 237
Abbey Road Studios, 2, 3, 5, 8, 15, 26, 29, 31, 35, 51, 64, 71, 95, 106, 107, 114, 120, 126, 143, 158, 173, 196, 220, 239
absorption, 6
acoustic guitar, 8, 17, 18, 24, 29, 58, 74, 76, 82, 83, 85, 94, 111, 177, 185, 200, 203–204
acoustic principles, 6
active (electronics), 56, 76, 179, 210, 222
A-D (analog-to-digital) converter, 28, 33–34
ADAT (Alesis Digital Audio Tape), 3, 48
AES (Audio Engineering Society), 108
AES/EBU, 48
Ainlay, Chuck, 122, 124, 127, 140, 222, 235, 237, 238
AKG, 17, 19, 21, 29, 133, 158
Alan Parsons Project, 18, 111, 130, 175
"All Our Yesterdays," 134, 150, 168, 172, 194, 220, 223, 225, 239
"All Right Now," 158
Allison Research, 99
ambience, 20, 24, 161, 210, 211
ambient, 24, 155, 161, 195, 214, 216, 227
Ampex, 2
analog, 32, 33, 34, 37, 40, 45, 46, 48, 51, 78, 79, 88, 91, 94, 95, 103, 108, 169, 191, 198, 212, 219, 220, 222, 228, 232, 238

analog console, 35, 36, 41, 43, 77, 110, 126
analog summing, 43, 65, 66
analog tape, 3, 31, 39, 43, 125, 126, 142, 235
analog versus digital, 31–36, 67, 70, 79
Aphex, 91
arrangement, 67, 84, 123, 125, 181, 239
Atari, 47
A-to-D converter. *See* A-D converter
attenuate, 74
attenuators, 21
audio, 2, 5, 8, 13, 21, 22, 25, 31, 32, 33, 34, 35, 39, 40, 42, 43, 48, 49, 50, 51, 52, 55, 57, 60, 61, 62, 63, 64, 66, 70, 71, 73, 77, 87, 91, 101, 106, 107, 108, 124, 144, 147, 148, 149, 150, 155, 168, 169, 170, 209, 227
audio interface, 46, 48, 50, 66
audio spectrum, 16, 90, 125
audio (recording) versus MIDI (recording), 168
Audio-Technica, 16, 17, 18, 20, 21, 25, 29
Auralex, 6, 11
Auratone, 57, 59
automation, 32, 66, 69, 71, 103, 219, 222–223, 231
Auto-Tune, 67, 137, 142
Aux (bus / sends), 37, 110

backing up, 47, 52, 126, 147, 150, 235, 238, 239
Badu, Erykah, 132, 133, 137, 139, 140, 145
balance, 3, 14, 15, 37, 38, 42, 61, 73, 78, 81, 83, 84, 87, 120, 121, 122, 124, 126, 134, 145, 164, 168, 171, 215, 217, 219, 222, 223, 225, 228, 229, 230, 231
balance engineers, 15
balanced signal, 178, 179, 214
B&W (Bowers & Wilkins), 64
Barta, Andrew, 191

bass, 5, 10, 36, 37, 43, 54, 56, 57, 58, 59, 61, 62, 63, 66, 73, 74, 75, 77, 80, 83, 84, 120, 158, 165, 171, 172, 173, 177–184, 208, 210, 223, 224, 225, 226, 227, 228, 232
bass drum, 21, 80, 85, 102, 110, 123, 125, 136, 155, 158, 163, 224. *See also* kick drum
bass guitar, 29, 33, 80, 84, 90, 92, 93, 111, 177–184, 185
bass player, 93, 120, 177–174, 227, 236
bass traps, 9, 11
Beatles, the, 2, 8, 24, 26, 27, 29, 62, 94, 143, 158, 180, 187, 196, 198, 225
Bell, Alexander Graham, 13
Berliner, Emile, 1, 14
Binson Echorec, 107, 113, 189, 194
bit, 39, 49, 51, 67
bit depth, 49
bit resolution, 39, 120
Blunstone, Colin, 130
Bolas, Niko, 43, 92, 96, 133, 141, 142, 146, 237
Bottrell, Bill, 42
Boxer, The, 196
brass, 14, 29, 36, 71, 83, 95, 239
Brown, Tony, 58, 127, 140, 228
Buff, Paul, 99, 103
bus, 32, 36, 37, 40, 41, 43, 95, 98, 231, 232
Butler, Artie, 182

capacitor mics, 17
Capitol Records, 106
carbon microphone, 14
cardioid, 19, 20, 137, 172, 190, 203, 204, 209, 210, 211, 212
center channel, 62–63
center image, 61, 225
channel strip, 35–36, 38, 40, 41, 42, 77, 88, 91, 99, 132, 162, 238
choir, 25, 172, 207–212
chorus (effect), 115, 116, 142
Clarke, Allan, 130
Clearmountain, Bob, 31, 78
click track, 122, 127, 163, 211, 214
clock, 49, 69
close-miking, 8, 24, 208
Cockney Rebel, 95
Cocker, Joe, 182
coincident pair (of mics), 25
Coles (microphone), 29, 160
Commodore 64, 65, 66

comping, 138, 139, 141–142
compression, 21, 34, 36, 39, 46, 73, 84, 87–98
compression ratio, 89
condenser mic, 17–18, 20, 21, 22, 28, 36, 82, 132, 158, 159, 160, 172, 190, 204, 209, 214
cone, 190, 191
console, 7, 17, 22, 23, 27, 28, 31–43, 46, 55, 56, 57, 59, 68, 72, 76, 77, 88, 99, 103, 110, 114, 115, 119, 120, 124, 126, 132, 162, 170, 178, 215, 216, 219, 220, 222, 223, 225, 228, 232, 236, 238
consolidation, 221, 232, 234
control room, 8, 11, 15, 25, 55, 60, 120, 122, 123, 124, 126, 130, 131, 132, 137, 140, 151, 207, 208, 210, 220, 235
controller, 41, 42, 67, 68, 69, 71, 72, 176, 219
converters, 28, 33, 34, 35, 48, 49, 64
Cooder, Ry, 98
Copeland, Kim, 129, 130, 131, 140
CPU, 47, 78
Cregan, Jim, 95
Cubase, 45, 71, 72, 209, 211
cymbals, 17, 24, 42, 81, 82, 85, 94, 101, 153, 154, 157–158, 160, 161, 164, 214, 215, 227

D-A (digital-to-analog) converter, 33, 34, 43, 48, 49, 64
Dark Side of the Moon, The, 2, 25, 31, 33, 55, 62, 80, 94, 101, 102, 109, 113, 189
DAW (Digital Audio Workstation), 2, 23, 32, 34, 36, 39, 40, 41, 43, 46, 48, 49, 51, 52, 56, 66–72, 78, 83, 91, 101, 103, 108, 110, 114, 115, 116, 117, 121, 122, 123, 126, 134, 141, 142, 144–151, 162, 168, 169, 170, 173, 175, 178, 191, 198, 211, 212, 219, 220, 222, 229, 238, 239
decibels, 11, 21, 75
de-essing, 90, 91
De Oliviera, Laudir, 182
DI box, 93, 120, 178, 179, 215
diaphragm, 14, 54, 185. *See also* large diaphragm condenser; small diaphragm condenser
Dickinson, Jim, 222
digital audio, 45, 46, 47, 49, 96
digital console, 31, 33, 34, 36, 41, 42, 103, 110, 114, 115, 228
digital delay line, 114
digital recording, 2, 3, 32, 49, 96, 166, 211
digital zero, 40, 231
digitized, 32, 34, 48
direct monitoring, 50

Disney, 2, 7, 62
dispersion, 54, 55
diffusion, 6, 109
distortion, 17, 27, 55, 73, 96, 115, 135, 142, 143, 144, 155, 188, 192, 230, 231, 237
Dodd, Richard, 97
Dolby, 101, 141
Dolby, Thomas, 66
dongle, 49–50
double-tracking, 114, 144, 196
Douglas, Jack, 139, 143, 230, 236
Douglass, Jimmy, 134, 137, 143, 221, 229, 233
Drawmer, 99
drumhead, 154–156
drums. *See* bass drum; kick drum; snare drum
drums, compression on, 94, 96, 97
drums, recording, 19, 23, 27, 29, 39, 77, 80, 81, 85, 90, 94, 102, 110, 120, 122, 123, 153–164, 181, 215, 223, 224, 225, 226, 227, 228, 229
D-to-A converter. *See* D-A converter
dubstep, 116, 117
dynamic mics, 18, 19, 20, 21, 29, 209, 214
dynamic range, 21, 39, 61, 87, 88, 90, 94, 96, 99, 153
dynamics, 18, 19, 21, 36, 37, 87–98, 99, 103, 134, 156, 160, 173, 174, 190, 192, 197, 204, 231

earbuds, 58, 59, 230
early reflections, 109
East, Nathan, 120, 123, 124, 127, 177, 178, 179, 180, 182
EastWest, 71, 175
echo, 1, 6, 9, 37, 41, 105–109, 113, 114–117, 181, 189, 191, 196, 199
echo chamber, 106–109, 196, 208
Echoplex, 114
Edison, Thomas, 1, 13, 14, 53
effect sends and returns, 37, 110
electret, 17, 18
electric guitar, 14, 17, 18, 21, 24, 29, 73, 76, 82, 94, 185–201, 215, 223, 225, 226, 227, 228
electric piano, 84, 165
electrodynamic loudspeaker, 54
Emerick, Geoff, 2, 62, 143, 158, 160, 225
EMI, 33, 95, 106, 212
envelope, 100, 102, 169, 176
EQ (equalization, equalizer), 23, 27, 34, 36, 37, 42, 43, 46, 55, 71, 73–86, 90, 91, 103, 115, 116, 120, 132, 134, 141, 146, 156, 157, 159, 164, 173, 174, 180, 181, 183, 215, 219, 222, 223, 227–228, 231, 238

Ethernet, 48, 70, 170
Eventide Harmonizer, 108, 114, 205
expander, 99–100
Expression College, 139, 236

Fairchild, 78, 88, 92, 133
feedback, 58–60, 69, 103, 113, 115, 116, 132, 156, 215
"Feelin' Alright," 182
Fender, 107, 178, 180, 187, 189, 190, 199
Fender Rhodes, 84, 169
Fields, John, 27, 31, 96, 97, 138, 187, 197
figure eight, 19–20, 25, 161, 209, 211, 212
filter, comb, 116
filter, high-pass, 75, 76, 77, 80, 82, 83, 84
filter, low-pass, 75, 82
filter, notch, 76, 85
filter, shelving, 82, 84
filtering, 22, 37, 69, 74, 75, 80, 143, 169
FireWire, 34, 42, 45, 48, 68, 70, 170
flanging, 116, 142, 181
flutter, 9
frequency-dependent, 90, 100
frequency domain, 7
frequency response, 16, 17, 19, 20, 21, 55, 73, 75, 210

gain reduction, 88, 89, 90, 93, 135
gate, 36, 71, 80, 99–104, 110, 162, 191, 216
gate effect, 71, 103
gated reverb, 100, 102, 110
Gaudi, 18
Gilmour, David, 102, 147, 189, 193, 194
gobo, 24
Grammy Museum, 1
gramophone, 1
graphic equalizer, 75
Green, Jackie, 16, 25, 26, 27
guitar. *See* acoustic guitar; bass guitar; electric guitar
guitar cabinet, 29, 60, 185, 190, 215

Hammond organ, 107, 166, 169, 173–175
Harper, Roy, 115
Harrison, George, 2, 198
Haverstick, Gavin, 6, 8, 11
Hawkins, Taylor, 155, 159, 163, 164
headphone mix, 8, 37, 60, 123, 124, 135, 136
headphones, 14, 24, 27, 37, 41, 58–59, 60, 61, 62, 79, 98, 115, 121, 124, 136, 137, 139, 141, 144, 149, 162, 183, 209, 210, 214, 230

hertz, 7, 74, 75
high frequency, 19, 49, 54, 100, 109, 112, 115
high-pass filter. *See* filter, high-pass
hi-hats, 29, 155, 157, 215
hold (noise gate parameter), 100, 102
horn, 13, 53–56
hum, 76, 77, 84, 94, 101, 179, 191, 199, 216
humbucker, 186–188
Humphrey, Paul, 182
hypercardioid, 19, 20, 203

in the box, 32, 34, 43, 88, 219, 222, 223
in-ear monitors, 59, 214, 215
input gain, 36
interface, 34, 42, 46, 48–50, 70, 72, 168, 170, 178, 209
Internet, 3, 46, 52, 56, 65, 116, 117
Internet recording, 147–151
isolation, 6, 7, 9, 10, 11, 24, 59, 120, 139
ITU configuration, 62–63
iTunes, 95

Jaffee, Rami, 120, 124, 125, 127, 167, 169, 171, 173, 174, 225
Johns, Glyn, 24, 43

Kaye, Carol, 93, 94, 177, 178, 179, 181, 182
Kellogg, E. W., 54
Kennedy, Kevin, 214, 215, 216
Kepex, 99, 101, 102
keyboard, 11, 36, 42, 43, 48, 65–72, 77, 111, 120, 136, 165–176, 181, 182, 214, 225, 226, 228
keyboard workstation, 34, 72, 125, 214
Keyfax, 71, 209
kick drum, 8, 18, 23, 26, 29, 61, 80, 81, 84, 85, 94, 101, 102, 103, 110, 153, 155–156, 158, 162, 181, 223, 226, 231
Knopfler, Mark, 124, 127

"Lady Madonna," 95, 173
laptop, 5, 45, 46, 119, 183, 209, 214, 216
large diaphragm condenser, 17, 29, 132
latency, 50–51, 114, 148, 150, 173
Lennon, John, 113, 143, 236
Leonard, Patrick, 42, 70, 133, 141, 168, 169
Leslie cabinet, 143, 173–175
Let It Be, 24
level, 11, 15, 17, 19, 20, 21–22, 32, 34, 36–43, 57, 61, 75, 82, 87–98, 99–103, 110, 115–117, 120, 124, 126, 130, 135, 136, 137, 143, 144, 159, 160, 164, 178, 183, 187, 193, 211, 217, 222, 224, 225, 226, 229, 230–231
Lexicon, 72, 108, 114
limiter, 36, 87–97, 130, 133, 134, 135, 141, 179, 238
Linn, Roger, 72
live-end/dead-end, 8
Local Control (MIDI), 68–69
lossless (audio codec), 63
Loudness Wars, 96–98, 231
loudspeaker, 13–14, 53–64, 158, 174, 214
low frequency, 6, 8, 54, 75, 77, 80, 84, 102, 115, 153
low-frequency oscillator (LFO), 116, 117
low-pass filter. *See* filter, low-pass
Lucca, Matt, 203, 204

Mac, 46, 50, 52, 147, 148
MADI (Multichannel Audio Digital Interface), 48
make-up gain, 90
Marcantonio, Steve, 97
Marshall (amps), 187, 188, 189, 190, 197, 215
Marshall, Robert, 149
Massenburg, George, 76
Massy, Sylvia, 18, 23, 57, 127, 162, 229, 231
mastering, 50, 52, 79, 80, 90, 213, 232, 239
mastering engineers, 52, 79, 231
Max/MSP, 72
"Maybe I'm Amazed," 173
McBride, John, 25, 26, 78, 132
McCartney, Paul, 31, 93, 173, 179, 180, 183
McDonald, Michael, 50, 51, 93, 111, 129, 130, 133, 135, 136, 138, 139, 142, 167, 170, 171
McDonald, Phil, 173
meters, 11, 39–40, 55, 61, 88, 89, 126, 183, 231, 232
mic input, 28, 34, 178, 209
mic placement, 24, 27, 76, 80, 81, 84, 204, 210, 132, 154, 157
mic pre, 23, 26, 28, 34, 36, 46, 49, 91, 132, 133, 164, 189, 200, 215, 238
mic technique (vocals), 21, 93, 135
microphones, 5, 13–30, 36, 45, 60, 76, 77, 80, 84, 87, 105, 107, 119, 132, 133, 134, 140, 146, 149, 150, 154, 156, 158, 185, 187, 189–192, 207, 208, 209–210, 211, 212, 214–215, 216, 217
midfield speakers, 55
MIDI (Musical Instrument Digital Interface), 32, 45, 47, 48, 51, 65–72, 113, 117, 122, 166, 168
MIDI Manufacturers Association, 72

MIDI recording versus audio recording, 168–169
Mid-Side (miking technique), 25, 208–211
Miles, John, 132
mix, 2, 3, 5, 7, 8, 46, 57, 61, 62, 70, 71, 77, 78, 79, 80, 83, 84–85, 87, 88, 92, 93, 97, 110, 124, 125, 143, 146, 159, 162, 183, 216, 237, 239
mix, compression on a, 95–96, 98
mixing, 31–43, 50, 54, 61, 62, 63, 94, 111, 164, 211, 214, 215, 217–234
mixing console. *See* console; analog console; digital console
mixing in the box. *See* in the box
mixing levels, 126, 183, 231–232
modeling (amp), 191
monitor engineer, 215
monitoring, 8, 38, 41, 53–64, 121, 136, 183, 196, 207, 210, 216, 219, 229
monitors, 37, 53–64, 79, 137, 183, 214, 215, 230, 238
mono, 2, 13, 23, 26, 31, 57, 61, 117, 162, 170, 174, 203, 225, 239
Moog, 169
Motown, 93, 111, 129, 179, 180, 182
moving coil principle, 14, 54
MP3, 60, 150, 230
multichannel, 34, 62, 124, 222
multitrack, 31, 39, 51, 52, 69, 99, 120, 215, 216, 222, 229, 233
Muse Research, 170

near-field (monitors), 55, 56, 57, 62, 79, 183
Neumann, 17, 29, 133, 134, 158, 172, 210, 211
noise, 5, 6, 10, 11, 17, 21, 24, 46, 58, 59, 85, 88, 94, 96, 97, 99–104, 153, 155, 174, 191, 193, 207, 211, 216
noise gate, 36, 71, 80, 99–104, 162
NS10 (Yamaha), 57, 158

Ocean Way Studios, 54
Olsson, P. J., 149, 150
omnidirectional (omni), 19–20, 27, 145, 161, 210
Optogate, 103
Orban, 91
orchestral recording, 2, 3, 8, 14, 21, 25, 35, 45, 70–71, 83, 119, 120, 123, 175, 207, 225, 238
organs, 51, 107, 165, 166, 171, 173–174
out-of-phase, 22–23, 36, 83, 116, 137
output level, 16, 17, 19, 20, 21, 38, 41, 88, 89, 100. *See also* level
overhead mics, 23, 29, 81, 82, 160, 162, 164, 215, 223, 226, 227

pad, 21
Padgham, Hugh, 102
palm mute, 179
pan, 22, 25, 68, 69, 71, 82, 83, 157, 160, 161, 170, 203, 210, 211, 212, 219, 223, 225–226, 229
panpot, 36, 37, 225
parametric EQ, 76–77, 81, 82, 84
passive (electronics), 56, 73, 179
Paton, David, 93
Paul, Les, 106, 186, 188, 199
PC (computer), 46, 70, 147
PCM formats (Sony), 2, 3
Pelonis, Chris, 7
percussion, 83, 85, 102, 117, 126, 162, 176, 223, 224, 225, 228
PFL (Pre-Fade Listen), 37, 38, 41
phantom center, 61, 225
phantom power, 17, 36, 179, 209
Phantom Recordings, 120
phase, 22–23, 25, 36, 55, 59, 83, 92, 116, 137, 162, 194, 212, 232
phasing, 114, 115, 116, 181, 192
Philips, 3, 108
Phillips, Sam, 107, 113
Phillips, Simon, 80, 120, 122, 124, 125, 126, 154, 155, 156, 157, 158, 159, 160, 162, 163, 164, 223
phonograph, 1, 13, 14, 53
piano, 18, 29, 50, 53, 54, 58, 66, 80, 84, 85, 95, 102, 105, 111, 120, 123, 125, 154, 165, 166, 167, 169, 170, 171, 172–173, 176, 210
piano, upright, 84, 172–173
Pierce, Tim, 101, 114, 117, 120, 124, 125, 127, 186, 187, 188, 189, 190, 191, 192, 193, 194, 195, 196, 197, 198, 199, 200
ping-pong delay, 111, 117
Pink Floyd, 2, 25, 31, 113, 147, 194, 224
pitching, 135–138, 141
plate (echo), 107–109
plug-ins, 5, 32, 39, 46, 47, 50, 51, 52, 67, 76, 78, 88, 90, 91, 114, 115, 143, 144, 196, 222
polar patterns, 19–20, 137, 161, 203, 214
polarized, 17
popping, 21–22, 84, 85, 96, 142, 167, 204
pop shield, 22, 204
Portastudio, 5
Poulsen, Valdemar, 1
PPM (Peak Program Meter), 39
preamp, 26, 28, 36, 82, 178, 179

pre-delay, 109, 116
Pre/Post, 37
PreSonus, 216
printing (EQ, processing), 70, 71, 79, 92, 97, 109, 111, 117, 181, 195
Pro Tools, 45, 46, 50, 66, 67, 72, 114, 117, 120, 143, 147, 170, 220, 228, 232
processing, 24, 32, 34, 43, 47, 50, 51, 62, 73, 77, 78, 89, 91, 94, 95, 105, 108, 109, 110, 114, 142, 181, 189, 215, 219, 222, 227–228, 238
producer, 2, 3, 8, 15, 18, 23, 26, 35, 51, 56, 57, 60, 61, 70, 71, 78, 96, 98, 117, 119, 125, 126, 127, 129, 136, 140, 142, 145, 148, 149, 150, 168, 170, 171, 175, 187, 199, 211, 222, 230, 232, 236, 237, 238, 239
proximity effect, 21, 132, 204
"Psychobabble," 111
Puig, Jack Joseph, 32, 86, 92, 93, 122, 124, 134, 140, 219, 223, 227, 232
Pultec, 73, 77, 78
punch-in / punch-out, 150, 170, 198
Putnam, Bill, 87, 105
Putnam, Bill Jr., 87, 92, 105, 108
PZM (Pressure Zone Microphone), 18, 173

Quadraphonic (Quad), 62
quantize, 67, 70, 126, 168

rackmount, 99, 215
Radiola, 54
RAM (random access memory), 47
Ramone, Phil, 147
RCA, 19, 26
release, 90, 93, 94, 100, 101, 102, 104, 175, 176
"Return to Tunguska," 147
reverb, 24, 36, 37, 46, 50, 57, 69, 73, 84, 199, 102, 105–112, 113, 114, 117, 120, 131, 139, 142, 143, 149, 161, 170, 178, 197, 203, 208, 225, 227, 228, 238
reverberant, 7, 8, 24, 107, 108, 110
Rhodes, Simon, 35, 71
ribbon mics, 19, 20, 29, 36, 82, 158, 174, 209
Rice, C. W., 54
Roland Space Echo, 114
room modes, 6, 9
Royer microphones, 174, 191
Rubin, Rick, 18, 231

sample, 5, 15, 45, 46, 65, 67, 71, 84, 95, 166, 167, 169, 172, 175, 223

sample rate, 48, 49–51
SansAmp, 94, 191, 192
Scheiner, Elliot, 111, 221, 224, 227, 231, 232
Sennheiser, 18, 190
separation, 24, 45, 103, 120, 123, 172, 203–204, 207, 210, 213, 215
Sequential Circuits, 65
Sgt. Pepper's Lonely Hearts Club Band, 2, 27, 184, 187, 196
Shanks, John, 49, 111, 117, 133, 137, 140, 141, 190, 192, 193, 197, 198, 199, 217
shelf, 75, 84
shelving, 82, 84
Shure, 16, 18, 29, 159, 160, 189, 214
sibilance, 84, 88, 90, 91, 93, 112, 142, 203
side chain, 90, 100
Sides, Allen, 54, 55, 57, 60, 61, 98
signal-to-noise ratio, 17, 21, 210
Sinatra, Frank, 132, 147
singing in tune, 135–137, 141
slapback echo, 107
SM57 (Shure), 18, 29, 159, 160, 189, 215
SM58 (Shure), 16, 18, 26, 29, 214
small diaphragm condenser, 17, 160
Smith, Dave, 65, 169
SMPTE time code, 69
snare drum, 100, 101, 110, 155, 156–157, 163
snare drum, miking, 17, 18, 21, 60, 159
snare drum, positioning, 61, 80, 82, 154, 223, 226
snare drum, tone, 74, 81, 84, 85, 155
soft knee, 89
software, 36, 40, 45–52, 67, 71, 72, 78, 88, 91, 99, 100, 108, 110, 137, 148, 149, 150, 168, 169, 191, 207, 216, 237
solid state, 17, 45, 88
solo (instrumental), 15, 29, 34, 37, 94, 95, 123, 127, 142, 150, 173, 188, 196, 197–199, 225, 226, 228, 230
solo (button), 38, 238
Sonny and Cher, 177
Sony, 2, 3, 191
Soquel High School, 172, 207, 208
sound balance, 3, 15, 61, 217
Sound Check 2 CD (Alan Parsons), 40, 231
sound engineers, 191
Sound Pressure Level (SPL), 61
soundproofing, 6, 10
Source-Connect, 148–150
S/PDIF (Sony/Philips Digital Interface Format), 48
Spector, Phil, 24, 110, 181, 236

speed of sound, 105
spill, 24, 58, 59, 99, 101, 137, 162, 215
spring reverb, 107
SSL, 32, 35, 77, 99, 220, 222
STC (sound transmission class), 10
steel drums, 29
stems, 37, 147, 164, 228–229
stereo, 2, 3, 16, 25, 26, 27, 31, 32, 34, 37, 39, 43, 52, 55, 61, 62, 64, 75, 78, 81, 83, 110, 111, 113, 116, 117, 124, 136, 137, 145, 157, 160, 170, 174, 175, 193, 195, 203, 210, 212, 214, 216, 219, 220, 223, 225, 226, 228, 231, 232
stereo bus, 36, 37, 41, 43, 95, 98, 232
stereo tape, 120
stomp box, 82, 94, 114, 189, 192
straight line mix, 229
Stratocaster, 186, 187
strings, 29, 39, 83, 95
sub-bass, 62, 85
subwoofer, 56, 62, 63
sum and difference technique, 212
Sun Studios, 107
surround, 26, 62–63, 170, 219
sync (synchronize), 2, 49, 69, 117, 148, 149, 214, 221
synth pad, 103, 125
synthesizer, 65, 67, 68, 72, 95, 165, 166, 169, 170, 172, 176, 201

talkback, 139, 149
tambourine, 39, 126
tape delay, 114–115
tape echo, 107, 108, 113, 115
tape loop, 114
tape op, 51, 198, 238, 239
Tascam, 3, 5
TC Electronics, 114
TDIF (Tascam Digital Interconnect Format), 48
Telefunken, 17, 18, 26, 49, 132
Telegraphone, 1
tempo-synced delay, 116
Thoener, David, 27, 32, 78, 124, 143, 228

threshold, 89, 90, 99, 100, 101, 102, 103, 162, 231
time domain, 7
"Tomorrow Never Knows," 143
toms, 23, 29, 80, 81, 85, 94, 110, 153, 154, 155, 156, 157, 164, 215, 223, 226
tracking, 58, 109, 119–127, 170, 171, 194, 228, 234
tremolo, 102, 103, 175, 192
Trident Studios, 155
trigger input, 100
tube amps, 3, 188, 192
tweeter, 11, 55, 56, 62, 86, 174
Twiddly.Bits, 71

U 47, 18, 29, 132, 133, 158
Universal Audio, 52, 78, 87, 88, 89, 91, 179
USB (Universal Serial Bus), 170, 209, 230, 239

Value for Money, 126, 183
VHS, 3
violin, 29, 54, 83, 105, 137, 199
vocal chain, 134
vocals, 22, 24, 26, 58, 60, 61, 63, 67, 78, 84, 85, 88, 90, 92, 93, 98, 103, 111, 129–146, 161, 203–205, 207–212, 222, 223, 225, 226, 230
vocals, backing, 78, 145, 173, 225, 228
vocals, live, 16, 18
volume, 6, 14, 21, 36, 39, 53, 58, 60–61, 67, 69, 71, 75, 87, 88–89, 95, 97–98, 101, 116, 117, 136, 145, 153, 156, 157, 158, 160, 166, 168, 191, 193, 215, 225
VU (Volume Units), 39–40, 231

Waters, Roger, 93
Watkins Copicat, 107, 113, 114
wet/dry signal, 110
woodwinds, 83, 95, 226
woofer, 54, 56, 86
Woolfson, Eric, 130
word clock, 49

Yamaha, 16, 57, 72, 114, 115, 125, 158, 168, 169, 180, 223

Also Available from Hal Leonard

ALAN PARSONS' ART & SCIENCE OF SOUND RECORDING DVD BOX SET

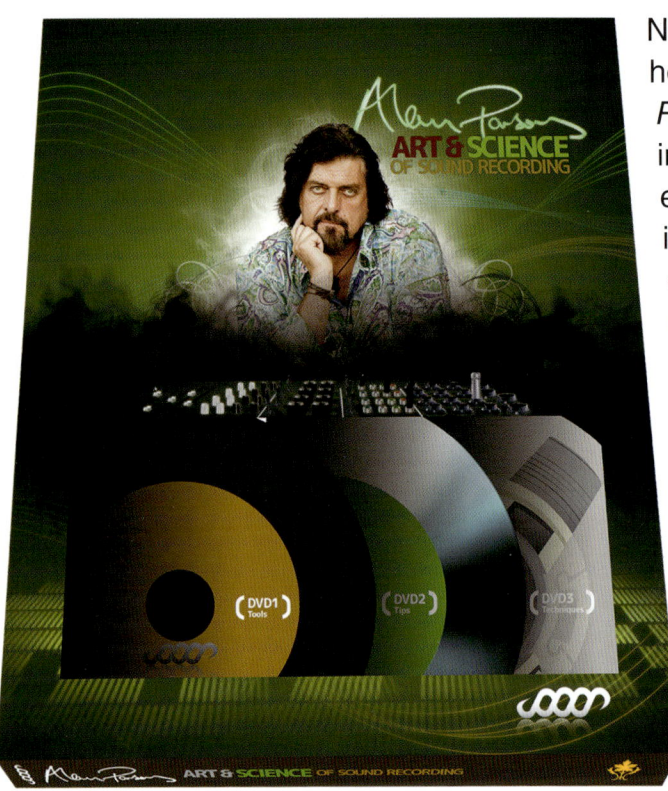

Nearly three years in the making, the monumental ten-hour video series *Alan Parsons' Art & Science of Sound Recording* is available in a three-DVD box set. Filmed in HD, this is the most powerful instructional series ever created for music production. Alan Parsons' illustrious career—as a recording engineer, producer, composer, and artist—acts as both backdrop and inspiration for the series.

Narrated by actor and musician Billy Bob Thornton, the DVDs are divided into twenty-four sections, covering everything from soundproofing to mixing and from recording guitar, keyboards, and drums to recording a choir. Fellow engineers and producers join Parsons, including Jack Joseph Puig, John Fields, Elliot Scheiner, and Jack Douglas. Artists and musicians interviewed include Michael McDonald, Taylor Hawkins, Nathan East, Rami Jaffee, Carol Kaye, and Erykah Badu.

This cutting-edge series applies classic, old-school recording experience to the modern recording scene, and it is certain to be a standard work on the subject for years to come. Together with *Alan Parsons' Art & Science of Sound Recording—The Book* and a fully interactive website, this DVD set forms a complete, practical course in modern recording.

U.S. $149.00
Published by Keyfax NewMedia, Inc.
HL00631668
ISBN: 9780615396392

HAL•LEONARD®
www.halleonard.com

Price and availability subject to change without notice.

0814